JOB SATISFACTION OF BANK EMPLOYEES

By

Dr. M. Nazer

M.Com., M.Phil., PGDCA., Ph.D., MBA
Associate Professor
Deptt. of Commerce,
Khadir Mohideen College
Adirampattinam
Tamil Nadu
(India)

&

Dr. P.K. Venkatachalam

Director
Deptt. of Management Studies
P.A. College of Engineering & Technology (PACET)
Coimbatore
Tamil Nadu
(India)

DISCOVERY PUBLISHING HOUSE PVT. LTD.

NEW DELHI-110 002

Published by:
Tilak Wasan

DISCOVERY PUBLISHING HOUSE PVT. LTD.
4383/4B, Ansari Road, Darya Ganj
New Delhi-110 002 (India)
Phone : +91-11-23279245, 43596064-65
Fax : +91-11-23253475
E-mail : parul.wasan@gmail.com
discoverypublishinghouse@gmail.com
web : www.discoverypublishinggroup.com

***First Edition:* 2012**

ISBN: 978-93-5056-103-4

Job Satisfaction of Bank Employees

Printed at:
Shree Balaji Art Press
Delhi

Dedicated

To

My Beloved Mother

Mrs. K.V. Kamashi

Preface

The introduction of New Economic Reforms of 1991 has brought about a shift in the operation of the Indian commercial banks due to stiff competition faced from the entry of new banks. This has necessitated the commercial banks for the better satisfaction of their customers which in turn has to absorb new technologies. However, the public sector banks are slow absorbers. Given that banks absorb huge government's fund which has got high opportunity cost, the poor performance of the banks reflects in the performance of the economy. Hence, an understanding of the customers' level of satisfaction becomes essential. It can also be noted that since the introduction of new technology in business has a bearing on the psychology of the employees to adopt to the changing needs of the business and satisfying the expectations of the customers an understanding of the opinion of the employees to the changing environment also becomes pertinent. The present study attempts to examine these issues in the micro level in the context of 14 public and 11 private sector banks in the urban areas of Coimbatore district. The objectives of the study were: (1) to study the type of banking services utilized by the customers of public and private sector banks, (2) to trace out the opinion of the customers of the public and private sector banks on the perceived and desired level of service quality of their banks, (3) to estimate the Service Quality Gap between the public and private sector banks, (4) to understand the opinion of the employees of public and private banks on the quality work life, (5) to identify the relationship between the socio economic status of the employees and their opinion on quality work life and (6) to offer suitable suggestions on the basis of the findings of the study.

To analyze the data collected from 280 customers of public sector banks and 220 private sector banks and 200 sample employees tools like, Simple Percentage Method, Simple Arithmetic Mean, Co-efficient of Variation and the techniques like Principal Component Analysis, Logit Model, and multiple regression models have been used. The analysis of the data has provided the conclusion that the service quality gap is negative for both public and private sector banks with a higher gap being recorded in the case of public sector than private sector banks. The employees felt that the dimension on stumbling block is the major factor influencing their productivity negatively.

This book is unique in its presentation and style. I have tried my best to present the matter in as clear and simple manner as possible to make it intelligible to even the reluctant student. This book is divided into Seven chapters.

In **Chapter I** a brief discussion about the entire project is provided. It also discusses in detail the statement of the problem identified. From the problem identified, the objectives are drawn in a logical sequence and provided. From the objectives, hypotheses which are germane to the study are drawn and provided. To study the objectives provided, the source of data, a discussion on the pilot study, the tools and techniques used in the present study are detailed. The chapter also provides the period of study and its limitations.

Chapter II provides a view on the concepts used in the study. A detailed review of the earlier studies carried out in the areas of banking performance, Quality Work Life (QWL) and the Service Quality has also been provided.

Chapter III has been devoted to the discussion on providing the history of Indian Banking and the profile of the study area.

In **Chapter IV** provides an analysis on demographic status, information about holding of account and operation of account.

In **Chapter V**, the significance of the difference between the services of the perceived and desired level of service quality of the sample banks have been examined.

In **Chapter VI**, the opinion of the employees on the Quality work Life (QWL) is discussed at length.

Chapter VII contains the summary, major findings, suggestions, emerging conclusions and the scope of future research.

I am confident that this book will be highly useful o the post graduate and undergraduate students and research scholars of Commerce, Economics and Management in addition several other finance related courses offered by various Indian universities and institutions.

Dr. M. Nazer
Dr. P.K. Venkatachalam

Chapter II provides a view on the concepts used in the study. A detailed review of the earlier studies carried out in the areas of banking performance, Quality Work Life (QWL) and the Service Quality has also been provided.

Chapter III has been devoted to the discussion on providing the history of Indian Banking and the profile of the study area.

In Chapter IV provides an analysis on demographic status, information about holding of account and operation of account.

In Chapter V, the significance of the difference between the services of the perceived and desired level of service quality of the sample banks have been examined.

In Chapter VI, the opinion of the employees on the Quality work Life (QWL) is discussed at length.

Chapter VII contains the summary, major findings, suggestions, emerging conclusions and the scope of future research.

I am confident that this book will be highly useful to the post graduate and undergraduate students and research scholars of Commerce, Economics and Management in addition several other finance related courses offered by various Indian universities and institutions.

Dr. M. Nazer

Dr. P.K. Venkatachalam

Acknowledgements

I owe a deep debt of gratitude and profound thankfulness to my Research Advisor *Dr. S. Shahul Hameed, M.Com., M.B.A., M.Phil., Ph.D., Research Advisor and Reader in Business Administration*, Khadir Mohideen College, Adirampattinam, for his guidance, valuable suggestions and constructive criticisms. Without his invaluable help and sustained interest and encouragement, this research work would not have been possible.

I am extremely thankful *Jnab Mohamed Aslam, Secretary and Correspondent*, Khadir Mohideen College, Adirampattinam for granting me permission for the successful completion of this endeavour.

I convey my heartfelt thanks to *Dr. A. Mohamed Abdul Khader, Principal*, Khadir Mohideen College, Adirampattinam and *Dr. O.M. Haja Mohideen, Head, Research Department of Business Administration*, Khadir Mohideeem College, Adirampattinam for granting me permission of the successful completion of this research work.

I am very much grateful to my co-guides *Dr. M. Nazer, Reader in Commerce*, Khadir Mohideen College, Adirampattinam and *Dr. A. Mohamed Siddique, Reader in Business Administration,* Khadir Mohideen College, Adirampattinam, for their constant support and encouragement for the successful completion of this research work.

I am very much grateful to *Dr. V. Radja Ramane, Reader in Economics,* Government Arts College, Coimbatore who has rendered a great help in carrying out my endeavour in the right perspective and without his inspiring advise and valuable suggestions in selecting and applying statistical tools in this place of research work, the thesis would not have been completed.

I am extremely thankful to *Shri Balchand Bothra, President,* SNMV College of Arts and Science, Coimbatore, and *Shri M.M. Bhuradia, Secretary,* SNMV College of Arts and Science, Coimbatore and *Dr. A.M.J. Philomin Raj, Principal,* for their permission and constant encouragement for the successful completion of this research work, respectively.

I convey my heartful thanks to my friend *Dr. M Gomestheswaran, Lecturer,* CMS College of Science and Commerce, for his help and encouragement for the successful completion of this endeavour.

On a personal note, I deeply acknowledge and warmly appreciate the encouragement given by my beloved Father. *P.S. Kailasanathen* and also my wife *Mrs. K. Chitra* and also my son *Master V. Anand Kailash.* I also thank my brothers *Mr. P.K. Shankaranarayan, Mr. P.K. Ganesh,* Sister *Mrs. Radha* and brother in law *Mr. S.V. Subramanian,* for their encouragement provided to me to do this research work.

I am also thankful to my friends and colleagues who have spared efforts in helping me throughout my research period. I also thank the authorities of various libraries who permitted me to provide their collections relevant to my study.

I gratefully remember the many indispensable individuals also who have worked behind the screen in completing this thesis.

Success the destiny of hard work and pain achieved only with the grace of *Lord Vinayaga* and *Goddess Manappully Bhagavathy*, I dedicate this humble endeavour of mine to the Almighty.

P.K. Venkatachalam

Contents

1 Introducton

Prelude

The importance of service sector contribution to economic well being has been gaining momentum world wide and India is not an exception to this global trends. In the Indian context, the service sector activities have received importance during the New Economic Reforms of 1991. Among the various service sector activities, the banking industry in India has received high priority. This is due to the reason that the banking sector is considered to be the lifeline of any economic activity as the contribution of this industry to the economy's growth is direct, considerable and commendable.

The history of Indian banking industry shows a metamorphosis in the growth of banks. The Indian commercial banks which were playing a role of catalyst with no profit motive and which had the motive of contributing to economic growth experienced a perceptible change in their activities after the introduction of New Economic Reforms of 1991. The liberalization process has compelled to bring about a considerable change in the services and activities of commercial banks which is due to the increased competition faced by the domestic public sector and private sector banks from the foreign banks. In this context, it was realized that the threat posed by the foreign banks to the Indian banks could be tackled only by adopting similar or better strategies as adopted by the foreign banks. In this context the need for adopting new technologies in service provision including the e-business was felt pertinent. However, the empirical evidence in the area of banking services indicated that while the private sector banks are the fast absorbers of these new technologies, the public sector banks are slow absorbers[1].

If the hypothesis of slow absorption of new technologies found true, this is expected to affect the performance of profitability of public sector banks. This is because, it is the level of service provision that determines the level of satisfaction of the customers of the banks. However, the adoption of new technologies also necessitated the acquiring new skills among the bank employees which in turn is said to bring about a change in the quality of work environment called 'Quality Work Life'[2]. Also, for the purpose of sustaining their customers, in tune with their expectations the banks have involved themselves in increasing their service provision quantitatively as well as qualitatively. However, given the stiff competition faced by the public and private sector banks of Indian origin, it can be noted that the deciding factor of service expansion and the level of satisfaction of the customers of the banks is not absolute but relative in nature.

The above discussion clearly indicates that globalization has brought about not only a paradigm shift in the functions and operations of the Indian commercial banks which took them apart from the traditional banking activities, but also it has a bearing on the psychology of the employees to adopt to the changing needs of the business and satisfying the expectations of the customers. With the differences in the business practices and the adoption of new technologies in business it is expected that they lead to differences in the performance of the banks. With the commercial bank being an active agent of economic change and the absorbers of huge amount of government's funds, if the performance of the banks is not up to the expectations, the negative impact could be felt not only the bank it terms of bankruptcy and closure, but also on the performance of the economy. This is a serious issue which requires an immediate concern particularly in the case of the developing countries like India as the economy's monetary transmission mechanism works only through commercial banks. Hence, an understanding of the adoptability of the employees to the changing needs of business environment and the resultant change in the opinion on Quality of Work Life and the customers' opinion on the services provided under new technology becomes pertinent. The present study attempts to examine these issues in the micro level in the context of a few sample banks of both public and private sector in nature which are operating in the urban areas of Coimbatore, a district which is industrially well developed and called as the 'Manchester of South India'.

Problem Design

The financial system is the lifeline of the economy. The changes in the economy get mirrored in the performance of the financial system. The banking system constitutes the core of financial sector which plays a crucial role in transmitting monetary policy impulses into the entire economic system.

In the Indian context, the government pursued policies of financial repression with great vigor during the 1970s and 1980s following nationalization of the major commercial banks. This was a period when the public sector commercial banks had rapid expansion of branches especially in the rural and semi urban areas and had reasonable success in the matters of deposit mobilization and disbursement of loans.

However, during this period efficiency considerations had taken a back seat. The operational efficiency of public sector commercial banks declined during the period mainly because of: (1) opening branches in un-remunerative regions; and (2) excess manpower and declining quality of loan portfolio.

However, in the early 1990s, the banking environment was transformed radically following bold initiatives from the RBI relating to dismantling of the entry barriers, interest rate deregulation, introduction of prudential accounting norms and the introduction of Basel I Capital Adequacy Norms. The relaxation of private sector entry in the banking sector led to the formation of nine new private sector banks and the entry of many foreign banks[3]. The liberal entry of foreign banks, operational freedom provided to the banks, deregulation of the interest rates, reduction in the statutory reserve requirements of Statutory Liquidity Ratio (SLR) and Cash Reserve Ratio (CRR), introduction of international norms of accounting in terms of capital adequacy, income recognition asset classification, and provisioning etc. have brought about competitiveness in the Indian Banking industry[4] which reduced the interest earnings of the commercial banks. This in turn has compressed the traditional source of income (Net Interest Margin = Interest Earned-Interest Expenses) [5]. Between 1991-92 and 1999-2000, the net interest margin of the commercial banks operating in India has declined from 3.31 per cent to 2.72 per cent[6]. Consequently, the commercial banks had to face the twin challenge of finding out new sources of income (mainly through off balance sheet activities and fee incomes) and containing overhead expenses.

Hence, given the reform initiatives of the government and the RBI in respect of banking, it became imperative on the part of the commercial banks of India to adopt the efficiency enhancement drivers for a better performance and for the long run survival of the banks. Moreover, with the entry of foreign banks and the continuous innovation that is taking place in the realm of information technology, the Indian commercial banks also have to make the increased use of electronic modes for their business transactions. Not only have the banks needed a greatly enhanced use of technology to the customer services but also needed technology for providing newer products and newer forms of services. Hence, technology absorption in banks has come to the forefront as an important technique of business and as a virtual necessity to face the imminent challenges[7]. A wide range of technology oriented services like, ATM, Internet Banking, Tele Banking, Core Banking Solutions, Credit/ Debit/Kisan/Smart Cards, Mobile Banking, Cash Management Services, Electronic Fund Transfer/ Electronic Clearing System have created a win win situation by extending great convenience and multiple options for customers while providing tremendous cost advantage to banks. The other advantages of the technology usage in banks include the flow of information much faster and more accurate and enable quicker analysis of data received. This in turn helps to make business decision faster and more efficient. It also enables development of appraisal and monitoring tools which would make credit management much more effective. The result would be a definite reduction in transaction costs, the benefits of which would be shared between banks and customers. Having understood the significant positive impact of technology oriented service on the bank's performance, the introduction of technology infusion is found visible in almost all in all banks and in all areas of banking operations[8].

Realizing this, the RBI committee on 'Technology Upgradation in the Banking Sector' has made a number of recommendations including the use of technology in the financial sector to ensure efficiency, stability, competition and above all service to the common person.[9]. While application of technology would help banks reduce their operating costs in the long run, the initial investments would be sizeable.

However, the process of computerization in the banking industry in India, particularly in the public sector banks is very slow. There are so many difficulties inherent in nationalized banks of which stiff opposition from the trade unions formed the paramount one. The directive by the Central Vigilance Commission (CVC) to PSU banks to achieve 100 per cent computerisation has imparted urgency to the process of technological advancement. While the foreign banks, followed by private sector banks are able to enjoy a head start in adopting 'core banking solutions', only a few public sector banks (PSU) too have fallen in this line rather vigorously. For example, as on March 31, 2007 of 27 PSU banks, as many as nine (with seven out of eight in the SBI group) had 100 per cent computerised branches; nineteen had more than 50 per cent.

Foreign banks have ATMs more than four times the number of their total branches (441 per cent) followed by new private sector banks (377 per cent). Total number of ATMs managed by PSU banks stands at 9992 (or 21 per cent of their total branches) which compares with 4985 managed by new private banks and 777 managed by foreign banks.[10]

In the process of transformation, the significant role played by Human capital was also realized. This is more so in the case of service sector organization like banking which does not require any input other than human resource to produce services.[10]. With banks having more or less equal technological strength, the differentiating factor is only the quality of human resources [11] and the level of satisfaction of staff will decide the quality of customer services. One cannot expect excellent result/service from a dissatisfied employee. His/her frustration and dissatisfaction with work will obviously get reflected in the way he/she treats the customers. This call for aligning the human resource strategy with the business goals at both the strategic and practical levels in order to fact the twin challenges unleashed by the new competitive business environment[12]. Maximum output or productivity can be achieved by optimizing capacity utilization as well as efficient utilization of each employee and by putting right person on the right job[13]. This requires the adoption of appropriate human resource strategies, policies and practices.

The above discussion clearly vindicates that the success of any banking institution depends on the customers' satisfaction on the service provision. However, the level of service provision of the bank employees depends greatly on the Quality of Work Life prevailing in the banking institution as it influences the employees' interest in serving their customers. The introduction of computers and the new technologies have changed the Quality of Work Life.

From the above discussion, the following issues emerge:

(1) What are the services the customers of public and private sector utilise the most?

(2) In a competitive environment, to what extent the customers of public and private sector banks are satisfied with the services of their banks.

(3) To what extent the there is a difference in the level of satisfaction between the public and private sector banks.

(4) What is the opinion of the bank employees on the Quality of Work Life prevailing in their banks?

(5) Is the socio-economic status of the bank employees has an influence over the opinion on Quality of Work Life?

Objectives of the Study

Based on the above mentioned issues, the following objectives were framed for the present study:

(1) To study the type of banking services utilized by the customers of public and private sector banks;

(2) To trace out the opinion of the customers of the public and private sector banks on the perceived and desired level of service quality of their banks;

(3) To estimate the Service Quality Gap between the public and private sector banks;

(4) To understand the opinion of the employees of public and private banks on the quality work life;

(5) To identify the relationship between the socio economic status of the employees and their opinion on quality work life;

(6) To offer suitable suggestions on the basis of the findings of the study.

Hypotheses of the Study

Based on the above issues the hypotheses formulated for the study are:

(1) There is a significant difference between the customers of the public and private sector banks on the perceived and desired level of service quality;

(2) The influence of the administrative policies of the bank on the employees' job satisfaction is higher and significant;

(3) There is a significant relationship between the factors determining the Quality of work Life and the Employees' socio-economic status;

(4) The impact of 'stumbling block' on the Quality of Work Life is significant.

Methodology of the Study

Source of Data

The methodology proposed in the present study is to analyze the issues mentioned above involves the measurement of the level of satisfaction of the employees on the Quality Work

Life (QWL) and the customers' opinion on the quality of services provided (SERV QUAL).

Primary Data

Sample Design

The present study has the dual objective of understanding the opinion of the bank employees on the quality of work life due to computerization on the one hand and the opinion of the customers on the Quality of services provided by the banks on the other.

A study on these lines requires the collection of primary data from both the employees and the customers of public and private sector banks. For this purpose, the urban areas of Coimbatore have been selected. For the purpose of analyzing these issues, identification of the public and private sector banks operating within the urban areas of Coimbatore was felt pertinent. This is because, Coimbatore is called the Manchester of South India. It is a highly industrialized district which contributes to around 45 per cent of the industries' output of the state of Tamilnadu. The high urbanization with heavy concentration of industries that include small, medium and large scale, the domestic and foreign transactions has necessitated the emergence of not only new banks that include private, public and foreign banks but also spread if bank branches. With heavy concentration of banks and bank branches computerization and customer care has emanated from fierce competition facing the banks.

A list of public and private sector banks operating within the urban areas of Coimbatore was prepared with the help of the unpublished records obtained from Canara Bank, the lead bank of Coimbatore district.

Table 1.1 exhibits that there are totally 46 banks which spread over the urban areas of Coimbatore. Of these, there are 26 public sector banks and the remaining 20 are private sector banks. (The foreign banks are excluded from the study as the study focuses on the performance of the public and private sector banks only). From these, 13 public sector banks and 11 private sector banks were selected randomly. Since the State Bank of India constitutes a major bank as it accounts for 21 per cent of the total market share, it was selected compulsorily. Hence, the sample banks include totally 14 public sector banks and 11 private sector banks which work out to a total number of banks of 25 which constitutes 50 per cent of the total population.

Table 1.1: List of Banks Located in the Urban Areas of Coimbatore District

Sl.No.	Name of the Bank	Type of Bank
1.	State Bank of India	Public Sector
2.	State Bank of Bikaner & Jaipur	Public Sector
3.	State Bank of Hyderabad	Public Sector
4.	State bank of Mysore	Public Sector
5.	State bank of Patiala	Public Sector
6.	State Bank of Saurashtra	Public Sector
7.	State bank of Travancore	Public Sector
8.	Allahabad Bank	Public Sector
9.	Andhra Bank	Public Sector
10.	Bank of Baroda	Public Sector
11.	Bank of India	Public Sector
12.	Bank of Maharashtra	Public Sector
13.	Canara Bank	Public Sector
14.	Central Bank of India	Public Sector
15.	Corporation Bank	Public Sector
16.	Dena Bank	Public Sector
17.	Indian Bank	Public Sector
18.	Indian Overseas Bank	Public Sector

Sl.No.	Name of the Bank	Type of Bank
19.	Oriental Bank of Commerce	Public Sector
20.	Punjab & Sind Bank	Public Sector
21.	Punjab National Bank	Public Sector
22.	Syndicate Bank	Public Sector
23.	Union Bank of India	Public Sector
24.	United Bank of India	Public Sector
25.	United Commercial Bank	Public Sector
26.	Vijaya Bank	Public Sector
27.	Bank of Rajasthan	Private Sector
28	Catholic Syrian Bank	Private Sector
29.	Dhanalakshmi Bank	Private Sector
30.	Federal Bank	Private Sector
31.	Karnataka Bank	Private Sector
32.	Karur Vysia Bank	Private Sector
33.	City Union Bank	Private Sector
34.	Lakshmi Vilas Bank	Private Sector
35.	Kodak Mahindra Bank Ltd.	Private Sector
36.	Sangli Bank	Private Sector
37.	South Indian Bank Ltd.	Private Sector
38.	Tamilnadu Mercantile Bank	Private Sector
39.	The Vysia Bank Ltd.	Private Sector
40.	Indus Ind Bank	Private Sector
41.	The ICICI Banking Corpn. Ltd.	Private Sector
42.	The Centurion Bank Ltd.	Private Sector
43.	HDFC Bank Ltd.	Private Sector
44.	IDBI Bank	Private Sector
45.	Axis Bank	Private Sector
46.	Bhrath Overseas Bank	Private Sector

Source: Unpublished Records of Canara Bank.

A list of public and private sector banks selected at random is given in the form of a table. (Table: 1.2).

Table 1.2: List of Banks Selected for the Study

Sl.No.	Name of the Bank	Type of Bank
1.	State Bank of India	Public Sector
2.	Dena Bank	Public Sector
3.	Indian Bank	Public Sector
4.	Indian Overseas bank	Public Sector
5.	Allahabad Bank	Public Sector
6.	Andhra Bank	Public Sector
7.	Bank of Baroda	Public Sector
8.	Bank of India	Public Sector
9.	Canara Bank	Public Sector
10.	Central Bank of India	Public Sector
11.	Corporation Bank	Public Sector
12.	Punjab National Bank	Public Sector
13.	Union Bank of India	Public Sector
14.	United Commercial Bank	Public Sector
15.	Karur Vysia Bank	Private Sector
16.	Tamilnadu Mercantile Bank	Private Sector
17.	Lakshmi Vilas Bank	Private Sector
18.	Karnataka Bank	Private Sector
19.	The ICICI Banking Corporation Ltd.	Private Sector
20.	HDFC Bank Ltd.	Private Sector
21.	South Indian Bank Ltd.	Private Sector
22.	Dhanalakshmi Bank	Private Sector
23.	Catholic Syrian Bank	Private Sector
24.	Federal Bank	Private Sector
25.	IDBI Bank	Private Sector

Source: Unpublished Records of Canara Bank.

The next step is the selection of samples from the selected sample public and private sector banks. To collect the primary data on the opinion on factors determining the quality of work life, a list of bank employees working in each of the selected sample banks was prepared and from the list 8 employees were selected randomly. Thus, 200 employees were selected with 112 employees from public sector banks and 88 employees from the private sector banks. The selected employee respondents were approached and the data pertaining to their age education, designation, years of experience, nature of work, type of employment, participation in trade union activities, salary, other facilities extended and the satisfaction on the various facilities extended, their family background like the size of the family, number of dependents, health situation of the employees and the family members etc were collected.

To identify the customers' level of satisfaction on the quality of services provided, 20 customers from each of the sample banks were selected randomly from the list of customers obtained from each of the sample banks. This gave a sample size of 500 samples. The selected customer respondents were met in person and their personal information; information relating to bank service utilization, opinion on perceived and desired levels of service quality was obtained.

Pilot Study

Before the field survey was conducted the consistency of the information to be collected had to be tested. For this purpose, a pilot survey was conducted. To carry out this, the already prepared questionnaires (one for customer and one for Employees) were taken to the filed namely the universe of the study. A few respondents were met and interacted. From their response, the questions which were found to be redundant were omitted. For questions for which it was felt that answers could not be obtained, they were put indirectly. This helped greatly to reframe the questionnaire and to obtain correct information.

Description of Variables

The study attempted to examine the customers' perceived and desired level of service quality on the one hand and the opinion on the Quality Work Life (QWL) of the sample bank employees on the other. To study these, the researcher has identified from the literature the relevant parameters.

Factors Considered Measuring Customers' Service Quality

To identify the opinion of the customers on the quality of services, 36 variables that are germane to measuring the service quality were identified under five broad dimensions and a seven point scale was constructed for each of these parameters. This is an improvement made over the five broad dimensions identified by Parasuram *et.al.*[14] The parameters identified is given below:

Sl. No.	Service Quality Variables
I.	**TANGIBILITY DIMENSION**
1.	Indication of display timings at appropriate counters:
2.	Indication of display boards at appropriate counters:
3.	Upkeep and cleanliness of the bank premises:
4.	Adequacy of space
5.	Location of the bank
II.	**ASSURANCE DIMENSION**
6.	Usage of computers and other modern technology to provide service:
7.	Image of your bank among the public:
8.	Usage of technical terms when speaking with you:
9.	Proficiency of the staff on the work they carry out for you:
10.	Confidence and perfection of the services provided to you:
III.	**RESPONSIVENESS DIMENSION**
11.	Attitude, responsiveness and courtesy of the staff:
12.	Responsiveness to your comments and suggestions:

Sl. No.	Service Quality Variables
13.	Transfer of money from your bank to other bank:
14.	Treatment of your need and urgency with care and seriousness:
15.	Response of the staff when there is a grievance:
16.	Dependability and accuracy of the services provided to you:
17.	Promptness of the services carried out:
IV.	**EMPATHY DIMENSION**
18.	Reaction of the bank staff if a scheduled appointment is missed by you
19.	Efforts taken by the bank staff to know about you and your needs:
20.	Recognition of the bank staff to call you by your name:
21.	Accessibility of the staff in the bank to contact by email:
22.	Conveying of information in the languages known to you:
23.	Accessibility of staff in the bank by telephone
24.	Accessibility of the branch manager or higher officials
25.	Accessibility and contact of staff in the bank:
26.	Care and Consideration given to your grievances
27.	Convenience of timing of the office hours of the bank.
28.	Prompt opening/closing of the branch as per time:
V.	**RELIABILITY DIMENSION**
29.	Interest and willingness to help you to provide prompt service:
30.	Time taken to process your grievances
31.	Attention given to the grievances and the follow up actions taken:
32.	Care and Consideration of your property and values entrusted for safe custody
33.	Appropriateness and update of the account statements provided to you:
34.	Neatness and legibility of the entries in the pass book:
35.	Quick provision of services:
36.	Skill of the staff to use computers and other modern technical devices

Parameters Considered to Measure Quality Work Life

To identify the opinion of the workers on the Quality Work life, from the literature, 37 parameters factors under eight broad categories that determine the quality of work life both positively and negatively were identified and a five point scale was constructed for each of these parameters. The parameters identified are given below:

Sl.No.	Variables Measuring Quality Work Life
I.	**DRIVING FORCE**
1.	Make Work Easier
2.	Increase Quality of Work
3.	Save Time
4.	Increase Output
5.	Reduce Repetitive Work
6.	Integrate Data Base
II.	**LEARNING**
7.	Read about computers
8.	Learn Computer Skills
9.	Adequately Trained
10.	Observed Others
III.	**APPLICATIONS**
11.	Analysis and Decisions
12.	Planning and Scheduling
13.	Report Generation
14.	Data Storage
15.	Letter Writing
IV.	**COMMON COMPLAINTS**
16.	Losing of Autonomy
17.	Boredom
18.	Isolation
19.	Delays

Sl. No.	Variables Measuring Quality Work Life
20.	Helplessness
21.	Health Problem
V.	**ORGANIZATIONAL INCENTIVE**
22.	Orientation Programmes
23.	Consultation/ Counselling
24.	Assurance
25.	Training Programmes
26.	Financial Incentives
VI.	**PROXIMITY**
27.	Extent of Work Computerized
28.	Use of Computers at Work
29.	Hours Spent on Computers
30.	Operating Computers Personally
31.	Computer's Help in Work
VII.	**STUMBLING BLOCKS**
32.	Power Failure
33.	Dead Locks/Shutdowns
34.	Virus Threat
35.	Fear of Loss of Data/Files
VIII.	**ECONOMIES**
36.	Saves Costs
37.	Reduce Paper Usage

Framework of Analysis

To analyze the collected primary data various statistical tools and techniques were used. The application of these tools and techniques were identified as relevant to the objectives of the study framed. The tools and techniques applied are listed below:

Simple Percentage Method

The relative share of each of the factors on service utilization has been calculated using the percentage method.

Simple Arithmetic Mean

The average score of each of the Quality Work Life variables and Service Quality dimensions, the arithmetic mean for each category has been calculated.

Standard Deviation

To measure the extent of dispersions in each of the variables on the opinion of Quality Work Life and various Service Quality Dimensions, standard deviation has been employed.

Co-efficient of Variation

For the purpose of comparison of the Quality Work Life and the Service Quality variables, a relative measure of dispersion namely, the coefficient of variation has been used.

Principal Component Analysis

The data collected from the bank officials on the opinion on the Quality work Life has been classified, tabulated and processed for factor analysis which is the most appropriate multivariate technique to identify the groups of determinants. Factor analysis identifies common dimensions of factors from the observed variables that link together the seemingly unrelated variables and provides insight into the underlying structure of the data[15]. In this study, Principal component Analysis has been used since the objective is to summarize most of the original information in a minimum number of factors for prediction purpose. A Principal Component analysis is a factor model in which the factors are based on the total variance. Another concept in factor analysis is the rotation factors. Varimax rotations are one of the most popular methods used in the present study to simplify the factor structure by maximizing the variance of a column of the pattern matrix. Another technique of 'latent root criteria' is also used.

Logit Model

To measure the extent of influence of the level of satisfaction on Job, a logit model has been used. From the literate it was identified that the free to use the known skill (Use of Skill), the responsibility given to the employees on the reliability (Responsibilities given), the security over the job (Security

Variables	Nature of the variable and the values assumed
Use of Skill (US)	Yes =(1), No (0)
Responsibilities Given (RG)	Yes =(1), No (0)
Security of Job (SJ)	Yes =(1), No (0)
Advancement (AD)	Yes =(1), No (0)
Recognition (RC)	Yes =(1), No (0)
Social Values (SV)	Yes =(1), No (0)
Work Environment (WE)	Yes =(1), No (0)
Salaries and other Benefits (SB)	Yes =(1), No (0)
Administrative Policies (AP)	Yes =(1), No (0)
Computerization of Work (CW)	Yes =(1), No (0)
Relationship with Co-officials and the Administrator (RW)	Yes =(1), No (0)

$$SJ = a_0US + a_1RG + a_2SJ + a_3\,AD + a_4\,RC + a_5\,SV + a_6\,WE + a_7\,SB + a_8AP + a_9CW + a_{10}\,RW$$

Where,

SJ = Satisfaction on Job
US = Use of Skill
RG = Responsibilities Given
SJ = Security of Job
AD = Advancement
RC = Recognition
SV = Social Values
WE = Work Environment
SB = Salaries and other Benefits
AP = Administrative Policies
CW = Computerization of Work
RW = Relationship with Co-officials and the Administrator

of Job), the chances for promotion without any recommendations or nepotism (Advancement), the recognition over the employee's efficiency (Recognition), the societal status gained by the job (Social Values), the congenial atmosphere of working (Work Environment), the pecuniary and fringe benefits (Salaries and other Benefits), the administrative policies (Administrative Policies), the intensity of computerization which is supposed to have either dissatisfaction for the technicality involved or satisfaction for the making the work easy (Computerization of Work), and the relationship with the co officials and administrator which helps in bringing a favourable work atmosphere (Relationship with co-officials and the Administrator) are the variables said to affect the level of jobs satisfaction.

However it can be noted that these variables are qualitative in nature and hence the dummy values are given to these variables.

Servqual Model

To measure the service quality of the banks, the 'SERVQUAL' model, as suggested by Parasuraman et.al.[16] was used. The variables included in the model are functional quality dimensions, outcome quality dimensions and the perception of overall service quality.

From the literature 36 service and technology related variables were identified which were broadly categorized under five broad dimensions which include:

(1) Tangibility; (2) Assurance; (3) Responsiveness; (4) Empathy; and (5) Reliability.

Significance of the Study

There are many studies carried out in the context of the banking. However, there are no studies that are carried out at the micro level to understand the relationship between computerization on the performance of the banking unit. In this context, the study is exploratory in nature.

The concept of Quality Work Life in the context of banking industry is of recent origin. The banking sector was treated top be the potential for creation of white collar jobs. The large scale branch networking and strong unionization as provided job security. However, the introduction of new technology has dismantled the traditional way of working. It has necessitated the acquiring of new skills by the employees. For a successful computerization, an understanding of the opinion of the work force on the changes in Quality of Work Life and the adoptability to the new environment becomes pertinent. Though it is theoretically known and empirically verified in the context of industrial and other service sector on the impact of job satisfaction on the productivity and performance of banks, in the Indian context there are no studies carried out to verify this issue in the context of changing technology-oriented banking environment. Hence, in this context this is empirical in nature. Identifying the relationship among the related variables is a maiden attempt too.

Similarly, there are studies which have examined the level of customer satisfaction in public and private sector banks. However, these studies have ignored the comparison of the service quality of the public sector banks with the private sector banks and hence could not identify the relative service quality performance of these banks. The present study bridges this research gap by estimating the perceived and desired levels of service quality, the difference between these two—the service quality gap- and also the differences in the service quality between the public and private sector. This is a maiden attempt indeed.

To measure these instruments, a nine point scale has been developed with the level of services scaled from 1 to 7 where, 1 means *low* and 7 means *high*. The scores thus obtained are used to calculate the total or mean of each of the dimensions.

Period of Study

The primary data were collected for a period of one year namely, 2007-08.

Scope of the Study

(1) The focus of this piece of research is to determine "what are the services the customers are utilizing frequently from their sample public and private sector banks".

(2) What is the level of satisfaction of the sample customers and what is the level of gap between what is being expected by the customers and what is being provided by the sample banks.

(3) What is the level of satisfaction of the bank employees with regard to the prevailing service quality?

Limitations of the Study

In spite of its strengths and uniqueness, the study hedges with certain limitations:

(1) The study pertains only to the urban areas of Coimbatore district and hence, generalization of the conclusions is limited.

(2) Any study on customer service cannot provide enduring findings over time as expectations of the customers and the type of services provided by banks, the technology upgradation change from time to time. Therefore, the findings of the study indicate only contemporary views of the bank employees and the customers and may not hold good for all time to come.

(3) Rural folks are excluded on the assumption that they may not be well informed and educated. Also, the technology has not percolated in the rural areas. This is because, though the nationalized banks have got spread in rural areas, the technology adoption and computerization is very poor. Since the private sector

banks operate under profit motive, there are no branches of private sector banks operating in the rural areas.

(4) The analysis of the views of the employees on the quality work Life is only to the present work environment and based on the present pecuniary and non pecuniary benefits. Hence, the findings and the conclusions arrived at in the present project may hold good only for the present policies of the bank management and the RBI and the work environment. Changes brought about in these aspects may bind to change the opinion of the employees in which case the suggestion provided would become obsolete.

Scheme of Report

The present project is divided into *Six Chapters*.

In *Chapter I,* a brief discussion about the entire project is provided. It also discusses in detail the statement of the problem identified. From the problem identified, the objectives are drawn in a logical sequence and provided. From the objectives, hypotheses which are germane to the study are drawn and provided. To study the objectives provided, the source of data, a discussion on the pilot study, the tools and techniques used in the present study are also detailed. The chapter also provides the period of study and its limitations.

Chapter II provides a view on the concepts used in the study. A detailed review of the earlier studies carried out in the areas of Quality Work Life (QWL) and Customer services, the Service Quality has also been provided.

Chapter III has been devoted to the discussion on the growth and development of Indian banking system.

In *Chapter IV,* a discussion on the various services provided by the sample banks and the extent of utilization of these services by the customers are discussed. The socio-economic status of the customer respondents is also discussed.

In *Chapter V* the customers' opinion on the perceived and desired level of service quality, the service quality gap and the significance of the difference between the perceived and desired level of service quality of the sample customers of public, private sector banks and all banks have been discussed in detail.

Chapter VI portrays the opinion of the employees on the Quality work Life (QWL). The relationship between the employees' opinion on the quality work life and their socio-economic status has been examined in detail.

Chapter VII contains the summary, major findings, suggestions, emerging conclusions and the scope of future research.

REFERENCES

1. Meenakshi Rishi and Sweta C. Saxena, 'Technological innovations in the Indian Banking Industry: The Late Bloomer', *Accounting, Business and Financial History*, Vol. 14 (3), November 2004, pp. 339–353.
2. D.S. Sangwan, 'Human Resource Management in Banks', *IBA Bulletin*, June, 2005, p. 11.
3. RBI, Trends and Progress of Banking in India, Banks, *ICFAI*, February, p. 9.
4. S.B. Singh, 'Indian Banking Vision', *The Journal of Indian Institute of Banking and Finance*, April-June, 2005, p. 6.
5. Biswajit Chatterjee and Ram Pratap Sinha, "Intermediation cost Efficiency: A Tale of Two Bank Groups', *The ICFAI Journal of Bank Management*, Vol. V (1), February 2006, pp. 7-38.
6. Ram Pratap Sinha, "Spread Efficiency of Indian Commercial Banks', *The ICFAI Journal of Bank Management*, Vol. V (4), November, 2006, pp. 39-58.
7. Nalini Prava Tripathy, Technology Banking: A Better Environment for Better Tomorrow, *The ICFAI Journal of Bank Management*, Vol. IV (4), November, 200, pp. 41-51.
8. Dharmendra Singh and Garima Kohli, 'Evaluation of Private Sector Banks in India: A SWOT Analysis', *Journal of Management Research*, Vol. 6 (2), August, 2006, p. 87.

9. Y.V. Reddy, Governor, *Reserve Bank of India at the Banking Technology Awards Function*, 2006 at the Institute for Development and Research in Banking Technology, Hyderabad on September 2, 2006.

10. D.S. Sangwan, '*Op. Cit.*

11. *Ibid*.

12. *Ibid*.

13. *Ibid*.

14. Parasuraman, V. Zeithaml and L. Berry, "A Conceptual Model of Service Quality and/its Implications for Future Research", *Journal of Marketing*, Vol.49 (Fall), 1985, pp. 40-50.

15. Richard A.Johnson and Dean W. Wichern, Applied Multivariate Statistical Analysis, Prentice Hall India Ltd., New Delhi, 1996.

16. Parasuraman, V. Zeithaml and L. Berry. *Op.Cit*.

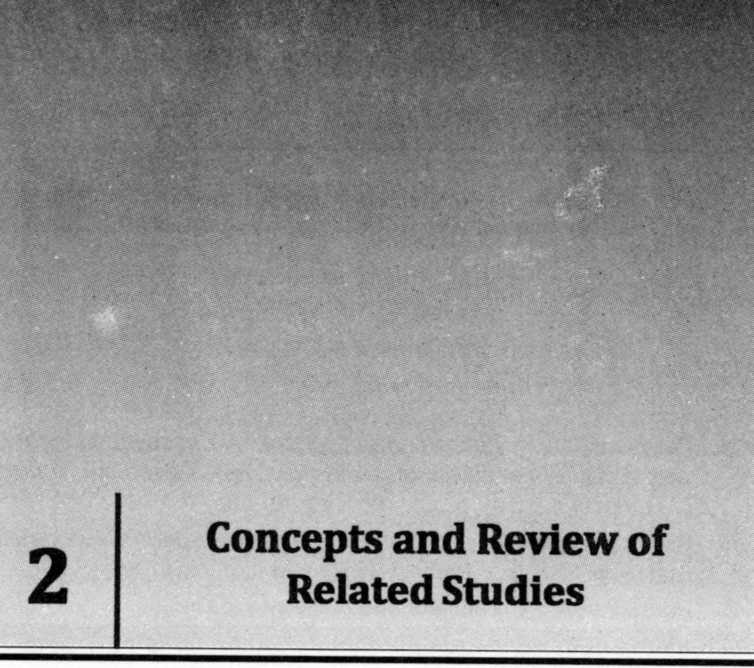

2 Concepts and Review of Related Studies

Introduction

The dual objective of the present piece of research is to examine the quality of work life of the employees and the customers' perception of the Service Quality (SERVQUAL). In the course of the discussion, the researcher has used certain concepts which are germane to the analysis. Hence, an understanding of these concepts becomes pertinent. The chapter is devoted towards this end. Also, a review of the available literature in the above mentioned two areas namely Quality Work Life and Customers' Service Quality has also been made. Hence, the present chapter has been divided into two sections. *Section I* deals with the concepts and the indicator relating to Quality of Work life and Customers' Service Quality. In *Section II* a review of related studies is being provided.

SECTION I

Concepts used in the Study

As mentioned above in the present section it is attempted to discuss the concepts germane to the analysis of Quality Work Life and Customers' Service Quality.

Concepts Relating to Banking and Services

(a) Computerization in Banks

Computerisation in banks is the introduction of computes for expansion, maintenance and processing of banking business, processing and reconciliation of inter branch transactions, processing statistical data and for research purpose. The four major objectives of computerisation in banking industry are: (1) Improvement in customer services; (2) Better house keeping; (3) Faster decision making; and (4) Increase in productivity and profitability.

(b) Mechanization in Banks

It is an endeavour to automate the operation of the banks. It is the Settlement provided for accounting machines electric/ electronic other than computer for the purpose of: (*a*) Current Account; (*b*) Savings Bank Account; (*c*) Cash Credit and Loan Accounts; (*d*) Other Deposit Account; (*e*) General Ledger Accounts; and (*f*) Salary and pay.

(c) Information Technology in Banks

In the field of banking, information technology implies the transaction processing and the integration of information system with communication technology and of innovative applications to product manufacturing, design and control. It is the through Information Technology the financial services like: (*a*) Automated Teller Machines; (*b*) Remote Banking Services; (*c*) Services not available through Remote Banking; (*d*) Smart Cards; (*e*) Internet banking; (*f*) Electronic Banking (electronic Transfer of funds, Electronic Clearing Services); (*g*) Tele-Banking (Automated Teller Machines); (*h*) Credit/Debit Cards; (*i*) Smart Cards; and (*j*) Electronic Cheques.

Factors Considered to Measure Quality of Work Life

The Quality of Work Life of the employees has been measured in terms of the selected indicators which can be divided under eight broad categories as Driving force, Learning, Applications, Common Complaints, Organization Incentives, Proximity, Stumbling Blocks and Economies are discussed as hereunder:

(a) Driving Force

In the event of any change it is essential for those who involved agreeing to the advantages of the same. It is these advantages that drive the users to continue to use. In the case of the introduction of computers in work place it is making the work easier, increased quality of work, time saving, reduction in repetitive work and the integration of data base among the various branches of the banks constitute the driving force. These factors have a direct bearing on the increased usage of computers or the driving force.

(b) Learning

For any technology to be accepted and utilized, the ability and confidence to use the same has to be present among those who are instrumental to implement/operate it. In the Indian context, a vast majority of the users/potential users still remain illiterate when it comes to computers. Employees' ignorance in the work place paves the way to incompetence, indifference and indignation. The various ways by which the employees can enhance their computer knowledge and skills are reading, listening, observing, practicing and formal education. Differences in the adoption of the above said method leads to differences in the level of skills in the usage of computers and as a result the employee's productivity.

(c) Applications

Apart from learning computers, the interest and involvement shown by the employees in the application of computers at work and their development has a greater bearing over the productivity and their work environment.

If computerization changed work atmosphere, the internet went one step ahead and revolutionized this change. The performance of the service sector institutions has been leveraged by the usage of internet and this is more so in the case of banking sector which has facilitated the introduction of e-banking. In the context of banking institutions, application of computers are mostly useful in the analysis and decision making of business, planning and scheduling, generation of reports, storage of data and letter writing. These applications make the day to day business of the banking firm more easy and time saving.

(d) Organizational Incentives

It is in the interest of the management that computerization takes place smoothly. To this end, they offer various kinds of incentives to the employees in the form of orientation Programmes, assurances, training, financial incentives, counselling and consultations. Status of these variables is absorbed from the respondents through scaled inventories. Many people have felt that the very provision of a computerized set up is an incentive to them to work on computers. Along with providing the ambience and the infrastructure, the managements have to ensure that the workers feel comfortable to work with computers ion all respects. Many organizations feel that these are wasteful indulgences. On the contrary the incentives are vital inputs that can earn employees' interest. They will also gain employee involvement which is crucial for the success of change implementation. This dimension tries to assess the amount of these incentives that the respondents have received so that they could adopt better to the system.

(e) Common Complaints

Introduction of new technologies has negative impact too on the quality of work life. This leads to monotonousness in work which in turn results in boredom. The employees have to spend their time with the computers always. This leads to isolation with no interaction with the coworkers. Since the employees have to spend their time only with the machines they have no time for interaction, they feel isolated and they also loose autonomy. Continuously watching the computers lead to health problems also.

(e) Proximity

This dimension includes the measurement of physical proximity to the machine that the respondents have at work. Extent of computer use at work, hours spent at the computers. Amount of help taken from computes to perform their work and extent of computerization in their work environment are taken into consideration. The actual closeness with the machine may be an indication of healthy adoption in the normal sense.

(f) Stumbling Blocks

Computerization has lot of advantages, but there are a few hurdles that one has to surmount successfully in order to be safe. The moment one downloads something from most web based email services, the service provider offers a virus scan. The set of real problems that arise due to computerization are covered in this factor. With the introduction of Core Banking the computers are prone to many numbers of viruses. Apart from this, frequent power failure, network failures, dead locks and fear of loss of data are inherent maladies in computer usage in banks for which proper safeguards are to be provided.

(g) Economies

Banks invest huge amount of money in computerization. The least they expect is a sizable reduction in the consumption of papers and other stationeries, thus reducing a sizable amount of money and economizing the cost. In the banking industry is more important factor as the business itself depends on maintaining the accounts of the customers.

Factors Relating to Service Quality (SERVQUAL)

The SERVQUAL method is a technique that can be used for performing a gap analysis of an organization's service quality performance against customer service quality needs.

SERVQUAL is an empirically derived method that may be used by a service-based organization to improve service quality. The method involves developing an understanding of target customers' perceived service needs and measuring their perceptions of service quality for the organization. The resulting gap analysis may then be used as a driver for service quality improvement.

SERVQUAL takes into account customers' perceptions of relative importance of service attributes, allowing an organization to prioritize and to direct resources at improving the most critical.

The methodology was originally based around 5 key dimensions:

(i) *Tangibles:* Appearance of physical facilities, equipment, personnel, and communication materials;

(ii) *Reliability:* Ability to perform the promised service dependably and accurately;

(iii) *Assurance:* Knowledge and courtesy of employees and their ability to convey trust and confidence;

(iv) *Empathy:* The caring, individualized attention the firm provides its customers. This has been modified later to cover a few more parameters[2]:

(v) *Responsiveness:* Willingness to help customers and provide prompt service.

SECTION II

Review of Related Studies

The present study attempts to examine the customer satisfaction and the quality of work life in the selected public and private sector banks operating in the urban areas of Coimbatore District. As found in the literature the introduction of new technology has resulted in stiff competition which in turn has led to the changes in the expectations of the customers on the services provided. Hence, an examination of the available literature in the areas of 'Technology (adoption) in Banks' and 'Service Quality and the Customer Satisfaction in banks' become essential. In the present chapter such an attempt is being made. The service quality of banks in developed countries like USA, UK and European countries is different from the service quality provisions of the Indian banking industry this may be due to the dual ownership namely, public and private sector banks, the differences in the technology absorption in banks and the above all the control of Reserve Bank of India. Similarly, the standard of living, the socio economic back ground of the customers is also different. These differences are expected to lead to differences in the service provision, and the opinion of the customers on the service provided. Hence, in the present chapter a review of the available studies is provided in terms of the foreign studies and Indian studies separately. However, this would also help to make methodological improvement in the present project.

Similarly, the introduction of new technologies in business brings about a change in the work environment of the bank staff. Hence, an understanding of the changes in the 'Quality of Work Life' becomes pertinent. Hence, in the present chapter it is attempted to provide a sketch on the literature available in the areas of: (1) technology in banks; (2) customer satisfaction in Banks; and (3) Quality of Work Life.

Technology in Banks

Desikan R.S.[1] discussed about the strategic use of IT for the banking industry. He suggested that moving into technological advancement is useful for cost reduction, differentiation of products and services from those of competitors, niche marketing, diversification and finally acceptance of greater risk. He also suggested that at most care should be taken by the policy makers for individual banks in evaluating proper options for selecting a strategy, which in the long run works to their advantage.

Shroff F.T[2] in his article stated the technological developments taking place in recent times and need for information technology in imparting better and effective service to customers. He has made an attempt to give an overview about present as well as the information technology in future. He also emphasized various benefits of information technology usage to banks.

K.C. Chowdhury[3] attempted to study selective problems which arise due to implementation of information technology in banks such as problems of computerization, standardization of software, infrastructure and power supply. He stated that customer wanted banking facilities to come to is office/house and banks have realized that the traditional hours of operation within the branch do not satisfy customers. Therefore banks have started electronic delivery systems such as ATM, Tele Banking, Credit Cards, Debit Cards and Smart Cards.

Doreswamy S.[4] discussed in his article Technology in Banking: Trends and implication about changes which are happening in banking industry with the introduction of information technology. He also discussed threats as well as opportunities to the banks in future. He concluded that in the emerging competitive environment, customer expectations and the imperative need for toning up operational efficiency to lead to better bottom in, banks have hardly an alternative.

G. Kathria[5] highlighted in his article Technology imperatives in banks the factors that drive the banks to upgrade technology such as liberalization new players in the market, customers growing expectations, house keeping problems and increased need to faster communication. He also stated that average numbers of clients served in India today is around two crores and inter branch entries are more than 50,000 per day. He also highlighted various benefits of computerization from customers' point of view and from bankers' point of view.

Ashish Sen[6] in his article Role of technology in banking highlighted that use of modern technology is being increasingly seen as an essential ingredient not only of good customer service, but also of a good house keeping. He also stated that Public Sector Banks are far behind in the usage of modern technology but Foreign Banks and newly established Private Sector Banks are fairly advanced in the use of technology and their customers are enjoying number of additional benefits He also explained various inter branch connectivity systems used in India and satellite based communication channels.

Bhide M.G.[7] revealed that customer expectations are changing. So banks are under pressure to offer today, what the customer would be excepting tomorrow. Information technology plays a major role in satisfying the future needs of the customer. He also stated that ATM, PC banking, internet banking, electronic delivery channel, MICR, BANKNET have cut down cost and increased the productivity of the banks. He concluded by saying that service institutions like banks have to evolve and implement strategies in fulfillment of their mission.

Girish Vaidya and Preetha Sundaram[8] in their article they highlighted that the world has never been more reliant on technology, which is increasing with the growing use of internet, electronic commerce and various banking innovations. Evolution of technology is taking place at an enormous pace and the approach to automation in banking must have an element of healthy 'Opportunism'. They also stated that a rigid approach could be non- functional and an excessively flexible approach result in loss of control over the strategy. They concluded by saying that technology if properly implemented after due strategy considerations provided a level playing field in a global environment.

Godse V.T.[9] in his article stated that the Indian banks have little choice were technology is concerned. He also stated that cross-selling of products is the only major strategy for survival of retail banking. He concluded that the Indian banks need to go in for IT policies commensurate with individual requirements, but keeping in view the standard of the competitive world.

Kamath R.J.[10] in his article Office Automation in India Banks revealed that computerization in banks in India has come to stay. By now many banks have gone ahead with their branch computerization activities. However the real benefit of computerization has not passed on to the customers. He also stated that office automation will help to speed up the services to the customers. Besides to this top management of banks will also be immensely assisted by MIS to take decisions fast.

Nandan K.[11] stated in his article that in the changed environment of aggressive competition, for competitive edge, banks have to exploit the capabilities of information technology. He also stated that in the changed environment modern technology have to be used to sustain consistent growth. In the modern market economy each player should have Unique Selling Proposition (USP) and technology is a great facilitator of this. Traditional banks have to face variety of challenges in absorbing technology such as re-deployment of excess manpower, hardware and software issues. The importance of computerized MIS in banks in various areas of operation is also stressed in the article.

Prabhu A.G.[12] in his article stated that the banking technology environment in India is not homogeneous with three distinct segment comprising foreign banks, public sector banks and new private sector banks. Depending upon their business goals and technology levels they would need to adopt both offensive and defensive Information Technology (IT) Strategies. He also stated that banks also need to be aware of the effect of technology choices and the skill sets needed to be implemented in technology are other areas which should engage their attention.

Ganti Subramanyam[13] in his article pointed out that more and more non-banks have gradually started giving banking functions. Financial liberalization, internationalization and technological advancement are going to further add to banks woes in their struggle to survive and thrive. Therefore he stated that Life Cycle banking in general and Relationship Banking in particular can provide the necessary anchor for banks to continuously leverage their position into restoring their banking role. He concluded by saying that banks need to rehear their distribution system to changing customer preferences.

Nandan M.[14] in his article stated that banking industry is facing number of challenges such as increased competition, improving, profitability, exceeding customer expectations and improving employees' productivity. He concluded that to face the above challenges it is mandatory for the banks to equip themselves with information technology tools that help the banks to respond positively, efficiently and confidently.

Jani Saainen[15] made a study with the objectives of analyzing how the new developments in Information Technology have affected banking services and methods particularly payment methods and also its implications for the bank customers. Questionnaire survey is carried out and questionnaires were sent to 100 respondents, 50 in Sweden and 50 in Finland. Some of the findings of the study are banking customers have received quite well the new payment methods and services. Credit cards, for instance, have been popular ones among customers, because of the ease of use in doing businesses. More over he also found out that in case of ATMs, customers have perceived this new service pretty well in both Sweden and Finland, where the amount of satisfied customer is bigger than the amount of unsatisfied ones.

Rangarajan[16] stated that deregulation and liberalization in the financial sector have stimulated financial innovation. He pointed out that banks are moving towards inter branch and intra bank connectivity and he concluded that IT is no longer considered as mere transaction processing or confined to MIS. IT should be used for product delivery, managing productivity, product design and to satisfy customer needs.

Rawani A.M. and M.P. Gupta[17] in their study found that public sector banks perceive the reason of IT application as to fulfill RBI/Government norms, where as majority of the respondents from foreign sector banks believe that IT application is need of the business. They also revealed that on all issues such as the management involvement, users involvement, users satisfaction, alignment of business with Information System, Public sector banks are lagging whereas foreign banks are leading. They concluded that there is a strong need to pay proper attention to these issues so as to survive in the changing IT led competitive environment.

Gupta M P and Rohet Sareen[18] in their study identified the key attributes of electronic money and its use by customers through a survey. The major findings shows that consumers still have a major mental block about payment on line, which they feel as insecure. Nearly equal number of customers said that they were ready for e-payment or that they were not ready for e-payment, corporations on the other hand were more positively inclined towards e-payment. A simple majority of respondents felt that e-payment could help in checking frauds and majority of the respondents were of the view that the Government must subsidize the e-payment infrastructure. They have concluded that electronic money systems are still in the relatively early stages of development and the timing of many future developments is likely to be slower than some people expect, for there are many obstacles to growth.

Hirve A.K. and P.K.Kulkarni[19] in their article analyzed that information technology has revolutionized the functioning of banks and financial institutions in the world over. They identified that any planning exercises for technology up gradation in banks needs to be customer centric due to service orientations. They addressed emerging issues because of technology up gradation such as internal process of banking operations not being in line with customers changing needs, lack of recognition of cost/ benefit aspect of technology investment, increasing incidence of vigilance cases, security concerns of IT and lack of organizational preparedness.

Karti Kerem and Tallinn[20] studied consumer behaviour and critical success factors in adoption of electronic banking in Estonia. He revealed that most important aspect in choosing internet bank for all client group was ease of use followed by functionality and easiness of finding information overall satisfaction with the service is high and the only aspect that was criticized is price level. He also observed further that the important factors discouraging the use of internet banking are lack of internet access and not having a chance to try out internet banking in the safe environment. He concluded that banks have to contribute to improve internet access and user skills by skills by participating in training projects and supporting public internet access points.

Rawani A.M. and M.P.Gupta[21] in their study made an empirical study to find out the role of Information Systems (IS) in public and private sector banks operating in India. 27 Public sector banks, 34 private sector banks and 43 foreign sector banks were taken as sample. Mean difference and chi—square test were employed to find out the role of IS in the banking sector. It is concluded that IS plays a supportive role in public sector banks and strategic role in private and foreign sector banks and the future impact of IS does not vary significantly with the banking groups.

Vepa Kamesam[22] discussed in his article about various initiatives undertaken by the RBI in IT field such as magnetic Ink Character Recognition (MICR) based cheque, Electronic Clearance Service (ECS), Security Settlement System (SSS), and Real Time Gross Settlement System (RTGS). She also advised bank to introduce computerization and keep internal software ready to speed up the banking services.

Kalpana Arora[23] pointed out that liberalization; deregulation and globalization have brought in a completely new operating environment to the banks. Emergence of new public sector, private sector and foreign sector banks on the scenario has made survival tough and challenging. She stated therefore that technology has a definitive role in facilitating transactions in the banking sector. Technology implementations have brought new banking products and services. She concluded that banks should implement information technology to achieve bank goals and not for the sake of technology adoption or because everybody else is doing it.

Lakshmi Prasad Padhy[24] stated that without large scale and sophisticated application of information technology, banking just cannot keep pace with the on going changes in the various sectors of economy. He concluded that information technology determines banks overall profitability, operational efficiency and competitive edge.

Sanjay S. Gaur, K.Abdul Waheed, Avish J. Kuzhimattathil and Ashish Mahajan[25] discussed the general IT adoption characteristics in Indian Banking and financial Institutions (BFSI) such as different kinds of IT delivery channels usage, operating systems, data bases usage and networking status during March-June 2002. This paper highlighted the benefits and hindrances/inhibitors of IT adoption and level of satisfaction of IT enabled business processes in Indian BFSI.

Shastri R.V. [26] in his article stated that liberalization policy and intense competition keeps every banker on his toes. Implementation of Information Technology (IT) helps for maintaining proper accounts especially in decision making process. He also stated that facilities like ATM, anywhere banking, Internet and mobile banking have imported customer service which in turn helps for better customer relations management. He also explained the challenges faced by banks because of IT implementation like employment problem and security concerns. He suggested that the customer delight is the primary goal of all future IT initiatives.

Anu Anna Thomas[27] in her article revealed that technology has changed the face of banking sector. It is helping the banks to ease cost pressure, improve quality and be competitive. While discussing about objectives of IT investment in banking she stated that it is to offer services to customer which will bring convenience and value to customer, retaining existing customer and to increase customer base. She also stated that the prudent technology investment decision is one which brings positive return on technology investment. According to her the major IT competitive edges in banks are improved distribution, enhanced operational efficiency, better management of risks and efficient payment system.

Prabhakar Rao Ch[28] in his article discussed about the revolutionary changes that witnessed in the financial sector around the world. He stated that net worked branches. ATMs, technology based payment and settlement system, technology vision of RBI, floating rate of interest have changed the Indian banking sector. He concluded that brick and mortar bank branches will disappear and customers will be able to operate their accounts through electronic devices.

Dharmalingam Venugopal[29] in his article revealed that after nationalization of banks, the banking activity has increased by leaps and bounds. They have introduced number of LIT oriented services to the customers. He also stated that to remain competitive, banks have to adopt core banking system which provides inter linkage between branches. He concluded that while formulating a technology policy, the banks should consider the vision of five to ten years and technology which is compatible to Base II norms.

Gulati V.P.[30] told that private sector banks have attained 100% computerization. Most of the public sector banks are also moving towards 100 per cent computerization. He stated that computerization is customer friendly. To attain customer-friendliness enterprise-wide automation must be aimed. He suggested that enterprise-wide automation will make customer as customer of a bank not branch. He suggested to develop separate software to the rural branches. He disagrees with the statement that technology is causing depersonalization. He emphasized that both brick and mortar type of banking and automation based banking should go together.

Pooja Malhotra and Balwinder Singh[31] stated that internet banking as a new delivery channel is receiving a great attention in the banking industry. This article describes the current state and future prospects of internet banking in India they concluded that the market of internet banking is still untapped.

Rabi N.Mishra[32] told that computerization in banking operation improves customer service, speed, efficiency and it reduces the transaction cost, meets the growing competition, and improves the quality of MIS. He also stated that improved facilities in banks have not reached beyond middle-class. He suggested that IT services to be introduced in the rural areas also. He observed that main constraint in the extension of It services to the rural area has been the non-availability of infrastructure. He concluded that complete withering away of brick and mortar banking may be a myth or may be at least, not the best interest of customer service.

Rajashekarr K.S. [33] stated that the new era in banking has started on account of information technology. He also stated that banking sector has undergone several changes with innovations like on-line banking, telephone banking, e-banking, internet, ATM and universal banking. He observed that the bank employees and customers of banking organization are not well aware of new technology on account of techno-phobia. So, he suggested that banks have to organize customer awareness programme and proper training should be given to the employees of banking organization. He concluded that much research should be carried out in the issues of techno-phobia, security, varied and new type of employment, opportunity cost of new technology customer awareness drive and the problem of training.

Customer Satisfaction in Banks

Rajagopal.S.[34] in his article discussed about the emerging competitive environment and increasing awareness have raised the expectation steeply among bank customers and demanding services like convenience banking, anywhere any time, any how banking (AAAB). He also observed some welcome developments like improvements in infrastructure, development in technology, changes in work culture and new provisions in legal framework. He concluded that with these positive trends, the Indian banking industry is poised to catch up with the rest of the world in the use of information technology.

Shetty J.V. [35] observed in his article that very soon the banks in India will be rated on the basis of their customer service. He also stated that successful bank of the future will be the one that excels in customer service and provides a range of services and products and does a continuous exercise in improving its potential to serve better.

One of the most systematic research programmes in service quality was conducted by Parasuraman, Berry and Zeithmal[36]. They developed a conceptual model on the "Service Quality Gap" which has received the maximum attention in the literature. It had been defined in terms of the measurement framework of "perception–minus-expectations". They had noted that the service quality is a relative measure and depends directly on expectations and performance.

Gronross[37] in his study emphasized that the service sector has captured significant interest in the attempt to identify factors that affect customer satisfaction. The main contention is that a satisfied customer is more likely to be loyal and be a long term client of the service providers. Relationship marketing argues that for a firm to be profitable, it must be attentive to those factors that affect satisfaction.

According to Bill Rossello[38] banks are becoming detached from the very customers they want to serve better, in the process of using the new technologies, satisfaction, building long-term relationship, and improve product and processes. High customer-care performers do several things which include dealing successfully with the common challenges to all customer service operations.

The need for bank technologies is to give customer service representatives and other contact employees a single, integrated information access point to all customer information to reduce customer response times, commented Ken Long[39]

According to Paul Calendrillo[40] retail banking industry face the problem of maintaining customer loyalty and tryst while at the same time they should push the sales process forward to help in satisfying all their customers' financial needs. The author emphasized that the trust can be built only by learning their customer's savings plan, financial goals, and about their planning to achieve them. When the banks try to sell non-traditional products and services, all employees have to redefine their rules as problem solvers.

Richord Koonce [41] has stated that banks are guilty of treating customers like commodities and as the cost of acquiring new customer is high, all banks should try tom retain the existing customers with proper service. Customer satisfaction and customer service are related terms but not the same thing. If a great deal of money and time are spent on improving customer service with little or no positive impact on customer satisfaction, the expenditure is wasteful observed Biff Motley. The author emphasized that the outcome of such expenses should be customer satisfaction for which customer services is a mean or a strategy. Sometimes customer service are very well thought out, based upon a detail understating of what customers expect, and supported with great resources and management attention. These are usually successful because they are very well focused. Often, however, such strategies are risky because they involve change.

Banks today provide choices and options to meet the needs to customers and community in its best way, by providing more services to enhance their reputation by means of personal touch said Brian Nixon[42].

Quality Customer Service, according to Janet Bigham Bernstel[43], is at present, moving as close as possible to the idea of one to one marketing, while the old fashioned service has been redefined to meet the modern world. The latest concept in banking is "Customer Relationship Management", whose crucial component is on a one-to-one marketing approach which ensures reshaping the way, business looks at products and people. The need to develop a system of holistic banking with a customer focus, through customer centric relationship has been stressed. The use of on-line banking for supporting customer service has been suggested.

The authors (Hille & Erik) [44] have observed that efficient and long term marketing can be achieved by focussing on present customers, instead of attracting the new ones. A prerequisite for banks to retain the present customers is to make them satisfied customers by establishing a long-term customer relationship and by offering the quality of service as perceived by the customers.

Tulley[45] found that the banks customers wanted a truly integrated relationship with their bankers. In early 1997, the Royal Bank of Canada conducted a gap analysis to identify the areas of its customers' relationship strategy that required greater focus. It was found that bank clients really wanted a banking relationship in which they were well understood, their needs were anticipated, and their business was valued—no matter where, when or how they interacted with their financial institutions.

An article by Thorsten Hennig-Thurau, Kevin P. Gwinner and Dwayne D. Gremler[46] integrates the two concepts of by positioning customer satisfaction and commitment as relationship quality dimensions that partially mediate the relationship between three relational benefits (confidence benefits, social benefits, and special treatment benefits) and the two out-come variables. The results provide support for the model and indicate that the concepts of customer satisfaction, commitment, confidence benefits, and social benefits serve to significantly contribute to relationship marketing out-comes in services.

Shanthi Saravane[47] had made a maiden attempt to examine the issues relating to delivery of customer services in Indian banks and provided an empirical analysis on the relationship between bank employees, job behaviour and its relationship with bank services delivery. She had found that lack of job motivation and lack of freedom at branch level, poor leadership qualities that prevailed among bank managers, job insecurity etc. have resulted in poor quality customer services in Indian banks.

Gupta[48] had described the working of consumer service centers, setup after 1985 in metro branches of Indian public sector banks. He also expressed that the main purpose of consumer service centers was to reduce delays in customer service delivery and improve administrative efficiency between banks.

Velankar[49] has in his paper stressed the importance of customer service in banks. He observed that different types of customers like rural, urban, metropolitan or corporate customers, pensioners have different expectations. Long term business relationships between bankers and customers service including retention of existing customers, encouragement of an efficient and responsive system for bank employees in order to promote time norms for certain common services etc. were suggested. It was also observed that the cost of retaining existing customers by bankers is cheaper than the cost of acquiring new customers when appropriate customer profiles for existing customer are maintained by banks. To him, the customer service included in its orbit courtesy, promptness, employee attitude, physical facilities, customer identification and recognition, speed, clarity and communication skills etc.

Puttaswamiah[50] in his book on "Customer Service in Canara Bank, Indicators of Measurement", has stated that the objectives of his study are to review and evaluate the performance of Canara bank in general and the customer service in particular and to identify and develop a set of parameters to review and evaluate the branches/Division/ Circles of the Bank in their service to customers. The author has evolved the indicators for measuring customer service on two broad categories namely macro indicators and micro indicators. Macro indicators are further subdivided into micro units. He also made an attempt to evaluate, to what extent the recommendation of Goiporia committee has been implemented in Canara bank.

To Shankar[51], customers need changes frequently due to competition. The customers' universe is vast, diverse and complex as never fully comprehensible. He concluded that the ability of an organization is to transform itself into a fine Belgian mirror that reflects the customers every need, mood and emotion and translating that input into a distinct long term marketing advantage.

Customer Services in Banks

Gadkari[52] had reviewed the general problems faced by bank

customers in India and also reviewed the working of customers' service centers. He had concluded that 'lack of awareness about bank customer service centers had made them a much under-utilization service'. He had also mentioned that a large number of customers complaint related to non-sanctioning of bank loans and irregularities in handling the loan cases by bankers have all highly correlated with the poor services and the poor performance of the banks.

Prabhakar[53] had analysed the nature and range of customer services provided by Indian banks. He had brought out the fact that in case of Indian Banks, "a major portion of complaints are from depositors—with the mass banking practice, a differential treatment is neither possible nor, permitted. The possibilities of dividing customers may be of some better service to important customers. The teller system partially serves this purpose". He had found that in India, there was a growing size of current and savings account holders who did not maintain the statutorily required minimum balances. Thus, the size of defaulters was high and growing, which caused additional work to bankers.

Ram Kumar[54] in his research paper had argued that the staff's impersonal and indifferent attitude was responsible for the poor quality of bank services in India. He had also pointed out that in India "people in general are still ignorant of bank facilities like, loans, advances, remittances, lockers, payment and collection which can indeed save time and effort in their day-to-day life.

Sushila Singhal's[55] study has identified about customer services in Indian Banks. The most important finding of this study was that the service quality of the private sector banks was better than the public sector banks. The private sector banks offer more services than the public sector banks and the infrastructure of the private sector banks are found top be better than the pubic sector banks.

A proper mix of technology with customer service can help the organization in a better way said Evan Mannakee[56]. A primary challenge for banks today is learning how to become financial advisors for customers rather than simply selling them products. Hence, the challenge for the banking industry is to more specifically anticipate customer needs and to actively position the products and services that will meet growing customer needs.

According to Patrick[57] banks are now moving to market themselves as quality service providers. He argues that improved internal marketing, training and customer service has erased many of the old problems and the customers have noticed the difference with customer service becoming a strategic imperative for the company. The improvised facilities made available to the customers also have a vital contribution to better customer service.

Saraf W.S. [58] in his article stated that the de-regulation of power, liberalization of regulated regime have brought totally a new era in the Indian banking. The competition has also put pressure on the banking to improve customer service and work for image building. He also stated that the following changes to be made like good information system, technology ands skills for decision making, improved customer service and friendly attitudinal pattern of the personnel at all levels to meet the competition.

Sunderesan[59] in his article viewed that Customer, Clerk and the Counter are a triumvirate in the banking industry and they integrate each other for the development of the institution. He also stated that nearly 15 per cent of the metropolitan customers are not satisfied with the services of their banks due to delay in the services. He expressed his grief that the public when using the services rendered by public utility services do not voice their grievances, when they are dissatisfied with the poor quality of services made available to them.

As viewed by Iyer[60] the customer choice and awareness have increased tremendously due to more open economy, the advent of information technology and media revolution and as a consequence hectic competition for resource by banks and non-banks. As the products are the same, the battle ground is service. As front line staff in the banks are the first contact point, they must have a perfect knowledge about the products and services which is highly dependent on proper and adequate training and motivation.

Though 'Service Quality' can be defined in many ways, Aravindhan *et.al.* [61] viewed it as 'Customer Satisfaction' as the definition of Service Quality. This is based on the logic that, measuring customer satisfaction gives a strategic advance in knowing where an organization stands in the market in terms of service quality. It provides an impetus the organization to act and to improve its position in the competitive environment.

According to Arvind Brahme[62] customer complaint is a universal phenomenon, with the banking industry being no exception. Handling of complaints is the core activity for successful development. The author has drawn a clear distinction between verbal and written complaints and found that 68 per cent of the customers are lost due to short comings in Customer Service. The author has quoted the check list given by Denis Walker for health check of the management. He concluded by stressing that there is a need for awareness and positive attitude and approach among the staff to win the customer and to curb growing complaints.

Diane Brady[63] in his study observed that as time goes on, the service gap between top customers and all the rest is wide due to increasingly rare customer service. He concludes by saying that, technology is creating a radical new business model that alters the whole dynamics of customer service.

Rohini Gupta Suri[64] in her study emphasized the need for marketing approach in the banking services. The objectives of her study were: (1) to know the existing services being rendered by the banks; (2) to highlight the problems being faced by the customers; (3) to determine the marketing effectiveness of Banking Services with special references to State Bank of India, Punjab National Bank and United Commercial Bank; (4) to know the complaints of the bank customers with regard to the bank services; and (5) to give suggestions in the light of the modern banking services with a view to making them market oriented/customer oriented. The study concluded that the services available in the bank are not being fully utilized by the customers, the available services are not supplied by the bank employees effectively. Hence, the study suggested for an effective service provision by the bank officials.

Service Quality in Banks

Jai Sharkar Ganesh, Mark J. Arnold and Kristy E. Reynolds[65] have conducted a study with the objectives of examining whether the three groups (Dissatisfied Switchers, Satisfied Switchers and Stayers) of customers differ in their overall satisfaction with the service provided by the current firm, to investigate the role of satisfaction with the various aspects of the service in differentiating among groups and to examine whether the group differ in their involvement with and loyalty behaviour towards the services. 200 respondents were selected for the study. Statistical tools such as correlation matrix, factor analysis, and discriminate analysis were used for analysis. The research finding says that dissatisfied switchers, satisfied switchers ands stayers differ significantly in terms of their satisfaction with the current service provider.

Metta Ongkasuwan and Worasri Tantichattaanon[66] analysed five dimensions of service quality *viz.*, performance, reliability serviceability, features and perceived quality dimensions. A survey using formal questionnaire followed by on site and telephone interview and web site visits is used as a research methodology. All thirteen banks in Thailand are studied and compared using formal questionnaire. It was observed that 31.79 per cent of respondents are aware of Internet banking services in Thailand. The result suggest that Bank of Asia has the highest rate and rank number one in terms of satisfaction on the five basic inquiries service on the internet banking services. It was suggested that all banks should provide 24 hours error free Internet bank services with quality and security to ensure their high level of performance to their customers.

Parimal Vyas[67] in his study analysed customer's satisfaction from the services provided by banks. The study is based on primary sources of customers from private banks, co-operative banks and foreign banks located in Baroda. He emphasized that the time taken to complete the banking transactions by the bank staff the main factor influencing the customer satisfaction.

Jabnoun, N, Al-Tamimi H. [68] developed and tested an instrument measuring service quality in UAE commercial banks based on SERVQUAL. The instrument was based on the five dimensions of SERVQUAL. Unlike SERVQUAL that measures the differences between excepted and perceived service quality, this instrument collected only perceptions data. Factor analysis results in three dimensions namely Human Skills, Tangibles, and Empathy. The three dimensions were reliable and valid. These dimensions were found to explain 67.5 per cent on the variations in overall service quality. The Human skills dimension consists mainly of items that were originally included in the reliability and assurance dimensions. Tangibles consisted of items that belonged originally to the same dimension of tangibles. Finally, the Empathy dimension consisted of items that were part of the two original dimensions of Empathy and Responsiveness. The authors also compared between the importance of the three dimensions and found Human Skills to be the most important.

Kshirsagar[69] opines that with customers demanding more flexible and conveniently situated distribution channels at all times and with technology enabling changes, and paradigm in financial services will shift from fixed locations to mobile shops as it has already taken place in the banking, electricity and telephone sectors.

Mushtaq A.Bhat and A.Gani[70] in their study stated that customers are increasingly aware of alternatives and their expectations are rising. Retaining customers and developing long term relationship is very important. In view of this widespread belief an attempt has been made by them to study service quality in commercial banks. The result lead to the conclusion that quality of foreign banks is comparatively much better than Indian banks and suggested that heavy investment by Indian banks in tangibility dimension to improve the quality of service to the customer.

Pathrose P.P[71] stated that ever escalating customer expectations coupled with widespread deregulation and globalization initiatives and severe competitive forces in the banking sector have added new dimensions to the challenges confronting banks in the areas of product design, product delivery, and pricing. He quoted that "simply catching up to where others have been is necessary to stay in the game, but the winners will be those who have the ability to invent fundamentally new games.

S.B.Singh[72] highlighted in his article that the human needs approach towards higher levels, the requirement of banking products and services also undergo changes leading to innovations. He also stated that marketing stages of Indian banking system can be classified as choice business, walk in business, competitive business, product oriented business and customer oriented business which are in response to basic physiological needs, safety and security needs, social needs, esteem, needs and self actualization needs.

G.S. Shergill and Bing Li[73] have done a study in New Zealand banks about trust and loyalty model. A structural equation model was developed and tested by them for identifying the determinants that influence customers trust and loyalty to I-Banking in New Zealand. They found out that shared value was the most critical factor impacting customers trust in I-Banking, compared with other two important factors called communication and opportunistic behavior control. They concluded that I-Banking needs to take satisfaction, trust, brand reputation and switching cost seriously, especially satisfaction, because it is the most important factor that influences customers' loyalty.

Edwyn Fernandes[74] in his study ascertained factors that influence customer satisfaction of internet banking services. He found that convenience, independence and security are the factors that influence customer satisfaction. To analyze the data he used factor influence customer satisfaction. To analyze the data he used factor analysis ands multiple regression analysis. He found that internet banking in UAE is yet to be properly utilized as a real added value tool to improve customer relationship.

Firdos T.Shroff [75] observed that customers have to wait for along time to avail services in brick and mortar era. But IT has introduced the concept of Universal Banking. He also stated that there can be no end to the variety of services that can be provided through the electronic channel. He also explained various benefits to the customers and to employees on account of internet. He also outlined the legal framework for electronic transactions.

P.T. Kuppuswamy[76] emphasized the need to give account statement very fast, calculation of interest on deposit and advances with zero error and introduction of ATM. He also emphasized the need of creating data base for the customers. He also suggested that to make India as developed in 2020 all the facilities to be created in rural areas. He disagrees that computerization replaced brick and mortar banking. He said that both brick and mortar banking and e-banking should function together.

Purwar A.K. [77] stated that bank has two types of customers, one who expects products and services with world class and on the other hand there are customers who are not comfortable with new technology. He also stated that modern technology to be introduced in rural areas also because rural population is no less techno- savvy than urban people. But he worries about losing of human touch in technology implementation. He stated that information technology reduces the cost of the transaction and it gives comfort to the customers. So, he suggested that both delivery channels to be given to the customers. So, he suggested that both delivery channels to be given to the customers. He concluded that "speed with social interaction" is need of the hour.

Parimal Vyas[78] analyzed the customer satisfaction on Information Technology in Banking Services. The study revealed that private banks and foreign banks have implemented e-banking effectively and nationalized banks were found to have lesser degree of computerization. He has used mean value and mean comparison to find out customer's overall experience in time taken to complete various types of transactions and to compare time taken for completing the transaction based banking services on selected criteria. He emphasized that Information Technology is not a matter of choice but it is a compulsion.

Parimal Vyas [79] the banking environment has become highly competitive, as traditional banking has undergone an absolute transformation. To survive in this competitive e-age and to provide continual customer satisfaction, the bankers are now looking for innovative use, absorption and adoption of Information Technology results into increase in overall profitability, operational efficiency and marketing effectiveness. A customers' satisfaction measurement study based on descriptive research design on the prevalent state of IT adoption among selected branches of sectoral banks located at Baroda was undertaken. The findings of the study revealed that there was effective implementation of e-banking services in case of Private Banks and Foreign banks, whereas, nationalized banks were found to have lesser degree of computerization. Therefore, IT is not a matter of choice but is a compulsion, which needs be harnessed by Indian banks to serve and satisfy the customers.

Rupa Rege Nitsure[80] stated that the biggest challenge that Indian banks face to day is to establish customer intimacy. Computerization certainly helps in identifying customer needs and designing tailor made products. But centralized operations and process automation using core banking application and internet based networks improves efficiency levels. She suggested that core banking system to be introduced to make a customer as customer of a bank rather than the customer of a branch. She also suggested that to maximize the value, our banks need to transform their branches from transaction processing centres into customer-centric service centres. She concluded that the surplus manpower due to automation can be used to advise on and to sell new financial instrument.

Upinder Dhar, Santosh Dhar and Abhinav Jain[81] analyzed in their exploratory study about different service quality factors in the private and public sector banks. They have used 150 respondents for the study and they have used correlation, factor analysis and z-test for analysis. The study revealed that competence, tangibility and record maintenance seems to be typical factors of private sector banks, because these three factor shave been found to be common in terms of the perception of employees and customers of private sector banks. Similarly, tangibility, reliability and access seems to be the typical factors of public sector banks, because these three factors have been found to be common in terms of the perception of employees and customers of public sector banks.

Chaitanya, V. Krishna[82] the customers have become more demanding and prefer innovative products and quality services at faster speed from the companies. This has made the job of financial service company much tougher and challenging, as they need to understand the customers changing needs, offer new products and services and most importantly they have to promote these. Therefore, in the present day context it has become even more important to learn the application of marketing theories of product, providing service quality, distribution and planning for a customer oriented marketing strategy.

Narendra Kumar and Mohan Kumar[83] analyzed the impact of computerization on customer service. Eight parameters were selected for the study. The study was conducted in public sector banks in Haryana and Delhi.460 bank customers were selected for the study. It is evident from the study that the computerization has brought improved customer service in bank branches. They also found that the increase in efficiency was higher in fully computerized bank branches.

Nazral Islam and Ezaz Ahmed[84] analyzed service quality of branch in Dhaka city of Bangladesh 404 bank clients were selected at random from nationalized, private and foreign commercial banks. Factor analysis was done to identify the service quality focus of the bank. In order to explore the relationship with the overall service quality, multiple regression analysis was used. Results show that most important service quality factor of banks is personal attention to the clients followed by error free records, safety in transaction and tangible physical facilities of the bank.

Shajahan S[85] in his study he analysed customer satisfaction on various modes of banking services. He conducted the study with 100 account holders of ICICI bank in Chennai. The study revealed that internet banking increased the level of satisfaction among bank customers. He opined that internet literacy is the major factor underlying online banking penetration in India.

Zillur Rahman[86] in his study measured the services quality of banks in India. He investigated the difference between customers' expectations and perceptions towards the quality of services. The study was conducted using the SERVQUAL instrument. The result indicates that the sample population has perceptual problems with their banking service experiences.

Ashwini K. Aswathi., Balaram Dogra[87] this study in an empirical investigation of service quality dimensions in the competitive service environment of retail banking in India. The results support the multidimensional structure of service quality, a three dimensional model emerges, with two functional quality dimensions and an outcome quality dimension. The findings highlight that industry specific outcome quality dimension for banking services is an important component of service quality in customer's perceptions, in explaining variance in overall service quality and in diagnosing the service shortfalls. The results provide an insight into the perceptions of service quality in retail banking customers, particularly on functional quality components and the outcome quality dimension.

Madhavaiah. C and Durga Rao. S[88] state that the success of any organization depends upon how far they meet the needs and preferences of the customers. Particularly, in the service sector it is more important for the service marketers to understand the service expectations of the customers and meeting them.

Job Satisfaction

Madam and Rajeswar Singh[89] have identified that the leadership quality of bank managers is an important determinant of the quality of services delivered. They had strongly recommended that the appropriate training programmes to be arranged to impart leadership skills and qualities for branch managers in order to motivate bank staff to work effectively.

Saxena[90] in his study had indicated that ignorance, over powering, neglecting colleagues by bank managers is bad, and it leads to low quality of bank services: (1) There are differences between different banks as to employees involvement, morale, attitude towards colleagues and customers; (2) the demographic and psychological variable were identified and their relationship with employees job performance and customer service was explained; and (3) She has also found that there, is no correlation between 'service efficiency' and 'customers satisfaction'.

Raghvan[91] had pointed out that one of the reasons for delays in the delivery of customer services was due to lack of work experience and the long time duration taken by the new recruits to learn the work through on-the-job training. He had recommended a five days week for customers and not to the bank staff.

Bhaskara B.G, T.V. Narasimha Rao and N.S. Viswanath[92] conducted a study with 300 bank customers and 150 bank employees in Bangalore Urban district with the objective of assessing and evaluating the needs of customers and the response of the process or the system, to the customer needs/ services. Chi-square and mean difference were used to test the 10 variables such as attitude, responsiveness, professional, commitment, job knowledge, procedures, infrastructure, technology etc. The study found that there are distinct and significant difference between what is there in practice to what is theoretically expressed at high significance levels. At zero probability level, there is no professional commitment, presence and punctuality in service. The employees perceived to have little knowledge and skill leading to inaccuracy and there is no competitive efficiency in service.

Robert Hall[93] stated that the workforce is the primary factor in influencing customer behaviour. This trend is bound to be welcomed on one hand by the customers and to improve the efficiency of performances by bank employees on the other. However, the 'Command and Control' approach of head quarters, acts as a potent de-motivator for the front-line workforce.

Uniqueness of the Present Study

The bank should find out through surveys what interest clients the best and then make those things available. Then the satisfaction will be much higher.

The studies reviewed above clearly indicated the importance of the customer service quality among the financial institutions. These studies have made use of various parameters to measure the service related variables. It can be noted that these studies could establish their view on service quality in isolation. However, it can not be denied that the level of satisfaction are strongly influenced by the socio-economic back ground of the customers, and non of the studies attempted to identify the extent of influence of these factors on the level of satisfaction on the service quality opinion. This study, apart from analyzing the service quality perception of the customers, would examine the extent of influence of socio-economic background on the satisfaction levels of the customers.

Similarly, there are studies which have attempted to examine the quality of work life of the employees of commercial banks. It can again be noted that these studies could examine the employees' satisfaction on their job. Again in the Indian context it can be noted that the internal factor namely, the work environment namely the internal factor and their socio-economic and demographic status namely the external factors are said to a significant influence on the level of satisfaction on their job. There no studies which attempted to examine the impact of these internal and external factors on the level of jobs satisfaction. The present study has filled this gap by examining the impact of internal and external factors on job satisfaction. In these regard the present project is a maiden attempt and exploratory in character. Through this, the study also contributes to the existing literature.

REFERENCES

1. Desikan R.S., Strategic Alignment of IT Future of Indian Banks, Becon,17th *Bank Economoists Conference*,1994, pp.195-199.
2. Shroff .F.T, Information Technology—A Tool for development, Becon, 17th *Bank Economists Conference*,1994, pp. 177-179.
3. Chowdhury K.C, Teconology in Banking: Problems and Prospects, *Vinimaya Special Issue*, Oct-Dec, 1996, pp. 51-56.
4. Doreswamy.S., Technology in Banking: Trends and Implications, *Vinimaya Special Issue*, Oct–Nov, 1996, pp. 38-44.
5. Kathiria G, Teconology Imperatives in Banks, *Vinimaya Special Issue*, Oct-Dec, 1996, pp. 45-50.
6. Ashish Sen, Role of Technology in Banking, *Vinimaya Special Issue*, pp. 70-74.
7. Bhide.M.G, Information Technology in Banks, *The Journal of Indian Institute of Bankers*, 1997, pp. 149-152.
8. Girish Vaidya and Preetha Sundram, Technology in Banking: A Global Perspective, *The Journal of Indian Institute of Bankers*, Oct-Dec, 1997, pp. 183-189.
9. Godse.V.T,Technology in Banking, *Vinimaya Special Issue*, 1996, pp. 101-105.
10. Kamath. R.J.,Office Automation on Indian Banks, *Vinimaya Special Issue*, 1997, pp. 89-100.
11. Nandan.K, Application of Information Technology in Banks for Competitive Edge, *Vinimaya Special Issue*, 1997, pp. 75-81.
12. Prabhu.A.G, Banking Technology in India: A Few Issues, *Vinimaya Special Issue*, 1997, pp. 83-88.
13. Ganti Subramanya, Banking in the Next Millennium, *Vinimaya Special Issue*, July-Sep, 1998, pp. 15-18.
14. Nandan.M.Nilekani, *Information Technology Strategy, Becon*,1998, pp. 186-189.
15. Jani Saaineen, Information Technology and Developments in the Banking Sector, 2000, www.cio.com..
16. Rangarjan.C., Banking in the High Tech Enviironment Banking and Finance, 2000, April pp. 7-12.
17. Rawani.A.M and M. P.Gupta, Information Technology Initiatives in Indian Banking Sector Paradigm, 2000, Jan-June, pp. 129-143.

18. Gupta.M.P.and Rohet Sareen, A Study of Consumer Concerns and Issues of Electronic Payment in India, *Global Business Review*, Jan,2001, pp. 101-119.

19. Hirve A.K. and Kulkarni P.R., Organizational Preparedness for Implementation of Technology Plans in Indian Banks, *Vinimaya Special Issue*, 2002, Jan-Mar, pp. 18-25.

20. Karti Kereem and Tallinn, Adoption of Electronic Banking: Underlying Consumer Behavior and Critical Success Factors, *Case of Estonia*, www.insofres,com, 2002, pp. 1-12.

21. Rawani A.M. and Gupta.M.P, Role of Information Systems in Banks: An Empirical Studying the Indian Context, *Vikalpa*, Oct-Dec, 2002, pp. 69-74.

22. Vepa Kamesam, Changing Faces of Banking: Banking with Technology Banking Finance, 2002, Jan, pp. 9-12.

23. Kalpana Arora, Indian Banking: Managing Transformation through Information Technology, *IBA Bulletin Special issues*, March, 2003, pp. 134-138.

24. Lakshmi Prasad Padhy, Banking: Challenges and Prospects, *Facts for You*, Feb, 2003, pp. 34-38.

25. Sanjay S.Gaur, Abdul Wheed.K., Avish J. Kuzhimattathil, and Ashish Mahajan, Perceived Benefits and Inhibitors of IT Adoption and Resulting Satisfaction, A Study in Indian BFSI Context, *The ICFAI Journal of Bank Management*, 2003, pp. 83-94.

26. Shastri.R.V., Recent Trends in Banking Industry, IT Emergence, *Charted Financial Analyst*, March, 2003, pp. 45-56.

27. Anu Anna Thomas, Prudent Technology Investment and Its Competitive Lead in the Banking Sector, *Professional Banker*, Aug, 2004, pp. 47-52.

28. Prabhakara Rao.Ch, Indian Banking in 2010: *IBA Bulletin Special Issue*, Jan, 2004, pp. 170-173.

29. Dharmalingam Venugopal, Technology in Banks, Some Thoughts for the Future, *Professional Banker*, 2004, Aug. pp. 30-32.

30. Gulati.V.P. Technology in Banks, *Professional Banker*, Aug, 2004, pp. 22-25.

31. Pooja Malhotra and Balwinder Singh, Internet Banking in India, *The Management Accountant*, Vol. 39, Nov, 2004, pp. 890-896.

32. Rabri N. Mishra, Technology in Banks, *Professional Banker*, Aug pp. 26-28.

33. Rajashekara.K.S (2004), Application of Information Technology in Banking, *Southern Economist*, Vol. 43, May, 2004, pp. 9-12.

34. Rajagoapal.S, Vision 2000 for Indian Banking: Demands and Challenges, *Vinimaya Special Issue*, Oct-Dec, 1996, pp.57-63.

35. Shetty.J.V. Customer Service in Banks, *Vinimaya Special Issue*, 1996, pp. 5-9.

36. Parasuraman, A, Berry, L. and Zeithmal, V.L., "A Conceptual Model of Service Quality and Its Implications for Future Research", *Journal of Marketing*, 1985, pp. 41-50.

37. Gronross, C. "Relationship Approach to Marketing in Service Context: The Marketing and Organizational Behaviour Interface", *Journal of Business Research*, Vol. 20, 1990, pp. 3-11.

38. Bill Rossello, "Customer Service Superstars", American Bankers Association, *ABA Banking Journal, New York*, Vol. 89, (10), October 1997, pp. 96-104.

39. Ken Long, "Quality of Customer Service Depends on Streamlined Access to Data", *Bank Systems and Technology, New York*, Vol.34 (10), October, 1997, pp. 66-67.

40. Paul Calendrillo, "Making the Customer More Right", *Bank Marketing*, Washington, Vol. 29, (5), May 1997, pp. 20-25.

41. Richord Koonce, "Do You Put Your Customers Through Hell?", *Bank Marketing, Washington*, Vol. 30 (2), February 1998, pp. 18-19.

42. Brain Nixon, "Community Banks and Customer Service", Community Banks and Customer Service", *Community Banker*, Washington, Vol. 9 (10), Oct.2000, pp. 8-19.

43. Janet Bigham Bernstel, "Is the Customer Stupid", *Bank Marketing*, Washington, Vol. 32 (11), Nov. 2000, pp. 14-20.

44. Hille, Erik "The 10 Rules for Evaluating An e-Mail Management Solution", and Customer Interaction Solutions: Nor Walk: Vol. 19, Issue 8, February 2001, pp. 50-54.

45. Tulley, John. "Establishing Unique Customer Relationship Using Data Warehousing", *The Canadian Manager*, Vol.26 (1), Spring 2001, pp. 12-13.

46. Thorsten Hennig-Thurau, Kevin P. Gwinner and Dwayne D. Gremler, Understanding Relationship Marketing Outcomes: An Integration of Relational Benefits and Relationship Quality, *Journal of Service Research*, Vol. 4, No. 3, 2002, 230-247.

47. Shanthi Saravane, Customers Service in Banks", 1984.
48. Gupta, D.C. "Commercial Banks and Customer Service", *Times of India*, January 25, 1987.
49. R.D.Velankar, "Customer Service—A Perspective", Becon, *17th Bank Economist Conference*, 1994, pp. 145-51.
50. Puttaswamiah, K. "Customer Service in Canara Bank, Indicators for Measurement", *Customer Service Section*, PD & GA Wing, Bangalore, 1996.
51. G. Shankar, "Total Customer Orientation: New Life Style", *Industrial Economists*, August 30 – September 14, 1999, p. 46.
52. S.Gadkari, "Problems of Bank Customers in India, *SBI Monthly Review*, January, 1985.
53. Prabhakara.S., An Insight into Service Attributes in Banking Sector, *Journal of Service Research* April-Sep, 2003, pp. 157-169.
54. Ram Kumar, E.R., "Banking- Services Without Smile", *Times of India*, January 8, 1987.
55. Sushila Singhal, Banks and Customers: A Behavioural Analysis", Shri Ram Centre for Industrial Relations and Human Resources, New Delhi, 1987, pp. 233.
56. Evan Mannakee, "Customer-focussed Technology Improved This Bank's Business", *Marketing News, Chicago*, Vol. 31 (23), Nov.10, 1997, pp. 14-15.
57. Patrick, Barrett, "Banks Lend an Ear to Service", Marketing, London, January 16, 1997, pp. 16-17.
58. Saraf.W.S.,Banking Technology: Agenda Ahead, *The Journal of Indian Institute of Bankers*, 1997, pp. 153-162.
59. Sunderesan, P.S. "Customer, Clerk and the Counter", *IBA Bulletin*, June 1997, pp. 24-27.
60. S.R.Iyer, "Customer Focus and Product Development", Towards Sound and Strong Banking", Becon-98, 1998, pp. 190-93.
61. Aravindhan, P. and Punniyamoorthy, M. Service Quality Model to Measure Customer Satisfaction" in Raghavachari, M. and Ramani K.V. (eds.) *Delivering Service Quality*", Macmillan Indian Ltd. New Delhi, 2000, pp. 104-10.
62. Arvind Brahme, "Customer Complaints', *Vinimaya*, Vol. XXI, (2), 2000-01, pp. 13-21.
63. Diane Brady, With Bureau Reports, "Why Service Stinks" *Business Week, New York*, Industrial/Technology Edition, Issue 3704, October 23, 2002, pp. 118-28.

64. Rohin Gupta Suri, "Services Marketing", Ammal Publications Pvt., Ltd., New Delhi, 2002.

65. Jai Shankar Ganesh, Mark J.Arnold and Krishty E.Reynolds, Understanding the Customer Base of Services Providers: An Examination of the Difference Between Switchers and Stayers, *Journal of Marketing*, July, 2000, pp. 65-87.

66. Metta Ongkasuwan Worasri Tantichattanon A Comparative Study of Internet Banking in Thailand, www.hot.or.th.com, 2002, pp. 1-18.

67. Parimal Vyas, Measurement of Customer Satisfaction: A Study of Banking Services Business Perspectives Jan-June Vol. 4, 2002, pp. 73-78.

68. Jabnoun N and Al-Tamimi H, Measureing Perceived Service Quality at UAE Commercial Banks, International *Journal of Quality and Reliability Management*, Vol. 20, No. 4, 2003, pp. 458-472.

69. Kshirsagar S.D., "Financial Services in India: A new Perspective", *Management Review*, June, 2003, pp. 37-44.

70. Mushtaq A.Bhat and Gani.A, Service Quality in Commercial Banks: A Comparative Study Paradigm, Jan-June, 2003, pp. 24-36.

71. Pathrose. P.P., Product Development and Marketing in Banks, *IBA Bulletin* Feb, pp. 2003, 32-34.

72. Singh.S.B, Marketing of Bank Services in India; An Integrated Approach, *Vinimaya Special issue*, Oct-Dec, 2003, pp. 26-33.

73. Shergill. G.S. and Bring Li, Internet Banking: An Emprical Investigation of a Trust and Loyalty Model for New Zealand Banks, www.konganpage.com pp., 2003,1-22.

74. Edwyn Fernades, Internet Banking: An Empirical Investigation into the Extent of Adoption by Banks and the Determinants of Customer Satisfaction in the UAE, www.arraudev.com, 2004, pp. 1-18.

75. Firdos T.Shroff, Impact of Technology on Banking: *IBA Bulletin Special Issue*, Jan, 2004, pp. 174-181.

76. Kuppuswamy. P.T., Technology in Banks: *Professional Banker*, 2004, Aug pp. 6-13.

77. Purwar. A.K., Technology in Banks, *Professional Banker*, Aug 2004, pp. 14-21.

78. Parimal Vyas, Measurement of Customer Satisfaction on Information Technology Adoption in Banking Services, PMJR, April –Oct, 2004, pp. 7-16.

79. Parimal Vyas, "Measurement of Customer Satisfaction on Information Technology Adoption in Banking Services", *Prestige Journal of Management and Research*, Vol. 8, No. 1-2, April-October, 2004.

80. Rupa Rega Nisture, Technology in banks, *Professional Banker*, Aug, 2004, pp. 28-32.,

81. Upinder Dhar,Santosh Dhar and Abninav Jain, Service with a Difference: A Comparative Analysis of Private and Public Sector Banks, *PMJR*, April, 2004, pp. 17-43.

82. Chaitanya, V. Krishna, "Metamorphosis of Marketing Financial Services in India", *Journal of Services Research*, Volume 5, Number 1 April-Sept., 2005, pp. 155-169.

83. Narendra Kumar and Mohan Kumar, A Study on Impact of Computerization on Customer Service, *South Asian Journal of Management*, March, 2005, pp. 20, 28.

84. Nazrral Isalam and Ezaz Ahmed, A Measurement of Ccustomer Service Quality of Banks in Dharka City of Bangladesh, *South Asian Journal of Management*, Jan–March, 2005, pp. 37-55.

85. Shajahan.S., A Study on the Level of Customers Satisfaction on Various Modes of Banking Services in India, *The ICFAI Jouranl of Bank Management*, Vol. IV, Feb, 2005, pp. 79-85.

86. Zillur Rahman, Service Quality : Gaps in the Indian Banking Industry: *ICFAI Journal of Marketing Management*, Vol. IV, Feb, 2005, pp. 37-47.

87. Ashwini K. Ashwathi and Balaram Dogra, "Measuring Service Quality in Banks An Assessment of Service Quality Dimensions" *Conference on Global competitiveness* IIM, Kozhikode, March 24-25, 2006,

88. Madhavaiah. C., and Durga Rao., "Effective Measurement of Customer Service in Banks", *Banking Finance*, Vol. XIX, No. 11, November, 2006 .

89. Madam and Rajeswar, Leadership Qualities among Bank Mangers, *SBI Monthly Review*, January, 1985.

90. Saxena, K.K. "Evaluation of Bank Marketing in India", *SBI Monthly Review*, January 1985, pp. 3-11.

91. Raghavan, R. "Customer Service and 5-Day Week", *Economic Times*, March 19, 1986, p. 5.

92. Bhaskara, B.G., Narishmmha, T.V. and Viswanath, N.S, Service Quality Management in Indian Banks,: Opportunities and Challenges, *South Economist*, 2000, pp. 11-15.

93. Robert Hall, "Restoring the Workforce to the Customer Equation", *Bank Marketing, Washington*, Vol. 33, (3), April 2001, pp. 14-15.

3 Development of Indian Banking Industry, Customer Satisfaction and Human Resources in Indian Banking Industry

Introduction

In the earlier chapter it was discussed that the banking industry constitutes the hub of economic development. The role of banking industry has transformed from the role of catalyst to a role of change agent. Hence, the progress of banking sector determines greatly the progress of the economy. Therefore, to contribute effectively for the growth of the economy, an improved performance of growth of the banking sector becomes a pre requisite. However, the advent of globalization has posed threat to the Indian banking industry and hence, for the purpose of survival providing services to the expectations and satisfaction of the customers has come to the forefront. This requires a qualitative and quantitative improvement in the banking industry and with human resources constituting the major input, improvement in the human resources increases the ability to provide better bank product and services. In the present chapter it is attempted to examine the progress of banking in the Indian context, the meaning of customer satisfaction in the context of banking industry and the human resource development in Indian banking industry are also discussed.

Developments in Indian Banking

On the eve of independence, Indian banking have inherited 2876 branches, serving an average population of 82000 with Rs. 860 cores deposits and Rs. 760 cores advances along with the responsibility of recuperating the war torn economy and unemployment.

Growth of Banking System in India

In order to understand present make up of banking sector in India and its past progress, it deserves to look at its development in a longer historical perspective. The past four decades and particularly the last decades witnessed cataclysmic change in the face of commercial banking all over the world. Indian banking system has also followed the same trend.

In over five decades since independence, banking system in India has passed through five distinct phase namely: (1) Evolutionary phase (prior to 1950); (2) Foundation phase (1950-1968); (3) Expansion phase (1968-1984); (4) Consolidation phase (1984-1990); and (5) Reformatory phase (since 1990).

Evolutionary Phase (Prior to 1950)

Enactment of the RBI Act gave birth to scheduled banks in India. The prominent among the scheduled banks is the Allahabad Bank, which was set up in 1865, with European management. The first bank which was established with Indian ownership and management was the Oudh Commercial Bank, formed in 1881, followed by the Ayodhya Bank in 1884, the Punjab National Bank in 1894 and Nedungadi Bank in 1899. Thus, there were five Banks in existence in the 19th century. During the period 1901-1914 twelve more banks were established, prominent among which were the Bank of Baroda (1906) the Canara Bank (1906) the Indian Bank (1907) the Bank of India(1908) and Central Bank of India (1911).

Thus the five big banks of today had come into being prior to the Commencement of the First World War, in 1913, and also in 1929 the Indian Bank faced serious crises. Several banks succumbed to these crises. Public confidence in banks received a jolt. There was a heavy rush on banks. An important point to be noted here is that no commercial bank was established during the First World War, while as many as twenty scheduled banks came into existence after independence—two in the public sector and one in the private sector. United Bank of India was formed in 1950 by the merger of four existing commercial banks. Certain non-scheduled banks were included in the second schedule of the Reserve Bank. In view these facts, the number of Scheduled banks rose to 81. Out of 81 Indian scheduled banks, as many as 23 were liquidated or merged into or amalgamated with other scheduled banks in 1968 leaving 58 Indian schedule banks.

Banking system in India came to be recognized in the beginning of 20th century as powerful instrument to influence the pace and pattern of economic development of the country. In 1921 need was felt to have a State Bank gifted with all support and resources of the Government with a view to helping industries and banking facilities to grow in all parts of the country. It is towards the accomplishment of this objective that the three Presidency Bank were amalgamated to form the Imperial Bank of India. The role of the Imperial bank was envisaged as to extend banking facilities, and to render the money resources of India more accessible to the trade and industry of this country, thereby promoting financial system which is an indisputable condition of the social and economic advancement of India.

Until 1935, when RBI came into existence to play the role of Central Bank of the country and regulatory authority for the banks, Imperial Bank of India played the role of a quasi central bank. It was by making it the sole repository of all its funds and when desired by it, the Government tried to influence the base of deposits and hence credit creation by Imperial Bank and by rest of the banking system.

Thus, the role of commercial banks in India remained confined to providing vehicle for the community's savings and attending to the credit needs of only certain selected and limited segments of the economy. Bank's operations were influenced primarily by commercial principle and not by developmental factor. Failure of banks was common as governance in privately owned joint stock banks left much to be desired.

Foundation Phase (1948-1968)

In those initial days, the need of the hour was to reorganize and to consolidate the prevailing banking network keeping in view the requirements of the economy. The first step taken to that end was the enactment of the Banking Companies Act, 1949 followed by rapid industrial finance. The role played by banks was instrumental behind industrialization with the impetus given to both heavy and small-scale industries. Subsequently after the adoption of social control, banks started taking steps in extending credit to agriculture and small borrowers. Finally on July 1969, 14 banks were nationalized with a view to extending credit to all segments of the economy and also to mitigate regional imbalances. Thus, the period of regulated growth from 1950 till bank nationalization witnessed a number of far-reaching changes in the banking system.

The banking scenario prevalent in the country during the period 1948-1968 presented a strong focus on class banking on security rather than purpose.

Expansion Phase (1968-1984)

The motto of bank nationalization was to make banking

services reach the masses that can be attributed as first banking revolution. Commercial banks acted as vital instruments for this purpose by way of rapid branch expansion, deposits, mobilization and credit creation. The penetration into the rural areas and agenda for geographical expansion in the form of branch expansion continued. The second dose of nationalization of 6 more commercial banks on April 15, 1980 further widened the phase of the public sector banks and therefore banks were to implement all the government sponsored programmes and change their attitude favour of social banking which was given the highest priority.

This phase witnessed socialization of banking in 1968. Commercial banks were viewed as agents of change and social control on banks. However, inadequacy of social control soon became apparent because all banks except the SBI and its seven associate banks were in the private sector and could not be influenced to serve social interests. Therefore, banks were nationalized (14 banks in 1969 and 6 banks in 1980) in order to control the heights of the economy in forming with national policy and objectives. This period saw the birth and the growth of what is now termed as directed lending by banks. It also saw commercial banking spreading to far and wide areas in the country with great pace during which a number of poverty alleviation and employment generating schemes were sought o be implemented through commercial banks. Thus, this period was characterized by the death of private banking and the dominance of social banking over commercial banking. It has realized that banks were organizations with social responsibilities but not social organizations. This period also witnessed the birth of Regional Rural Bank (RRBs) in 1975 and NABARAD in 1982 which had priority sector as their focus of activity.

Although the number of commercial banks has declined from 281 in 1968 to 68 in 1984, the number of scheduled banks shot up from 71 to 264 during the corresponding period, number of non-scheduled banks having registered perceptible decline from 210 to 4 during the period under reference. The rise in the number of scheduled banks was as stated above due to the emergence of RRBs.

The fifteen years following the banks' nationalization in 1969 were dominated by the banks expansion at path breaking pace. As many as 50000 bank branches were set up; three-fourths of these branches were opened in rural and semi urban areas. Thus, during this period a distinct transformation of far reaching significance occurred in the Indian banking system as it assumed a broad mass base and emerged as an important instrument of socio-economic changes. Thus, with growth came inefficiency and loss of control over widely spread offices. Moreover, retail lending to more risk prone areas at concessional interest rates has raised costs, affected the quality of assets of banks and put their profitability under strain. The competitive efficiency of the bank was at low ebb. Customer service became least available commodity. Performance of a bank/banker began to be measured merely in terms of growth of deposits, advances and other such targets and quality became a casualty.

Consolidation Phase (1985-1990)

A realization of the above weaknesses thrust the banking sector into the phase of consolidation. This phase began in 1985 when a series of policy initiatives were taken with the objectives of consolidating the gains of branch expansion undertaken by the banks, and of relaxing albeit marginally, the very tight regulation under which the system was operating. Although number of schedule banks increased from 264 in 1984 to 276 in 1990, branch expansion of the banks slowed down. Hardly 700 branches were set up during this period. For the first time, serious attention was paid to improving housekeeping, customer services, credit management, staff productivity and profitability of the banks and concrete steps were taken during this period rationalize the rates of bank deposits and lending. Measures were initiated to reduce the structural constraints which were then inhibiting the development of money market.

By this time about 90 per cent of commercial banks were in the public sector and closely regulated in all its facets. Prices of assets and liability were fixed by the RBI prices of service were fixed uniformly by the Indian Banking Association (IBA) composition of assets was also some what fixed in as much as 63.5 per cent of bank funds were mopped up by CRR and SLR and the remained was directed towards priority sector lending and small loaning; salary structure was negotiated by the IBA and validated by the Government. Thus, there was no autonomy in vital decisions. Commercial approach in operations and drive towards efficiency was almost non-existent. The result was that during this period, the banks ended up consolidating their losses rather than the gains.

Reformatory Phase (1991 and Onwards)

Indian banking system has been subject to widespread structural reforms initiated since June 1991. This phase can be regarded as second banking revolution. Reform measures such as introduction of new accounting and prudential norms, liberalization measures etc., are heading towards a truly competitive and well structured banking system resilient from an international perspective.

Continued financial profligacy of the government coupled with close monitoring and control rendered the financial system completely dependent and inefficient so much so that by the year 1991, the situation was ripe for drastic reforms. It was precipitated by the unprecedented economic crisis which engulfed the economy in 1991, for the first time in its history; India faced the problem of defaulting on its international commitments. The access to external commercial credit market was completely denied,

International credit rating had been downgraded and the international financial community's confidence in India's ability to manage its economy and had been severally eroded. The economy suffered from serious inflationary pressures, emerging scarcities of essential commodities and breakdown of fiscal discipline.

The government took swift action to restore international confidence in the economy and redress the imbalances. Various macro economic structural reformatory measures were undertaken in the field of foreign trade, tax system, industrial policy and financial and other sectors. The objective was to improve the underlying strength of the economy attempt to ensure against future crises and further the fundamental developmental objectives of growth with equity and self reliance.

Hence, Indian banking system has been subject widespread structural reforms initiated in June 1991. This phase can be regarded as second banking revolution. Reform measures such as introduction of new accounting and prudential norms, liberalization measures etc., are heading towards a truly competitive and well structured banking system resilient from an international perspective. These have spurred the dynamics of Indian banking sector in the entire field. The annual growth of branch expansion during 1990-2000 was 1.1 per cent. The population served per branch was 15000 as at March end 2000. During 1999-2000, the annual average growth rates of deposits and credit were 16.1 per cent and 14.8 per cent respectively. During 1990s, the growth of investments was 20.0 per cent as compared to 1.0 per cent during 1985-1990 and 18.8 per cent during 1980-85. The net profit of banking system grew by more from Rs. 55.33 corers as at March end 1990 to 7306.36 corers as at March end 2000.

Significance of Service Quality in Banks

Service quality has been described as a form of attitude related but not equivalent to satisfaction that results from the comparison of exceptions with performance. Quality in financial services has gained paramount importance by the increasing marketing profile of bank branch operations over time. The thrust on efficient customer service has increased manifold with the onset of competition from private players and the initiation of banking sector reforms in India since early 1990's (Narshimam Committee). The deregulation in Indian banking sector has resulted in reducing structural barriers to competition in domestic markets by abolishing interest rate ceiling on deposits and lending by financial intermediaries. Markets are now open to foreign competitor. Improved information technology has led to low cost, instantaneous communication and electronic fund transfers. This has further led to the integration of international markets. Moreover, due to increase in awareness and literacy ratio, the customer of today has come more learned about the risks, costs and return associated with various financial services. As consequences of all these changes, banks, one of the pioneer and premier financial institutions have had to face the brunt of intense competition both from their counterparts and several other upcoming privately owned finical institutions. The banks have now diversified into insurance, broking, advisory service, merchant banking and factoring and almost every other legitimate financial activity. In order to survive in the present day world of competition, the banks will have to formulate marketing strategies in a way to woo the customer towards them. Service delivery and customer delight is probably one of the most debatable issues gripping the banking industry in our country. Quality in financial services sector has gained paramount importance by the increasing marketing profile of bank branch operations over time. The thrust on efficient customer service has increased manifold with on onset of competition from private players and intimation of banking reforms in India since early 1990s.

Service is an invisible offering which is dependent on and inseparable from the person who extends it. Services in

Indian Banks are mostly branch based in the public sector banks, while the foreign banks are making strides into full scale technology enabled banking. Banking services constitute a hybrid type of offering that consists of both tangible goods like loan schemes, interest rate paid, kinds of accounts and the tangible services like behavior and efficient of the staff speed of transactions and ambience. Though, the commercial banks implement the marketing concept by the simultaneous use of internal marketing from company to employee, external marketing from company to customers and interactive marketing from employees to customers.

Human Resource Restructuring

Human resource management policy is need of the hour. The concept of human resource development audit is very important and can play a useful role in the banking industry. It is necessary to install HRM audit unit in banks to tune with corporate planning and strategies to assess the efficiency. Considering the above, Summantras Ghosal of London Business School described these elements in human capital, which are as under:

(1) *Intellectual Capital:* It consists, specialized knowledge, tacit knowledge of skills and learning capacity;

(2) *Social Capital:* For a company social capital is needed to achieve its goals. Its elements are network of relationship, sociability and trust worthiness;

(3) *Emotional Capital:* Specialized knowledge and a great network of friends are not enough to get things done. Individual and companies are also need emotional capital. It should have self confidence, ambition, courage and risk taking ability.

Effective Management of Human Resource

HRM policy should be thoroughly positive, motivating and transparent that should make every employee feel that they are the part of organization as well as decision-making process. Acknowledgement of updating activities and imperative need for management development in banks should be appreciated as there a gap between actual performance and potential performance. Moreover, existing HRM polices o the banks give preference to seniority over the skills in the promotion process and also there is no placement policy for skilled personnel. These policies create hindrance for effective skill development in banks. Hence, maintain the health of banking industry, skilled personnel with potential must be priority. It is necessary to establish the required infrastructure for an effective HRM that leads to higher economic growth rate and tremendous rise in productivity and efficiently in the globalize age.

Human beings are like raw materials and they re molded in to valuable assets when they are trained properly to increase their knowledge and skills. There should be seriousness and key philosophy about developing people. With the intensifying of competition market volatility and risks associated with it, the banks need a new breed of personnel, which has to be recruited, and or existing employees trained and re skilled to cope with the increasing demands in the changing business environment.

4 Service Utilization of Sample Customers of Commercial Banks
An Analysis

Introduction

Based on the logic extended in Chapter I, in the present chapter it is attempted to examine the customers' level of utilization of the services provided by the commercial banks. The reason behind making such an analysis is that the level of satisfaction of the customers on the services provided has been greatly determined by the extent of service utilization and eventual this determines the profitability and the performance of the banks. More specifically, a customer those utilize a large number of services in the banks, frequently and form a concrete idea about the level of satisfaction on the services of the bank. A customer who is highly satisfied with the services of the banks becomes a loyal customer of his bank and propagates for his bank. In a competitive banking environment this in turn increases the number of customers of the bank and eventually positively influences the performance and profitability of the bank.

However, in this context, it can also be noted that the level of satisfaction has been greatly influenced by the socio-economic status of the customers. This is because, as it has been empirically verified in the area of marketing on the customers' preference for goods and services, the differences in the socio-economic status leads to differences in the customers expectations and choice of preference for goods and services. Hence, before making an analysis of the customers' level of utilization of the services of their banks, it becomes essential to understand the socio economic status of the sample customers and the present chapter is directed towards this end.

To discuss these issues, the present chapter has been divided into two sections. Section I deals with the socio-economic status of the sample respondents. In Section II, the customers' service utilization has been discussed.

SECTION I

Customer Socio-economic Status: An Analysis of Customers' Profile

As discussed earlier, the socio-economic status of the customers plays a deterministic role in determining the level of satisfaction on the services provided. Hence, in the present section it is attempted to discuss the socio economic and demographic profile of the sample customers of sample public and private sector banks of the urban areas of Coimbatore District.

Distribution of Respondents by Age

As it could be seen in Table 4.1, among the 500 customer respondents selected, 34.60 per cent are in the age group of 35-45 years. Another 29.60 per cent respondents fall in the age group 25-35 years. There are 18.40 per cent respondents who fall in the age group of 45-55 years, while 11.80 per cent form the age category of below 25 years. The remaining 5.60 per cent of the sample respondents constitute the age group of above 55 years.

Table 4.1: The Distribution of Respondents by Age

Sl. No.	Distribution of Age	No. of Respondents	Percentage
1.	Below 25	59	11.80
2.	25-35	148	29.60
3.	35-45	173	34.60
4.	45-55	92	18.40
5.	Above 55	28	5.60
	Total	**500**	**100.00**

Source: Computed from Primary Data.

Thus from the analysis it can be concluded that a majority of the sample respondents fall in the age group of 35-45 years.

Distribution of Respondents by Sex

As given in Table 4.2, among the sample respondents, 60.20 per cent constitute males, while the remaining 39.80 per cent are female respondents.

Table 4.2: The Distribution of Respondents By Sex

Sl. No.	Distribution of Sex	No. of Respondents	Percentage
1.	Male	301	60.20
2.	Female	199	39.80
	Total	**500**	**100**

Source: Computed from Primary Data.

Thus from the analysis it can be concluded that a majority of the respondents are males.

Distribution of Respondents by Level of Monthly Income

As given in Table 4.3, 59 per cent of the sample respondents are graduates. Another 18.20 per cent of the respondents are Post Graduates. There are 12.60 per cent respondents who have completed their PUC/HSC. While 6.80 per cent respondents have obtained their Professional qualification, the remaining 3.40 per cent have no education.

Table 4.3: The Distribution of Respondents by Level of Monthly Income

Sl. No.	Distribution Income (in Rs.)	No. of Respondents	Percentage
1.	No formal Education	17	3.40
2.	PUC/HSC.	63	12.60
3.	Graduate	295	59.00
4.	Post Graduate	91	18.20
5.	Professional Qualification	34	6.80
	Total	**500**	**100**

Source: Computed from Primary Data.

Thus from the analysis it can be concluded that a majority of the sample respondents are graduates.

Distribution of Respondents by Level of Income of the Family

As it could be seen in Table 4.4, 47.40 per cent of the sample respondents have a family monthly income of Rs. 5000-10000. Another 28.60 per cent of the respondents have a monthly income of Rs. 10000-15000. There are 10.60 per cent respondents who have a monthly income of below Rs. 5000. While 10.20 per cent respondents earn an income level of Rs. 15000-20000 per month, the remaining 4.20 per cent earns an income of above Rs. 20000.

Thus from the analysis it can be concluded that a majority of the sample respondents have a monthly income of Rs. 10, 000-15,000.

Table 4.4: The Distribution of Respondents by Level of Family Income

Sl. No.	Distribution Income (in Rs.)	No. of Respondents	Percentage
1.	Below 5000	53	10.60
2.	5000-10000	237	47.40
3.	10000-15000	143	28.60
4.	15000-20000	51	10.20
5.	Above 20000	16	3.20
	Total	**500**	**100.00**

Source: Computed from Primary Data

Distribution of Respondents by Status of Occupation

It is evident from the table (see Table 4.5) that among the sample respondents selected businessmen account for 56.80 per cent while private sector employees form 29 per cent. Another 6.40 per cent are public sector employees. The next highest share in the occupational category is 'professionals' This category includes Professors, doctors, engineers,

Table 4.5: The Distribution Of Respondents by Occupational Status

Sl. No.	Distribution Income (in Rs.)	No. of Respondents	Percentage
1.	Public Sector Employees	32	6.40
2.	Professionals	28	5.60
3.	Private Sector employees	145	29.00
4.	Businessmen	284	56.80
5.	Self-employed	11	2.20
	Total	**500**	**100**

Source: Computed from Primary Data.

advocates and auditors. This forms 5.60 per cent of the total sample employee respondents. The remaining 2.20 per cent constitutes self employed.

Thus from the analysis it can be concluded that a majority of the sample respondents are businessmen.

SECTION II

Level of Service Utilsation of Customers in Sample Public and Private Sector Banks: An Examination

The above section provided a discussion on the socio economic profile of the 500 sample customer respondents. In the present section it is attempted to discuss the service utilization of the customers in their sample banks.

Distribution of Respondents by Type of Account Holdings

The paragraph given below discusses the type of account holdings of the 500 sample customers.

Table 4.6: The Distribution of Respondents by Type of Account Holdings

Sl. No.	Income (in Rs.)	No. of Samples	Percentage
1.	Savings A/C	284	56.80
2.	Current A/C	91	18.20
3.	Recurring Deposit A/C	91	18.20
4.	Fixed Deposit A/C	22	4.40
5.	NRI Deposit	12	2.40
	Total	**500**	**100.00**

Source: Computed from Primary Data

As it is given in Table 4.6, 56.80 per cent of the respondents maintain savings account with their banks.

Another 18.20 per cent of the respondents hold either current account or recurring deposit account in their bank. Fixed Deposit holders constitute 4.40 per cent of the respondents and the remaining 2.40 per of the respondents are NRI deposit holders.

Thus from the analysis it can be concluded that a majority of the respondents are savings account holder.

Distribution of Respondents by Years of Customership

The discussion given below provides a detailed discussion on the on the years of customership of the sample respondents in their banks. This analysis becomes essential as this constitutes the base for understanding the types of services provided and the extent of service utilization.

Table 4.7: The Distribution of Respondents by Years of Customership

Sl. No.	Customership in Years	No. of Samples	Percentage
1.	Less than One Year	31	6.20
2.	1-3 years	54	10.80
3.	4-5 years	179	35.80
4.	6-10 years	194	38.80
5.	11-15 years	16	3.20
6.	Above 15 years	26	5.20
	Total	**500**	**100.00**

Source: Computed from Primary Data.

As seen in Table 4.7, as high as 38.80 per cent of the respondents have their customership in their banks for 6-10 years. This has been closely followed by the respondents (35.80 per cent) who have 4-5 years of customership. There are 6.20 per cent of the respondents who have been the customers of their banks for less than one year and 5.20 per cent of the respondents are the customers of their banks for above 15 years. Another 10.80 per cent of the respondents happen to be the customers of their banks for 1-3 years. The remaining 3.20 per cent of the respondents happen to the customers of their banks for 11-15 years.

Thus from the analysis it can be concluded that a majority of the respondents are customers of the bank for the past 6-10 years.

Distribution of Respondents by Reason for Becoming Customer of the Sample Public and Private Sector Banks

As given in Table 4.8, among the various reasons for the respondents to open an account in a particular bank, 22.80 per cent of the sample respondents maintain their account for their better services provided. Another 14.80 per cent maintain their account in their present bank as it is nearest to their houses. There are 14.60 per cent who use the services

Table 4.8: Distribution of Respondents by Reason for Becoming Customer of the Bank

Sl. No.	Reason	No. of Samples	Percentage
1.	Nearest to House	74	14.80
2.	Nearest to Office	63	12.60
3.	Workplace Compulsion	24	4.80
4.	Familiarity	18	3.60
5.	Better Service	114	22.80
6.	Availability of Various Schemes	69	13.80
7.	Computerized Environment	73	14.60
8.	Cheap and Quick Service	65	13.00
	Total	**500**	**100.00**

Source: Computed from Primary Data.

of their banks for the computerized service provision Another 12.60 per cent respondents maintain their account in the present bank for the reason that it is nearest to their office. While there are 13.80 per cent respondents who maintain their account in the bank for the provision of wide category of services and schemes, 13 per cent utilize the services of the present bank for the cheap and quick services provided. While 4.80 per cent of the respondents avail the services of the banks due the work place compulsion, the remaining 3.60 per cent have opened their account due the familiarity of their bank.

Thus from the analysis it can be concluded that a majority of the respondents maintain their account for the better services provided.

Distribution of Respondents by Source of Awareness About Their Banks

The paragraph given below discusses the various sources through which the 500 sample respondents have acquired knowledge on their banks.

Table 4.9: The Distribution of Respondents by Source of Awareness

Sl. No.	Source	No. of Samples	Percentage
1.	Personal Knowledge	39	7.80
2.	Friends	173	34.60
3.	Relatives	101	20.20
4.	Business Circle	62	12.40
5.	New Paper and Magazines	65	13.00
6.	Radio/TV	53	10.60
7.	Internet	7	1.40
	Total	**500**	**100.00**

Source: Computed from Primary Data.

A close perusal of the data provided in Table 4.9 would indicate that as high as 34.60 per cent of the respondents have come to known of their banks through their friends. Another 20.20 per cent of the respondents have come to know of their present bank through their relatives. There are 13 per cent of the respondents who have come to know of the banks through newspapers, while 10.60 understand about the existence of their banks through radio/TV. Another 7.80 have come to know of their banks from their personal knowledge the remaining 1.40 per cent of the sample respondents have come to know of their banks through the knowledge from Internet.

Thus from the analysis it can be concluded that a majority of the respondents have come to know of their banks through friends.

Distribution of Respondents by Frequency of Operation

The frequency of usage of the services provided has a direct impingement on the opinion on the services provided and

Table 4.10: Distribution of Respondents by Frequency of Operation

Sl. No.	Frequency	No. of Samples	Percentage
1.	Daily	35	7.00
2.	Once in Alternate Days	76	15.20
3.	Once in a Week	147	29.40
4.	Twice in a week	74	14.80
5.	Once in a fortnight	51	10.20
6.	Once in a month	93	18.60
7.	As and when required	22	4.40
8.	Others	2	0.40
	Total	**500**	**100**

Source: Computed from Primary Data.

hence in the present paragraph it is attempted to examine the frequency of usage of facilities.

As given in Table 4.10, to as high as 29.40 per cent of the respondents, the frequency of operation stood highest with once in a week. Another 18.60 per cent of the respondents operate their account once in every month. There are 15.20 per cent of the respondents who have their account operated for once in alternative days. Another 14.80 12.60 per cent of the customers operate their account twice a week. While 10.20 per cent operate their account once in a fortnight, seven percent operate daily. There are 4.40 per cent of the respondents operate their account as and when needed, the remaining negligible portion of 0.40 per cent operates their accounts on seasons.

Thus from the analysis it can be conduced that a majority of the respondents operate their accounts once in a week.

Distribution of Respondents by Purpose of Visting Bank

The paragraph below discusses the 500 sample customers' purpose of visiting the banks.

As it could be seen in Table 4.11, a highest of 37.40 per cent of the respondents visits their banks to withdraw cash. This has closely been followed by the reason 'to make deposit'. For this purpose, as high as 18.60 per cent of the respondents visit their banks. There are 14.80 per cent of the respondents who visit their banks to deposit their cheques. While nine per cent of the respondents visit their banks to avail loans, 7.60 per cent visit the banks to take draft. There are 5.80 per cent of the respondents, who visit their banks to make enquiries, the remaining 2.40 per cent of the respondents visit their banks to get account statement.

Thus from the analysis it can be concluded that a majority of the respondents visit their banks to withdraw cash.

Table 4.11: The Distribution of Respondents by Major Purpose of Visiting Bank

Sl. No.	Reason	No. of Samples	Percentage
1.	To withdraw cash	187	37.40
2.	To make deposit	93	18.60
3.	To submit cheque	74	14.80
4.	To credit the proceeds	45	9.00
5.	To avail loan	29	5.80
6.	To make enquires	22	4.40
7.	To take Draft	38	7.60
8.	To get Account Statement	12	2.40
	Total	**500**	**100.00**

Source: Computed from Primary Data.

Respondents by Opinion on Time Taken by Banks to Make Deposits and Payments

The discussion given below provides a detailed idea on the time taken in the bank for payment and deposits of the 500 sample respondents.

Table 4.12: Distribution of Respondents by Opinion on Time taken to Make Deposits and Payments

Sl. No.	Duration	No. of Samples	Percentage
1.	Below 5 minutes	22	4.40
2.	5-10 minutes	59	11.80
3.	10-15 minutes	247	49.40
4.	Above 15 minutes	172	34.40
	Total	**500**	**100.00**

Source: Computed from Primary Data.

The time taken to provide a particular service by a bank employee constitutes a vital factor in determining the levels of satisfaction of the customers. Hence, in the present paragraph it is attempted to discuss the time taken to provide the major services of the banks namely, accepting deposits and making payments.

As given in Table 4.12, 49.40 per cent of the respondents felt that that it takes 10-15 minutes for an employee to provide the required service of the customer. Another 34.40 per cent viewed that it takes 15 minutes and above to provide the expected service. Nearly 11.80 per cent of the respondents felt that the bank employee takes 5-10 minutes to provide service expected. The remaining 4.40 per cent viewed that it takes less than five minutes for the employee to provide their services.

Thus from the analysis it can be concluded that according to a majority of the respondents it takes 10-15 minutes to provide the services of accepting deposits or making payments.

Respondents by Opinion on the Local Cheques Submitted for Realisation

The paragraph given below provides the opinion of the customers on the nature of cheques submitted to their banks for realization.

Table 4.13: Distribution of Respondents by Opinion on the Local Cheques Submitted for Realisation

Sl. No.	Duration	No. of Samples	Percentage
1.	Submitted	387	77.40
2.	Never Submitted	113	22.60
	Total	**500**	**100.00**

Source: Computed from Primary Data.

As it could be viewed in Table 4.13, among the sample respondents 77.40 per cent use to submit cheques for clearing regularly. The remaining 22.60 per cent do not use to submit cheques.

Thus from the analysis it can be concluded that to a majority of the respondents have utilized the facility of clearing the local cheques.

Respondents by Opinion on Time Taken to Realise Local Cheques

Table 4.14: Distribution of Respondents by Opinion on Time Taken to Realise Local Cheques

Sl. No.	Duration	No. of Samples	Percentage
1.	In One Day	15	3.88
2.	In Two Days	87	22.48
3.	In Five Days	173	44.70
4.	More than Five Days	112	28.94
	Total	**387**	**100.00**

Source: Computed from Primary Data.

Issue of cheque books in time expected by the customer is another important service expected to be provided by the banks. This also affects the customer satisfaction on the banking services.

As seen in Table 4.13, there are around 77.40 per cent of the respondents who avail the cheque services. It can also be seen in Table 4.14, among them, as high as 44.70 per cent viewed that it takes generally five days to get realized a local cheque. According to another 28.94 per cent it takes them two days to get the cheque amount credited. For 22.48 per cent of the respondents, the banks take two days to credit the cheque amount. Just for 3.88 per cent of the respondents it takes less than a day for the bank to get the cheque credited.

Thus from the analysis it can be concluded that to a majority of the respondents, it takes atleast five days to get their cheque amount realized.

Respondents by Opinion on the Outstation Cheques Submitted for Realisation

The paragraph given below provides the opinion of the customers on the nature of outstation cheques submitted to their banks for realization.

Table 4.15: Distribution of Respondents by Opinion on the Local Cheques Submitted for Realisation

Sl. No.	Duration	No. of Samples	Percentage
1.	Submitted	314	62.80
2.	Never Submitted	186	37.20
	Total	**500**	**100.00**

Source: Computed from Primary Data.

As it could be viewed in Table 4.15, 62.80 per cent use to submit their cheques regularly for clearing. The remaining 37.20 per cent never use to submit any outstation cheques for clearing.

Thus from the analysis it can be concluded that to a majority of the respondents utilize the facility of clearing the outstation cheques.

Respondents by Opinion on Time Taken to Realise Outstation Cheques

Clearing of outstation cheques in time is another important expected service of customers. The speed with which the cheques are cleared constitute an important factor that determines the level of satisfaction of the customers.

As in Table 4.16, there are around 38.54 per cent respondents who viewed that their outstation cheques are cleared within three days. There are 34.39 per cent respondents who viewed that their outstation cheques are cleared within two days. While to 16.56 per cent per cent respondent, the outstation cheques are cleared within five days, for the remaining 10.51 per cent the outstation cheques are said to be cleared in more than five days.

Table 4.16: Distribution of Respondents by Opinion on Time Taken to Credit Cheque Amount in Account

Sl. No.	Duration	No. of Samples	Percentage
1.	In two days	108	34.39
2.	In three Days	121	38.54
3.	In Five Days	52	16.56
4.	More than Five Days	33	10.51
	Total	**314**	**100.00**

Source: Computed from Primary Data.

Thus from the analysis it can be concluded that according to a majority of the sample respondents, it takes atleast three days for their banks to clear their outstation cheques.

Respondents by Opinion on Nature of Reminder Received in Advance on the Maturity of Deposits and Others

The discussion provided below gives a detailed idea on the opinion of the 500 sample customer respondents on the nature of reminder received in advance on the maturity of deposits and other account information.

As provided in Table 4.17, according to 76.40 per cent of the respondents, they do not receive any intimation from their banks on the maturity of their deposits and response to other doubts and grievances. While the remaining 23.60 per cent of the respondents viewed that they get reminders and other feed back letters for their accounts, maturity of deposits and letters that require a feedback.

Table 4.17: Distribution of Respondents by Opinion on Nature of Reminder Received in Advance on the Maturity of Deposits and Others

Sl. No.	Description	No. of Samples	Percentage
1.	Received Reminder	118	23.60
2.	Do not Receive Reminder	382	76.40
	Total	**500**	**100.00**

Source: Computed from Primary Data.

Thus from the analysis it can be concluded that according to a majority of the respondents their banks did not send any reminders for the maturity of their deposits or to any other related matters.

Respondents by Usage of ATM Facility

The discussion given below provides the number of sample respondents who have an ATM facility.

Table 4.18: Distribution of Respondents by Usage of ATM Facility

Sl. No.	Nature	No. of Samples	Percentage
1.	Yes	184	36.80
2.	No	316	63.20
	Total	**500**	**100.00**

Source: Computed from Primary Data.

As it could be seen in Table 4.18, of the 500 respondents only 36.80 per cent use the ATM facility while the remaining 63.20 per cent do not have.

Thus from the analysis it can be concluded that a majority of the respondents do not have ATM facility.

Respondents by Frequency of Usage of ATM Facility

The discussion given below provides an idea on the usage of available ATM facility.

As it could be seen in Table 4.19, as high as 40.22 per cent of the respondents use their ATM card once in every 15 days. Another 25 per cent of the respondents use their cards once in a week. 23.91 per cent of respondents they use their ATM cards every day. While 6.52 per cent of the respondents use their card once in a month, just 4.35 per cent of the respondents use the ATM card every day.

Table 4.19: Distribution of Respondents by Frequency of Usage of ATM Facility

Sl. No.	Frequency	No. of Samples	Percentage
1.	Every Day	44	23.91
2.	Once in a Week	46	25.00
3.	Once in Every 15 Days	74	40.22
4.	Once in a Month	12	6.52
5.	As and when required	8	4.35
	Total	**184**	**100.00**

Source: Computed from Primary Data.

Thus from the analysis it can be concluded that a majority of the respondents use their cards once in every 15 days.

Respondents by Usage of e Banking Facility

The proceeding paragraph provides the usage of e Banking facility by the sample customers.

As given in Table 4.20, a highest of 60.20 per cent of the respondents are not using the e-banking facilities. The remaining 39.80 per cent of the respondents use the e Banking facilities.

Table 4.20: Distribution of Respondents by Usage of e Banking Facility

Sl. No.	Reason	No. of Samples	Percentage
1.	Using	199	39.80
2.	Not Using	301	60.20
	Total	**500**	**100.00**

Source: Computed from Primary Data.

Thus from the analysis it can be concluded that a majority of the respondents are either not using the e Banking facility or it is not available.

Respondents by Frequency of Usage of e Banking Facility

The paragraph given below provides a discussion on the usage of e Banking facility by the sample respondents.

Table 4.21: Distribution of Respondents by Frequency of Usage of e Banking Facility

Sl. No.	Frequency	No. of Samples	Percentage
1.	Every Day	67	33.67
2.	Once in a Week	38	19.10
3.	Once in Every 15 Days	63	31.66
4.	Once in a Month	12	6.03
5.	As and when required	19	9.55
	Total	**199**	**100**

Source: Computed from Primary Data.

A close perusal of the data given in Table 4.21 would indicate that as high as 33.67 per cent of the respondents use their e Banking facility every day. Another 31.66 per cent each of the respondents use their e banking facility once in a every 15 days. There are 19.10 per cent of the respondents who use the facility once in a week.. While 9.55 per cent of the respondents use the e banking facilities as and when they require, the remaining 6.03 per cent use the e Banking services once in a month.

Thus from the analysis it can be concluded that a majority of the respondents use the e banking facilities every day.

Respondents by Usage of Credit Card Facility

The proceeding paragraph provides the usage of e Banking facility by the sample customers.

Table 4.22: Distribution of Respondents by Usage of Credit Card Facility

Sl. No.	Reason	No. of Samples	Percentage
1.	Using	212	42.40
2.	Not Using	288	57.60
	Total	**500**	**100.00**

Source: Computed from Primary Data.

As given in Table 4.22, a highest of 57.60 per cent of the respondents are not using the Credit card facility. The remaining 42.40 per cent of the respondents are using the credit card facility.

Thus from the analysis it can be concluded that a majority of the respondents are not using the credit card facility.

Respondents by Frequency of Usage of Credit Card Facility

In the paragraph given below provides a detailed discussion on the frequency of usage of credit card facilities by the sample respondents.

A close perusal of the data given in Table 4.23 indicates that a highest of 33.49 per cent of the respondents use the credit card facility once in a month. Another 24.53 per cent of the respondents use their credit cards once in a week. There are 19.81 per cent of the respondents who use their credit cards every day. While 13.68 per cent of the respondents use their credit cards once in every 15 days, 8.49 per cent of the respondents use their cards as and when required.

Table 4.23: Distribution of Respondents by Frequency of Usage of Credit Card Facility

Sl. No.	Frequency	No. of Samples	Percentage
1.	Every Day	42	19.81
2.	Once in a Week	52	24.53
3.	Once in Every 15 Days	29	13.68
4.	Once in a Month	71	33.49
5.	As and when required	18	8.49
	Total	**212**	**100.00**

Source: Computed from Primary Data.

Thus from the analysis it can be concluded that a majority of the respondents use their credit card facility once in a month.

Respondents by Frequency of Usage of Debit Card Facility

The below paragraph discusses in details the frequency of usage of debit card facility by the sample customers.

As it could be noted in Table 4.24, 44.29 per cent of the respondents use their debit cards once in a every 15 days. Another 25.71 per cent of the respondents use their debit cards once in a month. There are 17.14 per cent of the respondents who use their debit cards once in a week. While 7.14 per cent of the respondents use their credit cards once in every day, the remaining 5.71 per cent of the respondents use their debit cards as when they require. It could also be seen in the table, of the 500 respondents, only 70 respondents, that is 14 per cent of the respondents have debit cards.

Table 4.24: Distribution of Respondents by Frequency of Usage of Debit Card Facility

Sl. No.	Frequency	No. of Samples	Percentage
1.	Every Day	5	7.14
2.	Once in a Week	12	17.14
3.	Once in Every 15 Days	31	44.29
4.	Once in a Month	18	25.71
5.	As and when required	4	5.71
	Total	**70**	**100.00**

Source: Computed from Primary Data.

Thus from the analysis it can be concluded that only a minority of the sample respondents use the debit card facilities and the highest duration of usage among the debit card holders is once in every 15 days.

Respondents by Opinion on the Banks Working on Sundays

The discussion provided below gives a detailed discussion on the respondents' opinion on the banks working on Sundays.

Among the various services provided, the making the services to the convenience of the customers is one of the important service that can satisfy the customers to a greater extent. One such way of increasing the working hours is to make the banks to operate on Sunday. This would facilitate the customers to utilize the day effectively as it is a holiday for a majority of the customers including the businessmen. Based on this view, in the present paragraph it is attempted to discuss the opinion of the customers about the working of their banks on Sundays.

Table 4.25: Distribution of Respondents by Opinion on the Banks Working on Sundays

Sl. No.	Frequency	No. of Samples	Percentage
1.	Working	74	14.80
2.	Not Working	426	85.20
	Total	**500**	**100.00**

Source: Computed from Primary Data.

As it could be seen in Table 4.25, according to 85.20 per cent of the respondents their banks are not working on Sundays, while according to the remaining 14.80 their bank branches are working on Sundays.

Thus, from the analysis it could be concluded that according to a majority of the respondents, the banks where they are customers, are not working on Sundays.

Respondents by Opinion on the Frequency of Usage of Convenient Banking

The paragraphs provided below details the customer respondents' opinion on the frequency of usage of convenient banking facility.

Table 4.26: Distribution of Respondents by Opinion on the Frequency of Usage of Convenient Banking

Sl. No.	Frequency	No. of Samples	Percentage
1.	Once in every day	8	3.77
2.	Once in a week	42	19.81
3.	Once in every 15 days	74	34.91
4.	Once in a month	58	27.36
5.	As and when required	30	14.15
	Total	**212**	**100.00**

Source: Computed from Primary Data.

Convenient banking is a recent concept which has been introduced after being observed the operation of the foreign banks and the stiff competition faced from. According to this the working hours of the banks are extended even after the usual time and the additional hours of working goes up to 7.30 to 8.00 p.m., depending on the type of bank. This again facilitates the customers to utilize the services of the banks effectively.

As it could be seen in Table 4.26, among the 500 sample respondents, just 212 respondents, that is 42.40 per cent of the respondents are using the convenient banking. Among the sample respondents of 212, the highest of 34.91 per cent use the facility once in every 15 days. Another 27.36 per cent use the facility once in a month. There are 19.81 per cent of the respondents who use the facility once in a week, while 14.15 per cent of the respondents use the facility as and when they require. The remaining meagre percentage of 3.77 per cent uses the facility once in every day.

Thus from the analysis provided above it can be concluded that a majority of the respondents use the convenience banking facility once in every 15 days.

5 Customers' Perceived and Desired Level of Service Quality in Public and Private Sector Banks

An Examination

INTRODUCTION

The preceding chapter provided a detailed view on the extent of utilization of the services of the commercial banks by the sample customers. As discussed earlier, the extent of utilization of the services greatly determines the level of satisfaction of the customers. Given that the extent of service utilization has been examined, in the present chapter it is attempted to discuss the level of satisfaction on the services provided. This is because, with the increasing competition among the banks, it is only the increased service provision and the facilities extended that can help any bank to improve it performance and the profitability position. Hence, it becomes essential on the part of any banking institution to satisfy the expectations of the customers, if at all if the bank wants to survive in the market. Hence, there is a pertinent need for the banks to understand what is the level of services expected from the customers? What is the level of services provided? What is the difference (gap) between the two? In fact, the banks are in a position to compare their services with the services of their competitors as the customers are very much aware of the services provided by various banks and they choose that bank which provides better services or services to their expectations. Technically, the customers select that banks where the difference between the expected and the desired level of satisfaction on the services is at its minimal. Hence, in the analysis of the customers' satisfaction it becomes pertinent to understand not only the desired and perceived levels of services from the banks but also the difference between the two. Based on this view in the present chapter it is attempted to discuss the customers" perceived and desired level of service quality on the various dimensions in the context of selected public and private sector banks. To understand the overall level of satisfaction of the customers, the perceived and desired level of satisfaction has been discussed for both the public and private sector banks combined together. For the purpose of convenience, this chapter has been divided into three sections. *SECTION I* deals with the perceived level of service quality. The desired level of services has been dealt in *SECTION II.* The service quality gap has been discussed in *SECTION III.*

SECTION I

Perceived Level of Service Quality

The perceived level of level of satisfaction indicates the customers' observation on the quality of services supplied or provided by the bank. It is the quality of service extended and obtained by the customers. A higher score indicates the higher level of customers' perception on the service of the bank and eventually a higher level of satisfaction.

Perceived Level of Service Quality: All Sample Banks

In the subsequent paragraphs it is attempted to examine the customers' perceived level of service quality of all the sample banks. This helps to understand the overall satisfaction level of the customers on the perceived level of service quality.

Tangibility Dimension on Perceived Level of Service Quality: All Banks

As it could be seen in Table 5.1, under the tangibility dimension, the highest average score of 1.74 has been recorded by the factor on 'Image of your bank among the public'. The next lowest score has been recorded by the factor on 'Usage of computers and other modern technology to provide service' (1.73). The order of other factors is in the order of: Location of the bank (1.71), Adequacy of space (1.7), Upkeep and cleanliness of the bank premises (1.69), Indication of display boards at appropriate counters (1.68) and Indication of display timings at appropriate counters (1.59). The average score of all the factors considered under Tangibility dimension is 1.69. In terms of coefficient of variation, a measure of dispersion of the variable has indicated that the least variation is being record by the factor on 'Image of your bank among the public' with 110.92 per cent. The order of other factors in terms of increasing coefficient of variation is: 'Usage of computers and other modern technology to provide service' (112.14%), Location of the bank (116.37%), 'Adequacy of space' (116.47%), 'Upkeep and cleanliness of the bank premises' (119.53%), 'Indication of display boards at appropriate counters' (122.02%) and 'Indication of display timings at appropriate counters' (131.45%). The overall coefficient of variation for the entire dimension stood at 118.34 per cent.

From the above discussion it can be understood in the case of tangibility dimension, the customers view the factor on 'Image of your bank among the public' as the most important perceived level of service quality.

Assurance Dimension on Perceived Level of Service Quality: All Banks

As it could be seen in the table, the factor on 'Confidence and perfection of the services provided to you' recorded the highest score of 1.89. The order of other factors in terms of average score is: 'Proficiency of the staff on the work they carry out for you' (1.854) and 'Usage of technical terms when speaking with you' (1.79). The average score of the entire dimension stood at 1.88. In terms of coefficient of variation, the least value of 98.40 per cent has been recorded by the factor on 'Confidence and perfection of the services provided to you'. The order of other factors in terms of the increasing coefficient of variation is: Proficiency of the staff on the work they carry out for you (100.79%) and 'Usage of technical terms when speaking with you' (106.47%). The overall coefficient of variation recorded for the entire dimension stood at 98.74 per cent.

From the above discussion it can be understood that under assurance dimension, the customers view the factor on 'Confidence and perfection of the services provided to you' as the most important perceived service quality variable.

Responsive Dimension on Perceived Level of Service Quality: All Banks

As it could be seen in the table under the responsiveness dimension, the factor on 'Attitude, responsiveness and courtesy of the staff' (1.98) recorded the least score. The order of the other factors is: 'Responsiveness to your comments and suggestions' (2.18), 'Transfer of money from your bank to other bank' (2.16), 'Treatment of your need and urgency with care and seriousness' (2.15), 'Response of the staff when there is a grievance' (2.12), 'Dependability and accuracy of the services provided to you' (2.09) and Promptness of the services carried out (2.03). The overall average score of the entire dimension stood at 2.1. In terms of coefficient of variation, the order of the factors is: 'Responsiveness to your comments and suggestions' (75.23%), 'Transfer of money from your bank to other bank' (76.39%), 'Treatment of your need and urgency with care and seriousness (78.6%), 'Response of the staff when there is a grievance' (80.66%), 'Dependability and accuracy of the services provided to you' (83.25%), 'Promptness of the services carried out' (86.21%) and 'Attitude, responsiveness and courtesy of the staff' (90.40%). The overall coefficient of variation for the entire dimension on responsiveness is 81.43 per cent. The above discussion indicates that the order of the average and the order of the dispersion are found to be different and the factor which has recorded the highest average has experienced one of the highest dispersion indicating that the customers' perceived level on this factor is highly dispersing and they do not have uniform opinion with regard to this variable.

Empathy Dimension on Perceived Level of Service Quality: All Banks

As seen in the Table 5.1 (*See on page 109-112*) under the empathy dimension, the factor on 'Prompt opening/closing of the branch as per time' recorded the highest score of the customers' perception with 2.62. The order of other factors is: 'Care and Consideration given to your grievances' (2.54), 'Convenience of timing of the office hours of the bank' (2.5), 'Accessibility and contact of staff in the bank' (2.49), 'Accessibility of the branch manager or higher officials' (2.46), 'Accessibility of staff in the bank by telephone' (2.43), 'Conveying of information in the languages known to you' (2.4), 'Accessibility of the staff in the bank to contact by email' (2.34) and 'Recognition of the bank staff to call you by your name' (2.28), 'Efforts taken by the bank staff to know about you and your needs' (2.21) and 'Reaction of the bank staff if a scheduled appointment is missed by you' (2.18). The overall score of the empathy dimension stood at 2.4. In terms of coefficient of variation, the least dispersion is being recorded in the case of the factor on 'Prompt opening/closing of the branch as per time' (53.44 per cent), followed by 'Care and

Consideration given to your grievances' (56.30%), 'Convenience of timing of the office hours of the bank' (58.00%), 'Accessibility and contact of staff in the bank' (58.63%), 'Accessibility of the branch manager or higher officials' (59.76%), 'Accessibility of staff in the bank by telephone (60.91%), 'Conveying of information in the languages known to you' (62.08%), 'Accessibility of the staff in the bank to contact by email' (65.81%), 'Recognition of the bank staff to call you by your name' (69.30%), 'Efforts taken by the bank staff to know about you and your needs' (73.30%) and 'Reaction of the bank staff if a scheduled appointment is missed by you' (75.23%). The overall coefficient of variation recorded a value of 62.92 per cent.

Reliability Dimension on Perceived Level of Service Quality: All Banks

As seen in the Table, the reliability dimension indicates that among the various factors considered, the factor on 'Skill of the staff to use computers and other modern technical devices' formed the highest score with 3.01. The next highest score of 3.00 has been recorded by 'Quick provision of services'. The order of the other factors is: 'Neatness and legibility of the entries in the pass book' (2.94), 'Appropriateness and update of the account statements provided to you' (2.93), 'Time taken to process your grievances' (2.87), 'Care and Consideration of your property and values entrusted for safe custody' (2.82), 'Attention given to the grievances and the follow up actions taken' (2.74) and 'Interest and willingness to help you to provide prompt service' (2.68). The average score of the entire dimension stood at 2.87. In terms of coefficient of variation also this order has been maintained with 'Skill of the staff to use computers and other modern technical devices' (38.34%) with registering the lowest coefficient of variation. The order of other factors in terms of increasing variance is: Quick provision of services' (39.47%), 'Appropriateness and update of the account statements provided to you' (41.27%), 'Neatness and legibility of the entries in the pass book' (41.52%), 'Time taken to process your grievances' (43.10%), 'Care and Consideration of your property and values entrusted for safe custody' (44.82%), 'Attention given to the grievances and the follow up actions taken' (48.95%) and 'Interest and willingness to help you to provide prompt service' (50.58%). The average level of variance stood at 43.35 per cent for the entire dimension.

Thus from the analysis it can be concluded that under the tangibility dimension the perceived level of service quality has registered the highest value and the least coefficient of variation in the case of Image of your bank among the public' which indicates that the public perceive the image of the bank as the highest factor of preference among the tangibility dimension. Under the assurance dimension the perceived level of service quality has registered the highest value and the least coefficient of variation in the case of 'Confidence and perfection of the services provided to you' which indicates that the public perceive perfection in the service provided as the highest factor of preference among the assurance dimension. Under the responsiveness dimension the perceived level of service quality has registered the highest value in the case of the factor on 'Promptness of the services carried out' which indicates that the public perceive perfection in the service provided as the highest factor of preference among the assurance dimension.

In terms of average as well as in terms of coefficient of variation, the factor on 'Prompt opening/closing of the branch as per time' recorded the highest score and the least dispersion indicating the consistency of the customers' perception. The factor on skill of the staff to use computers and other modern technical devices' recorded the highest score as well as the minimum variance indicating the consistency of the customers towards the preference for this factor. It can also be inferred from the table that by preferring this factor the most, the customers have well understood the skill of the staff as a major determining of the employees' productivity in serving them better and faster.

Table 5.1: Distribution of Sample Respondents by Opinion on the Perceived Level of Service Quality on Tangibility Dimension: All Banks

Sl. No.	Factor	Average Sample Size	Total Score	Average Score	C.V.
1	2	3	4	5	6
	TANGIBILITY DIMENSION				
1.	Indication of display timings at appropriate counters:	500	797.00	1.59	131.45
2.	Indication of display boards at appropriate counters:	500	838.00	1.68	122.02
3.	Upkeep and cleanliness of the bank premises:	500	846.00	1.69	119.53
4.	Adequacy of space	500	851.00	1.70	116.47
5.	Location of the bank	500	856.00	1.71	116.37
6.	Usage of computers and other modern technology to : provide service	500	863.00	1.73	112.14
7.	Image of your bank among the public:	500	870.00	1.74	110.92
	TOTAL		**845.86**	**1.69**	**118.34**
	ASSURANCE DIMENSION				
8.	Usage of technical terms when speaking with you:	500	895	1.79	106.47
9.	Proficiency of the staff on the work they carry out for you:	500	927	1.85	100.79

(Contd...)

1	2	3	4	5	6
10.	Confidence and perfection of the services provided to you:	500	943	1.89	98.40
	TOTAL		**921.66**	**1.84**	**98.74**
	RESPONSIVE DIMENSION				
11.	Attitude, responsiveness and courtesy of the staff:	500	992	1.98	90.40
12.	Responsiveness to your comments and suggestions:	500	1088.00	2.18	75.23
13.	Transfer of money from your bank to other bank:	500	1079.00	2.16	76.39
14.	Treatment of your need and urgency with care and seriousness:	500	1073.00	2.15	78.60
15.	Response of the staff when there is a grievance	500	1062.00	2.12	80.66
16.	Dependability and accuracy of the services provided to you:	500	1046.00	2.09	83.25
17.	Promptness of the services carried out:	500	1016.00	2.03	86.21
	TOTAL		**1050.86**	**2.10**	**81.43**
	EMPATHY DIMENSION				
18.	Reaction of the bank staff if a scheduled appointment is missed by you	500	1092	2.18	75.23

(Contd...)

1	2	3	4	5	6
19.	Efforts taken by the bank staff to know about you and your needs:	500	1106	2.21	73.30
20.	Recognition of the bank staff to call you by your name:	500	1138	2.28	69.30
21.	Accessibility of the staff in the bank to contact by email:	500	1168	2.34	65.81
22.	Conveying of information in the languages known to you:	500	1202	2.40	62.08
23	Accessibility of staff in the bank by telephone	500	1213	2.43	60.91
24	Accessibility of the branch manager or higher officials	500	1228	2.46	59.76
25	Accessibility and contact of staff in the bank:	500	1243	2.49	58.63
26	Care and Consideration given to your grievances	500	1269	2.54	56.30
27	Convenience of timing of the office hours of the bank.	500	1251	2.50	58.00
28	Prompt opening/closing of the branch as per time:	500	1309	2.62	53.44
	TOTAL		**1202**	**2.40**	**62.92**
	RELIABILITY DIMENSION				
29	Interest and willingness to help you to provide prompt service:	500	1338	2.676	50.58
30	Time taken to process your grievances	500	1434	2.868	43.10

(Contd...)

1	2	3	4	5	6
31.	Attention given to the grievances and the follow up actions taken:	500	1372	2.744	48.95
32.	Care and Consideration of your property and values entrusted for safe custody	500	1411	2.822	44.82
33.	Appropriateness and update of the account statements provided to you:	500	1466	2.932	41.27
34.	Neatness and legibility of the entries in the pass book:	500	1469	2.938	41.52
35.	Quick provision of services:	500	1499	2.998	39.47
36.	Skill of the staff to use computers and other modern technical devices	500	1503	3.006	38.34
	TOTAL		**1436.5**	**2.873**	**43.35**

Source: Computed from Primary Data.

Distribution of Sample Respondents by Opinion on the Perceived Level of Service Quality Dimensions: Public Sector Banks

In the subsequent paragraphs it is attempted to examine the customers' view on the perceived level of service quality of public sector banks.

Tangibility Dimension on Perceived Level of Service Quality: Public Sector Banks

As it could be seen in Table 5.2 (*See on page 118-121*), under the tangibility dimension, the highest average score of 1.72 has been recorded by two factors namely, Upkeep and cleanliness of the bank premises and Usage of computers and other modern technology to provide service. The order of the other factors is: Adequacy of space (1.70), Image of your bank among the public (1.70), Location of the bank (1.69) and Indication of display timings at appropriate counters (1.65). The average score of all the factors considered under Tangibility dimension is 1.71. In terms of coefficient of variation, a measure of dispersion of the variable has indicated that the least variation is being record by the factor on 'Usage of computers and other modern technology to provide service (112.21 per cent). The order of other factors in terms of increasing coefficient of variation is: 'Indication of display boards at appropriate counters (112.5 per cent), Image of your bank among the public (113.53 per cent), Adequacy of space (114.71 per cent), Upkeep and cleanliness of the bank premises (115.7 per cent), Location of the bank (117.16 per cent) and Indication of display timings at appropriate counters (123.64 per cent). From the above discussion it can be understood that the order of the variable in terms of average is the order of the dispersion. This means that the factor with higher score could register the lowest coefficient of variation.

Assurance Dimension on Perceived Level of Service Quality: Public Sector Banks

As it could be seen in the Table 5.2, the factor on 'Confidence and perfection of the services provided to you' recorded the highest score of 1.90. The order of other factors in terms of average score is: 'Proficiency of the staff on the work they carry out for you' (1.83) and 'Usage of technical terms when speaking with you' (1.79). The average score of the entire dimension stood at 1.89. In terms of coefficient of variation, the least value of 96.84 per cent has been recorded by the factor on 'Confidence and perfection of the services provided to you'. The order of other factors in terms of the increasing coefficient of variation is: Proficiency of the staff on the work they carry out for you (102.19 per cent) and 'Usage of technical terms when speaking with you' (104.47 per cent). The overall coefficient of variation recorded for the entire dimension stood at 96.30 per cent. From the above discussion it can be understood that the order of the variable in terms of average is the order of the dispersion. This means that the factor with higher score could register the lowest coefficient of variation.

Responsive Dimension on Perceived Level of Service Quality: Public Sector Banks

As it is given in the Table 5.2, under the responsiveness dimension, the factor on 'Response of the staff when there is a grievance (2.29) has recorded the highest average score. This indicates that the customers of the public sector banks found that the employees of their banks are highly responding to their request. The order of other factors is: Dependability and accuracy of the services provided to you (2.26), promptness of the services provided to you (2.26), Transfer of money from your bank to other bank (2.16), Treatment of your need and urgency with care and seriousness (2.16), Attitude, responsiveness and courtesy of the staff (2.04) and Responsiveness to your comments and suggestions (0.76). In terms of coefficient of variation, the order of the factors is: 'Dependability and accuracy of the services provided to you (68.14%) has recorded the least score. This implies that the sample respondents have almost a similar opinion on the dependability of the service provided. The order of the other factors in terms of increasing value of coefficient of variation is: 'Response of the staff when there is a grievance (69.43%), Promptness of the services carried out (71.69%), Treatment of your need and urgency with care and seriousness (75.46%), Transfer of money from your bank to other bank (77.31%), Attitude, responsiveness and courtesy of the staff (84.31%), Responsiveness to your comments and suggestions (269.74%), The overall coefficient of variation for the entire dimension on responsiveness is 84.85 per cent. The above discussion indicates that the order of the average and the order of the dispersion are found to be different and the factor which has recorded the highest average has experienced one of the highest dispersion indicating that the customers' perceived level on this factor is highly dispersing and they do not have uniform opinion with regard to this variable.

Empathy Dimension on Perceived Level of Service Quality: Public Sector Banks

As given in the Table 5.2, under the empathy dimension, the factor on 'Prompt opening/closing of the branch as per time' recorded the highest score of the customers' perception with 2.60. This indicates that the customers of the public sector bank viewed the timely opening and timely closing of the bank as the highest factor on the empathy dimension. The order of other factors is: 'Convenience of timing of the office hours of the bank (2.59), Accessibility and contact of staff in the bank (2.54), Care and Consideration given to your grievances (2.53),Accessibility of the branch manager or higher officials (2.44), Accessibility of the staff in the bank to contact by email (2.4), Accessibility of staff in the bank by telephone (2.39), Recognition of the bank staff to call you by your name: (2.36), Conveying of information in the languages known to you (2.34), Reaction of the bank staff if a scheduled appointment is missed by you (2.28) and Efforts taken by the bank staff to know about you and your needs (2.14).

The overall score of the empathy dimension stood at 2.42. In terms of coefficient of variation, the least dispersion is being recorded in the case of the factor on 'Convenience of timing of the office hours of the bank (54.44%). This indicates that the customers' opinion on the service time of the banks is convenient. Accessibility and contact of staff in the bank (55.12%), Care and Consideration given to your grievances (55.34%), Prompt opening/closing of the branch as per time (55.38%), Accessibility of the branch manager or higher officials (60.25%), Accessibility of the staff in the bank to contact by email (61.25%), Accessibility of staff in the bank by telephone (61.92%), Recognition of the bank staff to call you by your name (63.56%), Conveying of information in the languages known to you (64.10%), 'Reaction of the bank staff if a scheduled appointment is missed by you (68.86%) and Efforts taken by the bank staff to know about you and your needs (72.43%). The overall dispersion stood at 60.74 per cent.

Reliability Dimension on Perceived Level of Service Quality: Public Sector Banks

As seen in the Table–5.2, the reliability dimension indicates that among the various factors considered, the factor on 'Quick provision of services (3.14), Neatness and legibility of the entries in the pass book (3.03), 'Skill of the staff to use computers and other modern technical devices' (3.02), Interest and willingness to help you to provide prompt service (2.92), 'Care and Consideration of your property and values entrusted for safe custody (2.91), Time taken to process your grievances (2.84), Attention given to the grievances and the follow up actions taken (2.82), Appropriateness and update of the account statements provided to you (2.63). The average score of the entire dimension stood at 2.91. In terms of coefficient of variation also this order has been maintained with 'Quick provision of services (36.62 per cent), Skill of the staff to use computers and other modern technical devices

(37.09 per cent), Neatness and legibility of the entries in the pass book (39.27 per cent), Care and Consideration of your property and values entrusted for safe custody (41.24 per cent), Time taken to process your grievances (43.31 per cent), Interest and willingness to help you to provide prompt service (43.84 per cent), Attention given to the grievances and the follow up actions taken (45.39 per cent), Appropriateness and update of the account statements provided to you: (48.29 per cent). The overall standard deviation stood at 41.92 per cent.

Thus from the analysis it can be concluded that under the tangibility dimension the perceived level of service quality among the public sector banks has registered the highest value in the case of' Upkeep and cleanliness of the bank premises and Usage of computers and other modern technology to provide service" which indicates that the public perceive the image of the public sector bank as the highest factor of preference among the tangibility dimension. The public sector banks under the assurance dimension on the perceived level of service quality, the highest value and the least coefficient of variation has been achieved by 'Confidence and perfection of the services provided to you' which indicates that the customers of public sector banks perceive perfection in the service provided as the highest factor of preference among the assurance dimension. The responsiveness dimension the perceived level of service quality has registered the highest value in the case of the factor on 'Response of the staff when there is a grievance'. However, the dispersion is found to be the least ion the case of 'Dependability and accuracy of the services provided to you' which indicates that the public perceive dependability of the service provided as the highest factor of preference among the assurance dimension. In terms of average, the factor on 'Prompt opening/closing of the branch as per time' recorded the highest score while in terms of coefficient of variation, the

Table 5.2: Distribution of Sample Respondents by Opinion on the Perceived Level of Service Quality Dimensions: Public Sector Banks

Sl. No.	Factor	Average Sample Size	Total Score	Average Score	C.V.
1	2	3	4	5	6
	TANGIBILITY DIMENSION				
1.	Indication of display timings at appropriate counters:	280	461.00	1.65	123.64
2.	Indication of display boards at appropriate counters:	280	477.00	1.70	114.71
3.	Upkeep and cleanliness of the bank premises:	280	481.00	1.72	115.70
4.	Adequacy of space?	280	477.00	1.70	114.71
5.	Location of the bank	280	473.00	1.69	117.16
6.	Usage of computers and other modern technology to provide service:	280	482.00	1.72	112.21
7.	Image of your bank among the public:	280	475.00	1.70	113.53
	TOTAL	**280**	**475.14**	**1.69**	**115.20**
	ASSURANCE DIMENSION				
8	Usage of technical terms when speaking with you:	280	500.00	1.79	104.47

(Contd...)

1	2	3	4	5	6
9.	Proficiency of the staff on the work they carry out for you:	280	511.00	1.83	102.19
10.	Confidence and perfection of the services provided to you:	280	533.00	1.90	96.84
	TOTAL	**280**	**514.66**	**1.83**	**96.30**
	RESPONSIVENESS DIMENSION				
11.	Attitude, responsiveness and courtesy of the staff:	280	570.00	2.04	84.31
12.	Responsiveness to your comments and suggestions:	280	212.00	0.76	269.74
13.	Transfer of money from your bank to other bank:	280	606.00	2.16	77.31
14.	Treatment of your need and urgency with care and seriousness:	280	606.00	2.16	75.46
15.	Response of the staff when there is a grievance:	280	640.00	2.29	69.43
16.	Dependability and accuracy of the services provided to you:	280	634.00	2.26	68.14
17.	Promptness of the services carried out	280	614.00	2.19	71.69
	TOTAL	**280**	**554.57**	**1.98**	**84.85**
	EMPATHY DIMENSION				
18.	Reaction of the bank staff if a scheduled appointment is missed by you	280	637.00	2.28	68.86

(Contd...)

1	2	3	4	5	6
19.	Efforts taken by the bank staff to know about you and your needs	280	599.00	2.14	72.43
20.	Recognition of the bank staff to call you by your name	280	661.00	2.36	63.56
21.	Accessibility of the staff in the bank to contact by email	280	671.00	2.40	61.25
22.	Conveying of information in the languages known to you	280	654.00	2.34	64.10
23.	Accessibility of staff in the bank by telephone	280	668.00	2.39	61.92
24.	Accessibility of the branch manager or higher officials	280	684.00	2.44	60.25
25.	Accessibility and contact of staff in the bank	280	711.00	2.54	55.12
26.	Care and Consideration given to your grievances	280	707.00	2.53	55.34
27.	Convenience of timing of the office hours of the bank	280	726.00	2.59	54.44
28.	Prompt opening/closing of the branch as per time	280	729.00	2.60	55.38
	TOTAL	**280**	**677.00**	**2.42**	**60.74**
	RELIABILITY DIMENSION				
29.	Interest and willingness to help you to provide prompt service:	280	818.00	2.92	43.84
30.	Time taken to process your grievances	280	794.00	2.84	43.31
31.	Attention given to the grievances and the follow up actions taken:	280	790.00	2.82	45.39

(Contd...)

1	2	3	4	5	6
32.	Care and Consideration of your property and values entrusted for safe custody	280	815.00	2.91	41.24
33.	Appropriateness and update of the account statements provided to you:	280	735.00	2.63	48.29
34.	Neatness and legibility of the entries in the pass book:	280	847.00	3.03	39.27
35	Quick provision of services:	280	879.00	3.14	36.62
36	Skill of the staff to use computers and other modern technical devices	280	845.00	3.02	37.09
	TOTAL	**220**	**815.38**	**2.91**	**41.92**

Source: Computed from Primary Data.

factor on 'Convenience of timing of the office hours of the bank' recorded the least dispersion. The factor on Quick provision of services' formed the highest score as well as the minimum variance indicating the consistency of the customers towards the preference for this factor. It can also be inferred from the table that by preferring this factor the most, the customers expect the bank employees to provide quick and speedy service.

Distribution of Sample Respondents by Opinion on The Perceived Level of Service Quality Dimensions: Private Sector Banks

In the subsequent paragraphs it is attempted to examine the customers' opinion on the perceived level of service quality of private sector banks.

Tangibility Dimension on Perceived Level of Service Quality: Private Sector Banks

As it could be seen in Table 5.3 (*See on page 127-130*), under the tangibility dimension, the highest average score of 1.80 has been recorded by the factor on 'Image of your bank among the public.' The next lowest score has been recorded by the factor on 'Location of the bank (1.74). The order of other factors is: 'Usage of computers and other modern technology to provide service (1.73), Adequacy of space (1.70), Upkeep and cleanliness of the bank premises (1.66), Indication of display boards at appropriate counters (1.56) and 'Indication of display timings at appropriate counters (1.53). The average score on the tangibility dimension of the private sector banks stood at 1.67. In terms of coefficient of variation, a measure of dispersion of the variable has indicated that the least variation is being record by the factor on 'Image of your bank among the public (106.67%), Usage of computers and other modern technology to provide service (113.29%), Location of the bank (114.94%), Adequacy of space (119.41%), Upkeep and cleanliness of the bank premises (122.89%), Indication of display boards at appropriate counters (136.54%) and Indication of display timings at appropriate counters (140.52%). The coefficient of variation for the entire dimension stood at 121.56 per cent. From the above discussion it can be understood that the order of the variable in terms of average is the order of the dispersion. This means that the factor with higher score could register the lowest coefficient of variation.

Assurance Dimension on Perceived Level of Service Quality: Private Sector Banks

As it could be seen in table 5.3, the factor on 'Proficiency of the staff on the work they carry out for you' recorded the highest score of 1.89. The order of other factors in terms of average score is: 'Confidence and perfection of the services provided to you (1.86), and 'Usage of technical terms when speaking with you' (1.80). The average score of the entire dimension stood at 1.87. In terms of coefficient of variation, the least value of 96.84 per cent has been recorded by the factor on 'Proficiency of the staff on the work they carry out for you (98.94%). The order of other factors is: 'Confidence and perfection of the services provided to you' (101.08%) and 'Usage of technical terms when speaking with you' (108.33%). The overall coefficient of variation recorded for the entire dimension stood at 101.07 per cent. From the above discussion it can be understood that the order of the variable in terms of average is the order of the dispersion. This means that the factor with higher score could register the lowest coefficient of variation.

Responsive Dimension on Perceived Level of Service Quality: Private Sector Banks

As it is given in Table 5.3, under the responsiveness dimension, the factor on 'Responsiveness to your comments and suggestions (3.65) has recorded the highest average score. This indicates that the customers of the public sector banks found that the employees of their banks are highly responding to their suggestions. The order of other factors is: 'Promptness of the services carried out (2.15), 'Treatment of your need and urgency with care and seriousness' (2.07), 'Dependability and accuracy of the services provided to you' (2.02), 'Transfer of money from your bank to other bank' (2.00), 'Response of the staff when there is a grievance' (1.97) and 'Attitude, responsiveness and courtesy of the staff:' (1.92). The average score on the responsiveness dimension stood at 2.26. In terms of coefficient of variation, the order of the factors is: 'Responsiveness to your comments and suggestions (35.07%) has recorded the least score. This implies that the sample respondents have almost a similar opinion on the dependability of the service provided. The order of the other factors in terms of increasing value of coefficient of variation is: 'Promptness of the services carried out (80.47%), Treatment of your need and urgency with care and seriousness (87.44%), Dependability and accuracy of the services provided to you (88.12%), Transfer of money from your bank to other bank (91.00%), Response of the staff when there is a grievance (91.88%) and Attitude, responsiveness and courtesy of the staff (97.40%). The average score for the dimension on responsiveness as a whole stood at 76.55 per cent.

The above discussion indicates that the order of the average and the order of the dispersion are found to be the same indicating the consistency of the customers in terms of perceived level of service quality of the private sector bank.

Empathy Dimension on Perceived Level of Service Quality: Private Sector Banks

As given in the Table, under the empathy dimension, the factor on 'Prompt opening/closing of the branch as per time' recorded the highest score of the customers' perception with 2.64. This indicates that the customers of the private sector bank viewed the timely opening and timely closing of the bank as the highest factor on the empathy dimension. The order of other factors is: 'Care and Consideration given to your grievances (2.55), 'Conveying of information in the languages known to you (2.49), Accessibility of staff in the bank by telephone (2.48), 'Accessibility of the branch manager or higher officials' (2.47), 'Accessibility and contact of staff in the bank (2.42), Convenience of timing of the office hours of the bank (2.39), 'Efforts taken by the bank staff to know, about you and your needs' (2.3), 'Accessibility of the staff in the bank to contact by email' (2.26), 'Recognition of the bank staff to call you by your name' (2.17) and 'Reaction of the bank staff if a scheduled appointment is missed by you' (2.07). In terms of coefficient of variation, the least dispersion is being recorded in the case of the factor on 'Prompt opening/closing of the branch as per time' (51.14%), 'Care and Consideration given to your grievances' (57.65%), 'Conveying of information in the languages known to you' (59.44%), 'Accessibility of the branch manager or higher officials' (59.51%), 'Accessibility of staff in the bank by telephone' (59.68%), 'Convenience of timing of the office hours of the bank' (62.76%), 'Accessibility and contact of staff in the bank' (63.22%), 'Accessibility of the staff in the bank to contact by email' (71.68%), 'Efforts taken by the bank staff to know about you and your needs' (74.35%), 'Recognition of the bank staff to call you by your name' (77.42%) and 'Reaction of the bank staff if a scheduled appointment is missed by you' (84.06%).

Reliability Dimension on Perceived Level of Service Quality: Private Sector Banks

As seen in Table 5.3, the reliability dimension indicates that among the various factors considered, the factor on

'Appropriateness and update of the account statements provided to you' (3.32) formed the highest score. This is being followed by other factors in the order: 'Skill of the staff to use computers and other modern technical devices' (2.99), 'Time taken to process your grievances' (2.91), 'Neatness and legibility of the entries in the pass book' (2.83), 'Quick provision of services' (2.82), 'Care and Consideration of your property and values entrusted for safe custody' (2.71), 'Attention given to the grievances and the follow up actions taken' (2.65) and Interest and willingness to help you to provide prompt service (2.36). The average score on the reliability dimensions stood at 2.82 in the case of the dimension on reliability. In terms of coefficient of variation also this order has been maintained with 'Appropriateness and update of the account statements provided to you' (34.04%), The order of other factors is: Skill of the staff to use computers and other modern technical devices (39.80%), Time taken to process your grievances (42.61%), 'Quick provision of services (43.26%), 'Neatness and legibility of the entries in the pass book (44.52%), Care and Consideration of your property and values entrusted for safe custody (49.45%), 'Attention given to the grievances and the follow up actions taken' (53.58%) and 'Interest and willingness to help you to provide prompt service' (61.44%). The overall standard deviation stood at 45.39 per cent.

Thus from the analysis it can be concluded that under the tangibility dimension the perceived level of service quality among private sector banks has registered the highest value in the case of 'Image of your bank among the public" which indicates that the public perceive the image of the private sector bank as the highest factor of preference among the tangibility dimension. The private sector banks under the assurance dimension on the perceived level of service quality, the highest value and the least coefficient of variation has been achieved by 'Proficiency of the staff on the work they

Table 5.3: Distribution of Sample Respondents by Opinion on the Perceived Level of Service Quality Dimensions: Private Sector Banks

Sl. No.	Factor	Average Sample Size	Total Score	Average Score	C.V.
1	2	3	4.	5	6
	TANGIBILITY DIMENSION				
1.	Indication of display timings at appropriate counters:	220	336.00	1.53	140.52
2.	Indication of display boards at appropriate counters:	220	344.00	1.56	136.54
3.	Upkeep and cleanliness of the bank premises:	220	365.00	1.66	122.89
4.	Adequacy of space?	220	374.00	1.70	119.41
5.	Location of the bank	220	383.00	1.74	114.94
6.	Usage of computers and other modern technology to provide service:	220	381.00	1.73	113.29
7.	Image of your bank among the public:	220	395.00	1.80	106.67
	TOTAL	**220**	**368.29**	**1.67**	**121.56**
	ASSURANCE DIMENSION				
8.	Usage of technical terms when speaking with you:	220	395.00	1.80	108.33

(Contd...)

1	2	3	4	5	6
9.	Proficiency of the staff on the work they carry out for you:	220	416.00	1.89	98.94
10.	Confidence and perfection of the services provided to you:	220	410.00	1.86	101.08
	TOTAL	**220**	**407.00**	**1.85**	**101.07**
	RESPONSIVENESS DIMENSION				
11.	Attitude, responsiveness and courtesy of the staff:	220	422.00	1.92	97.40
12.	Responsiveness to your comments and suggestions:	220	804.00	3.65	35.07
13.	Transfer of money from your bank to other bank:	220	440.00	2.00	91.00
14.	Treatment of your need and urgency with care and seriousness:	220	456.00	2.07	87.44
15.	Response of the staff when there is a grievance:	220	433.00	1.97	91.88
16.	Dependability and accuracy of the services provided to you:	220	445.00	2.02	88.12
17.	Promptness of the services carried out	220	474.00	2.15	80.47
	TOTAL	**220**	**496.29**	**2.26**	**76.55**
	EMPATHY DIMENSION				
18.	Reaction of the bank staff if a scheduled appointment is missed by you	220	455.00	2.07	84.06

(Contd...)

1	2	3	4	5	6
19.	Efforts taken by the bank staff to know about you and your needs	220	507.00	2.30	74.35
20.	Recognition of the bank staff to call you by your name	220	477.00	2.17	77.42
21.	Accessibility of the staff in the bank to contact by email	220	497.00	2.26	71.68
22.	Conveying of information in the languages known to you	220	548.00	2.49	59.44
23.	Accessibility of staff in the bank by telephone	220	545.00	2.48	59.68
24.	Accessibility of the branch manager or higher officials	220	544.00	2.47	59.51
25.	Accessibility and contact of staff in the bank	220	532.00	2.42	63.22
26.	Care and Consideration given to your grievances	220	562.00	2.55	57.65
27.	Convenience of timing of the office hours of the bank	220	525.00	2.39	62.76
28.	Prompt opening/closing of the branch as per time	220	580.00	2.64	51.14
	TOTAL	**220**	**524.73**	**2.39**	**64.85**
	RELIABILITY DIMENSION				
29.	Interest and willingness to help you to provide prompt service:	220	520.00	2.36	61.44
30.	Time taken to process your grievances	220	640.00	2.91	42.61

(Contd...)

1	2	3	4	5	6
31.	Attention given to the grievances and the follow up actions taken:	220	582.00	2.65	53.58
32.	Care and Consideration of your property and values entrusted for safe custody	220	596.00	2.71	49.45
33.	Appropriateness and update of the account statements provided to you:	220	731.00	3.32	34.04
34.	Neatness and legibility of the entries in the pass book:	220	622.00	2.83	44.52
35.	Quick provision of services:	220	620.00	2.82	43.26
36.	Skill of the staff to use computers and other modern technical devices	220	658.00	2.99	39.80
	TOTAL	**220**	**621.13**	**2.82**	**45.39**

Source: Computed from Primary Data.

carry out for you' which indicates that the customers of private sector banks perceive profession in the service provided as the highest factor of preference among the assurance dimension. Under the responsiveness dimension the perceived level of service quality has registered the highest value and the lowest dispersion. In terms of average and in terms of coefficient of variation, the factor on 'Responsiveness to your comments and suggestions' recorded the highest score and least coefficient of variation. Under empathy dimension the perceived level of service quality has registered the highest value the factor on 'Prompt opening/closing of branch as per time'. The factor on Appropriateness and update of the account statements provided to you' (34.04%), formed the highest score as well as the minimum variance indicating the consistency of the customers towards the preference for this factor, under Reliability dimension. It can also be inferred from the table that by preferring this factor the most, the customers expect the bank employees to provide updated information on their accounts.

SECTION II

Desired Level of Satisfaction: All Banks

The earlier section provided a detailed view on the customers' perceived level of service quality. In the present section, it is attempted to discuss the customers' desired level of services. The desired level of level of satisfaction indicates the customers' expected quality of services from the bank. It is the quality of services desired to be supplied by the banks to the customers. A higher score indicates the higher level of customers' expectation on the service of the bank.

Desired Level of Service Quality: All Sample Banks

In the subsequent section it is attempted to examine the customers' desired level of satisfaction of all the banks selected as samples.

Tangibility Dimension on Desired Level of Service Quality: All Banks

As it could be seen in Table 5.4 (*See on page 137-140*), under the tangibility dimension, the highest average score of 1.80 has been recorded by the factor on 'Indication of display timings at appropriate counters' (4.41). The next lowest score has been recorded by the factor on 'Indication of display boards at appropriate counters (4.32). The order of other factors is: 'Upkeep and cleanliness of the bank premises (4.31), Adequacy of space (4.30), 'Location of the bank (4.29), Usage of computers and other modern technology to provide service (4.27), 'Image of your bank among the public (4.26). The average score on the tangibility dimension of the private sector banks stood at 4.31. In terms of coefficient of variation, a measure of dispersion of the variable has indicated that the least variation is being record by the factor on 'Image of your bank among the public (25.59%), this is being followed by other factor in the order as: 'Usage of computers and other modern technology to provide service (26.00%), 'Adequacy of space (26.98%), 'Location of the bank (27.27%), 'Upkeep and cleanliness of the bank premises' (27.84%), 'Indication of display timings at appropriate counters (28.12%) and 'Indication of display boards at appropriate counters (28.94%). The average level of coefficient of variation is recorded as 27.15 per cent. From the above discussion it can be understood that the order of the variable in terms of average and the order of the dispersion are widely dispersed. This is unlike the order found in the case of the perceived level. This means that the customers' order of perceived level of service quality is different from the order found in the case of desired level.

Assurance Dimension on Desired Level of Service Quality: All Banks

As it could also be seen in the table, the factor on 'Usage of technical terms when speaking with you' constituted the highest score with 4.21. The order of other factors in terms of average score is: 'Proficiency of the staff on the work they carry out for you (4.15) and 'Confidence and perfection of the services provided to you (4.11). The average score of the entire dimension stood at 4.16. In terms of coefficient of variation, the least value of 26.13 per cent has been recorded by the factor on 'Usage of technical terms when speaking with you'. The order of the other factors is: 'Proficiency of the staff on the work they carry out for you:' (26.51%) and 'Confidence and perfection of the services provided to you (26.76%). The average coefficient of variation stood for the entire dimension at 26.44 per cent. From the above discussion it can be understood that the order of the variable in terms of average is the order of the dispersion. This means that the factor with higher score could register the lowest coefficient of variation.

Responsive Dimension on Desired Level of Service Quality: All Banks

As it is given in Table 5.4, under the responsiveness dimension, the factor on 'Attitude, responsiveness and courtesy of the staff (4.02) has recorded the highest average score. This indicates that the customers of the public sector banks found that the employees of their banks are highly responding to their request, courteous towards the customers. The order of other factors is: Responsiveness to your comments and suggestions (3.97), Transfer of money from your bank to other bank (3.91), Treatment of your need and urgency with care and seriousness (3.88), Response of the staff when there is a grievance (3.85), Dependability and accuracy of the services provided to you (3.84), Promptness of the services carried out (3.82). The average score for the dimension as a whole on responsiveness dimension stood at 3.9. In terms of coefficient of variation, the order of the factors is: Dependability and accuracy of the services provided to you (26.82%), Attitude, responsiveness and courtesy of the staff (26.87%), Responsiveness to your comments and suggestions

(26.95%), Promptness of the services carried out (26.96%), Response of the staff when there is a grievance (27.79%), Treatment of your need and urgency with care and seriousness (28.09%) and Transfer of money from your bank to other bank (28.13%). The average coefficient of variation for the dimension on responsiveness as a whole stood at 27.44 per cent. The above discussion indicates that the order of the average and the order of the dispersion are found to be different with Attitude, responsiveness and courtesy of the staff occupying the highest score while the and the least coefficient of variation is being recorded by the factor on 'Dependability and accuracy of the services provided to you' indicating the inconsistency of the customers' opinion in terms of perceived level of service quality of the private sector bank.

Empathy Dimension on Desired Level of Service Quality: All Banks

As given in Table 5.4, under the empathy dimension, the factor on 'Reaction of the bank staff if a scheduled appointment is missed by you' recorded the highest score of 3.82. This indicates that the customers of the sample sector bank want the bank employees to be attentive to their problems even they are busy. The order of other factors is: 'Efforts taken by the bank staff to know about you and your needs (3.79), 'Recognition of the bank staff to call you by your name' (3.72), 'Accessibility of the staff in the bank to contact by email' (3.66), 'Conveying of information in the languages known to you:' (3.60), 'Accessibility of staff in the bank by telephone' (3.57), 'Accessibility of the branch manager or higher officials' (3.54), 'Accessibility and contact of staff in the bank' (3.51), 'Convenience of timing of the office hours of the bank' (3.50), 'Care and Consideration given to your grievances' (3.46) and 'Prompt opening/closing of the branch as per time' (3.38). The average score for the dimension as a whole on responsiveness dimension stood at

3.6.In terms of coefficient of variation, the least dispersion is being recorded in the case of the factor on 'Efforts taken by the bank staff to know about you and your needs' (26.91%), followed by the other factors in their order: 'Reaction of the bank staff if a scheduled appointment is missed by you' (27.23%), 'Recognition of the bank staff to call you by your name' (27.42%), 'Accessibility of the staff in the bank to contact by email' (27.87%), 'Conveying of information in the languages known to you' (28.33%), 'Accessibility of staff in the bank by telephone' (28.85%), 'Accessibility of the branch manager or higher officials' (29.38%), 'Accessibility and contact of staff in the bank' (29.63%), 'Convenience of timing of the office hours of the bank' (30.00%), 'Care and Consideration given to your grievances' (30.64%) and 'Prompt opening/closing of the branch as per time' (32.25%). The average coefficient of variation stood at 28.89 per cent.

Reliability Dimension on Desired Level of Service Quality: All Banks

As seen in Table (5.4), the reliability dimension indicates that among the various factors considered, the factor on 'Interest and willingness to help you to provide prompt service (3.32) formed the highest score. This is being followed by other factors in the order: 'Attention given to the grievances and the follow up actions taken' (3.26), 'Care and Consideration of your property and values entrusted for safe custody' (3.18), 'Time taken to process your grievances' (3.13), 'Appropriateness and update of the account statements provided to you' (3.07), 'Neatness and legibility of the entries in the pass book' (3.06), 'Quick provision of services' (3.00) and 'skill of the staff to use computers and other modern technical devices (2.99). The average score for the entire reliability dimensions stood at 3.13. In terms of coefficient of variation also this order has been maintained with 'Interest and willingness to help you to provide prompt service' (32.83%), 'Attention given to the grievances and the follow up actions taken' (34.97%), 'Care and Consideration of your property and values entrusted for safe custody (35.22%), 'Time taken to process your grievances' (35.78%), 'Appropriateness and update of the account statements provided to you' (37.46%), 'Neatness and legibility of the entries in the pass book' (38.24%), 'Skill of the staff to use computers and other modern technical devices' (38.80%) and 'Quick provision of services' (39.33%). The average coefficient of variation stood at 36.42 per cent for the reliability dimension as a whole.

Thus from the analysis it can be concluded that under the tangibility dimension the desired level of service quality among the sample banks has registered the highest value in the case of 'Indication of display boards at appropriate counters' while in terms of the coefficient of variation, the factor on 'Image of your bank among the public' formed the least dispersion indicating the consistency in the idea of the customers. The All banks under the assurance dimension on the perceived level of service quality, the highest value and the least coefficient of variation has been achieved by 'Usage of technical terms when speaking with you' which indicates that the customers of private sector banks perceive profession in the service provided as the highest factor of preference among the assurance dimension. Under the responsiveness dimension the 'Attitude, responsiveness and courtesy of the staff' has registered the highest value. Under the empathy dimension and reliability dimension the highest factor of preference have recorded 'Reaction of the bank staff if a scheduled appointment is missed you' and 'Interest and willingness to help you to provide prompt service' respectively.. It can also be inferred from the table that by preferring this factor the most, the customers expect the bank employees to provide prompt service.

Desired Level of Satisfaction: Public Sector Banks

In the subsequent paragraphs it is attempted to provide a view on the customers' opinion on the desired level of satisfaction on the services of public sector banks.

Table 5.4: Desired Level of Satisfaction: All Banks

Sl. No.	Factor	Average Sample Size	Total Score	Average Score	C.V.
1	2	3	4	5	6
	TANGIBILITY DIMENSION				
1.	Indication of display timings at appropriate counters:	500	2203.00	4.41	28.12
2.	Indication of display boards at appropriate counters:	500	2162.00	4.32	28.94
3.	Upkeep and cleanliness of the bank premises:	500	2154.00	4.31	27.84
4.	Adequacy of space?	500	2149.00	4.30	26.98
5.	Location of the bank	500	2144.00	4.29	27.27
6.	Usage of computers and other modern technology to provide service:	500	2137.00	4.27	26.00
7.	Image of your bank among the public:	500	2130.00	4.26	25.59
	TOTAL		**2154.14**	**4.31**	**27.15**
	ASSURANCE DIMENSION				
8.	Usage of technical terms when speaking with you:	500	2105.00	4.21	26.13
9.	Proficiency of the staff on the work they carry out for you:	500	2073.00	4.15	26.51

(Contd...)

1	2	3	4	5	6
10.	Confidence and perfection of the services provided to you:	500	2057.00	4.11	26.76
	TOTAL		**2078.33**	**4.16**	**26.44**
	RESPONSIVENESS DIMENSION				
11.	Attitude, responsiveness and courtesy of the staff:	500	2008.00	4.02	26.87
12.	Responsiveness to your comments and suggestions:	500	1984.00	3.97	26.95
13.	Transfer of money from your bank to other bank:	500	1954.00	3.91	28.13
14.	Treatment of your need and urgency with care and seriousness:	500	1938.00	3.88	28.09
15.	Response of the staff when there is a grievance:	500	1927.00	3.85	27.79
16.	Dependability and accuracy of the services provided to you:	500	1921.00	3.84	26.82
17.	Promptness of the services carried out	500	1912.00	3.82	26.96
	TOTAL		**1949.14**	**3.90**	**27.44**
	EMPATHY DIMENSION				
18.	Reaction of the bank staff if a scheduled appointment is missed by you	500	1908.00	3.82	27.23

(Contd...)

1	2	3	4	5	6
19.	Efforts taken by the bank staff to know about you and your needs	500	1894.00	3.79	26.91
20.	Recognition of the bank staff to call you by your name	500	1862.00	3.72	27.42
21.	Accessibility of the staff in the bank to contact by email	500	1832.00	3.66	27.87
22.	Conveying of information in the languages known to you	500	1798.00	3.60	28.33
23.	Accessibility of staff in the bank by telephone	500	1787.00	3.57	28.85
24.	Accessibility of the branch manager or higher officials	500	1772.00	3.54	29.38
25.	Accessibility and contact of staff in the bank	500	1757.00	3.51	29.63
26.	Care and Consideration given to your grievances	500	1731.00	3.46	30.64
27.	Convenience of timing of the office hours of the bank	500	1749.00	3.50	30.00
28.	Prompt opening/closing of the branch as per time	500	1691.00	3.38	32.25
	TOTAL		**1798.27**	**3.60**	**28.89**
	RELIABILITY DIMENSION				
29.	Interest and willingness to help you to provide prompt service:	500	1662.00	3.32	32.83
30.	Time taken to process your grievances	500	1566.00	3.13	35.78

(Contd...)

1	2	3	4	5	6
31.	Attention given to the grievances and the follow up actions taken:	500	1628.00	3.26	34.97
32.	Care and Consideration of your property and values entrusted for safe custody	500	1589.00	3.18	35.22
33.	Appropriateness and update of the account statements provided to you:	500	1534.00	3.07	37.46
34.	Neatness and legibility of the entries in the pass book:	500	1531.00	3.06	38.24
35.	Quick provision of services:	500	1501.00	3.00	39.33
36.	Skill of the staff to use computers and other modern technical devices	500	1497.00	2.99	38.80
	TOTAL		**1563.50**	**3.13**	**36.42**

Source: Computed from Primary Data

Tangibility Dimension on Desired Level of Service Quality: Public Sector Banks

As it could be seen in Table 5.5 (*See on pages 146 to 149*), under the tangibility dimension, the highest average score of 5.80 has been recorded by the factor on 'Indication of display timings at appropriate counters' (5.54). The next lowest score has been recorded by the factor on 'Location of the bank (5.49). The order of other factors is: 'Image of your bank among the public' (5.48), 'Upkeep and cleanliness of the bank premises' (5.45), 'Usage of computers and other modern technology to provide service' (5.45), 'Adequacy of space' (5.44) and 'Indication of display boards at appropriate counters (5.43). The average score for the tangibility dimension under desired level of service quality for the public sector banks stood at 5.47. In terms of coefficient of variation, a measure of dispersion of the variable has indicated that the least variation is being record by the factor on 'Image of your bank among the public' (19.34%). This is being followed by other factor in the order as: 'Usage of computers and other modern technology to provide service' (19.82%), 'Adequacy of space (20.59%), 'Location of the bank' (20.77%), 'Upkeep and cleanliness of the bank premises' (21.83%), 'Indication of display timings at appropriate counters' (21.84%) and 'Indication of display boards at appropriate counters' (22.10%). The average coefficient of variation for the entire dimension stood at 20.84 per cent. From the above discussion it can be understood that the order of the variable in terms of average and the order of the dispersion are widely dispersed. This is unlike the order found in the case of the perceived level. This means that the customers' order of perceived level of service quality is different from the order found in the case of desired level.

Assurance Dimension on Desired Level of Service Quality: Public Sector Banks

As it could be seen in the Table 5.5, the factor on 'Usage of technical terms when speaking with you formed the highest score with 5.32. The order of the scores stood at: Proficiency of the staff on the work they carry out for you' (5.31) and Confidence and perfection of the services provided to you' (5.21). The average score stood for the entire dimension stood at 5.28. In terms of coefficient of variation, the least value of 19.74 per cent for the factor on 'Usage of technical terms when speaking with you. The order of other factors in terms of increasing coefficient is: 'Proficiency of the staff on the work they carry out for you' (20.15%) and 'Confidence and perfection of the services provided to you' (20.92%). The average coefficient for the entire dimension on assurance stood at 20.27 per cent. From the above discussion it can be understood that the order of the variable in terms of average is the order of the dispersion. This means that the factor with higher score could register the lowest coefficient of variation.

Responsive Dimension on Desired Level of Service Quality: Public Sector Banks

As it is given in the Table 5.5, under the responsiveness dimension, the factor on 'Responsiveness to your comments and suggestions' (5.11) secured the highest score. This is being followed by the factor on 'Attitude, responsiveness and courtesy of the staff' (5.05). The order of other factors is: 'Transfer of money from your bank to other bank' (4.88), 'Treatment of your need and urgency with care and seriousness' (4.88). Promptness of the services carried out' (4.82). 'Dependability and accuracy of the services provided to you' (4.75) and 'Response of the staff when there is a grievance' (4.73). The average score for the entire dimension on responsiveness stood at 4.89. In terms of coefficient of variation, the order of the factors is: Responsiveness to your comments and suggestions' (19.18%), 'Promptness of the services carried out' (19.92%), 'Attitude, responsiveness and courtesy of the staff' (20.20%), 'Dependability and accuracy of the services provided to you' (20.21%), Treatment of your need and urgency with care and seriousness (20.29%), 'Transfer of money from your bank to other bank (21.72%) and Response of the staff when there is a grievance (22.20%). The average dispersion recorded a level of 20.45 for the entire dimension. The above discussion indicates that the order of the average and the order of the dispersion are found to be the same with the factor on Responsiveness to your comments and suggestions' occupying the highest score and the least coefficient of variation.

Empathy Dimension on Desired Level of Service Quality: Public Sector Banks

As given in the Table, under the empathy dimension, the factor on 'Efforts taken by the bank staff to know about you and your needs' (4.91) formed the highest. The order of other factors is: 'Reaction of the bank staff if a scheduled appointment is missed by you' (4.74), 'Conveying of information in the languages known to you' (4.66), 'Recognition of the bank staff to call you by your name' (4.63), 'Accessibility of staff in the bank by telephone' (4.60), 'Accessibility of the staff in the bank to contact by email' (4.59), 'Accessibility of the branch manager or higher officials' (4.53), 'Care and Consideration given to your grievances' (4.42), 'Accessibility and contact of staff in the bank' (4.40), 'Convenience of timing of the office hours of the bank' (4.34) and Prompt opening/closing of the branch as per time' (4.32). The average score for the dimension on empathy stood at 4.56. In terms of coefficient of variation, the least dispersion is being recorded in the case of the factor on 'Efforts taken by the bank staff to know about you and your needs' (16.70%). This is being followed by the factors like: 'Conveying of information in the languages known to you' (20.60%), 'Reaction of the bank staff if a scheduled appointment is missed by you' (21.10%), 'Accessibility of the staff in the bank to contact by email' (21.13%), 'Recognition of the bank staff to call you by your name' (21.170%),

'Accessibility of staff in the bank by telephone' (21.52%), Accessibility of the branch manager or higher officials (22.52%), Care and Consideration given to your grievances (22.85%), Accessibility and contact of staff in the bank (23.18 per cent), 'Convenience of timing of the office hours of the bank (25.12%) and Prompt opening/closing of the branch as per time (26.16%). The average coefficient of variation for the entire dimension stood at 21.93 per cent.

Reliability Dimension on Desired Level of Service Quality: Public Sector Banks

As seen in the Table 5.5, the reliability dimension indicates that among the various factors considered, the factor on Appropriateness and update of the account statements provided to you' (4.30) recorded the highest. This is being followed by the factors like: 'Attention given to the grievances and the follow up actions taken' (4.05), Time taken to process your grievances' (4.03), Care and Consideration of your property and values entrusted for safe custody (3.93), Interest and willingness to help you to provide prompt service (3.92), Skill of the staff to use computers and other modern technical devices (3.80), Neatness and legibility of the entries in the pass book (3.79) and Quick provision of services (3.64). The average score for the entire dimension stood at 3.93. In terms of coefficient of variation also this order has been maintained with Appropriateness and update of the account statements provided to you (21.63%) occupying the least score, followed by the factors in the order: Time taken to process your grievances (27.05%), Attention given to the grievances and the follow up actions taken (27.90%), Care and Consideration of your property and values entrusted for safe custody (28.50%), Skill of the staff to use computers and other modern technical devices (30.00%), Interest and willingness to help you to provide prompt service (30.87%), Neatness and legibility of the entries in the pass book (31.93%) and Quick provision of services (34.62%). The average coefficient of variation stood at 29.01 per cent for the reliability dimension as a whole.

Thus from the analysis it can be concluded that under the tangibility dimension the desired level of service quality among the public sector banks has registered the highest value in the case of 'Indication of display timings at appropriate counters' while in terms of the coefficient of variation, the factor on 'Image of your bank among the public' formed the least dispersion indicating the consistency in the idea of the customers. The public sector banks under the assurance dimension on the perceived level of service quality, the highest value and the least coefficient of variation has been achieved by 'Usage of technical terms when speaking with you' which indicates that the customers of public sector banks perceive profession in the service provided as the highest factor of preference among the assurance dimension. Under the responsiveness dimension the factor on 'Responsiveness to your comments and suggestions' has registered the highest value. In terms of average and coefficient of variation, the factor on 'Efforts taken by the bank staff to know about you and your needs' is in favourable position when compared to all other factors, under empathy dimension.. The factor on 'Appropriateness and update of the account statements provided to you' formed the highest score as well as the minimum variance indicating the consistency of the customers towards the preference for this factor. It can also be inferred from the table that by preferring this factor the most, the customers expect the bank employees to provide an updated account.

Desired Level of Satisfaction: Private Sector Banks

In the subsequent paragraphs it is attempted to provide a view on the customers' opinion on the desired level of satisfaction on the services of private sector banks.

Table 5.5: Desired Level of Satisfaction: Public Sector Banks

Sl. No.	Factor	Average Sample Size	Total Score	Average Score	C.V.
1	2	3	4	5	6
	TANGIBILITY DIMENSION				
1.	Indication of display timings at appropriate counters:	280	1219.00	5.54	21.84
2.	Indication of display boards at appropriate counters:	280	1194.00	5.43	22.10
3.	Upkeep and cleanliness of the bank premises:	280	1199.00	5.45	21.83
4.	Adequacy of space?	280	1197.00	5.44	20.59
5.	Location of the bank	280	1207.00	5.49	20.77
6.	Usage of computers and other modern technology to provide service:	280	1198.00	5.45	19.82
7.	Image of your bank among the public:	280	1205.00	5.48	19.34
	TOTAL		**1202.71**	**5.47**	**20.84**
	ASSURANCE DIMENSION				
8.	Usage of technical terms when speaking with you:	280	1170.00	5.32	19.74
9.	Proficiency of the staff on the work they carry out for you:	280	1169.00	5.31	20.15

(Contd...)

1	2	3	4	5	6
10.	Confidence and perfection of the services provided to you:	280	1147.00	5.21	20.92
	TOTAL		**1162.00**	**5.28**	**20.27**
	RESPONSIVENESS DIMENSION				
11.	Attitude, responsiveness and courtesy of the staff:	280	1110.00	5.05	20.20
12.	Responsiveness to your comments and suggestions:	280	1124.00	5.11	19.18
13.	Transfer of money from your bank to other bank:	280	1074.00	4.88	21.72
14.	Treatment of your need and urgency with care and seriousness:	280	1074.00	4.88	20.29
15.	Response of the staff when there is a grievance:	280	1040.00	4.73	22.20
16.	Dependability and accuracy of the services provided to you:	280	1046.00	4.75	20.21
17.	Promptness of the services carried out	280	1061.00	4.82	19.92
	TOTAL		**1075.57**	**4.89**	**20.45**
	EMPATHY DIMENSION				
18.	Reaction of the bank staff if a scheduled appointment is missed by you	280	1043.00	4.74	21.10

(Contd...)

1	2	3	4	5	6
19.	Efforts taken by the bank staff to know about you and your needs	280	1081.00	4.91	16.70
20.	Recognition of the bank staff to call you by your name	280	1019.00	4.63	21.17
21.	Accessibility of the staff in the bank to contact by email	280	1009.00	4.59	21.13
22.	Conveying of information in the languages known to you	280	1026.00	4.66	20.60
23.	Accessibility of staff in the bank by telephone	280	1012.00	4.60	21.52
24.	Accessibility of the branch manager or higher officials	280	996.00	4.53	22.52
25.	Accessibility and contact of staff in the bank	280	969.00	4.40	23.18
26.	Care and Consideration given to your grievances	280	973.00	4.42	22.85
27.	Convenience of timing of the office hours of the bank	280	954.00	4.34	25.12
28.	Prompt opening/closing of the branch as per time	280	951.00	4.32	26.16
	TOTAL		**1003.00**	**4.56**	**21.93**
	RELIABILITY DIMENSION				
29.	Interest and willingness to help you to provide prompt service:	280	862.00	3.92	30.87
30.	Time taken to process your grievances	280	886.00	4.03	27.05

(Contd...)

1	2	3	4	5	6
31.	Attention given to the grievances and the follow up actions taken:	280	890.00	4.05	27.90
32.	Care and Consideration of your property and values entrusted for safe custody	280	865.00	3.93	28.50
33.	Appropriateness and update of the account statements provided to you:	280	945.00	4.30	21.63
34.	Neatness and legibility of the entries in the pass book:	280	833.00	3.79	31.93
35.	Quick provision of services:	280	801.00	3.64	34.62
36.	Skill of the staff to use computers and other modern technical devices	280	835.00	3.80	30.00
	TOTAL		**864.63**	**3.93**	**29.01**

Source: Computed from Primary Data.

Tangibility Dimension on Desired Level of Service Quality: Private Sector Banks

As it could be seen in Table 5.6 (*See on pages 154 to 157*), under the tangibility dimension, the highest average score of 4.47 has been recorded by the factor on 'Indication of display timings at appropriate counters:' The next lowest score has been recorded by the factor on Indication of display boards at appropriate counters' (4.40), Upkeep and cleanliness of the bank premises (4.34), Adequacy of space (4.33), Usage of computers and other modern technology to provide service (4.27), Location of the bank (4.26), and Image of your bank among the public (4.20). The average score for the tangibility dimension under desired level of service quality for the public sector banks stood at 4.32. In terms of coefficient of variation, a measure of dispersion of the variable has indicated that the least variation is being record by the factor on 'Image of your bank among the public' (26.90), 'Usage of computers and other modern technology to provide service' (26.93), Adequacy of space (27.71), Upkeep and cleanliness of the bank premises' (28.11), Location of the bank (28.40), Indication of display timings at appropriate counters' (28.86) and Indication of display boards at appropriate counters' (29.77). The total dispersion for the entire dimension stood at 28.24. From the above discussion it can be understood that the order of the variable in terms of average and the order of the dispersion are widely dispersed. This is unlike the order found in the case of the perceived level. This means that the customers' order of perceived level of service quality is different from the order found in the case of desired level in the case of private sector banks also. However, these conclusions matches with the conclusion arrived in the case of the analysis on the public sector banks indicating the similar preference of both the public sector and private sector banks.

Assurance Dimension on Desired Level of Service Quality: Private Sector Banks

As it could be seen in the Table 5.6, the factor on 'Usage of technical terms when speaking with you' constituted the highest score with 4.25. The order of other factors is: Confidence and perfection of the services provided to you' (4.14), 'Proficiency of the staff on the work they carry out for you' (4.11). The average level of score stood at a value of 4.17. In terms of coefficient of variation, the least dispersion of 27.05 per cent has been recorded by the factor on 'Confidence and perfection of the services provided to you'. The order of the other factors is: 'Proficiency of the staff on the work they carry out for you' (27.49%) and 'Usage of technical terms when speaking with you' (27.53%). The average dispersion stood at 27.34. From the above discussion it can be understood that the order of the variable in terms of average and the order of the dispersion are not uniform indicating a wider dispersion.

Responsive Dimension on Desired Level of Service Quality: Private Sector Banks

As it is given in the Table, under the responsiveness dimension, the factor on 'Attitude, responsiveness and courtesy of the staff recorded the highest score of 4.08. This is being followed by the factor on Response of the staff when there is a grievance' with a score of 4.03. The order of other factors is: 'Transfer of money from your bank to other bank' (4.00), 'Dependability and accuracy of the services provided to you' (3.98), 'Treatment of your need and urgency with care and seriousness' (3.93), 'Responsiveness to your comments and suggestions' (3.91) and 'Promptness of the services carried out' (3.87). The average score of the entire dimension constituted 3.97. In terms of coefficient of variation, the order of the factors is: 'Response of the staff when there is a grievance' (27.30%), 'Dependability and accuracy of the services provided to you' (27.89%), 'Attitude, responsiveness and courtesy of the staff' (28.19%), 'Promptness of the services carried out' (28.42%), 'Transfer of money from your bank to other bank' (28.75%), 'Responsiveness to your comments and suggestions' (29.92%) and 'Treatment of your need and urgency with care and seriousness' (30.53 per cent). The average level of coefficient of variation stood at 28.72 per cent. The above discussion indicates that the factor on Attitude, responsiveness and courtesy of the staff' recorded the highest score while in terms of coefficient of variation the factor on 'Response of the staff when there is a grievance' recorded the least.

Empathy Dimension on Desired Level of Service Quality: Private Sector Banks

As given in the Table 5.6, under the empathy dimension, the factor on 'Reaction of the bank staff if a scheduled appointment is missed by you' (3.93) recorded the highest score. The order of the other factors is: 'Recognition of the bank staff to call you by your name' (3.83), 'Accessibility of the staff in the bank to contact by email' (3.74), Efforts taken by the bank staff to know about you and your needs' (3.70), 'Convenience of timing of the office hours of the bank' (3.61), 'Accessibility and contact of staff in the bank' (3.58), 'Accessibility of the branch manager or higher officials' (3.53), 'Accessibility of staff in the bank by telephone' (3.52), 'Conveying of information in the languages known to you' (3.51), 'Care and Consideration given to your grievances' (3.45) and Prompt opening/closing of the branch as per time' (3.36). The average score on the entire dimension on empathy stood at 3.61. In terms of coefficient of variation, the least dispersion is being recorded in the case of the factor on 'Reaction of the bank staff if a scheduled appointment is missed by you' (27.23%), 'Recognition of the bank staff to call you by your name' (27.94%), 'Convenience of timing of the office hours of the bank' (27.98%), 'Accessibility of the staff in the bank to contact by email' (28.61%), 'Accessibility of the branch manager or higher officials' (29.75%), 'Accessibility and contact of staff in the bank' (30.17%) and 'Accessibility of staff in the bank by telephone' (30.40%), 'Prompt opening/closing of the branch as per time' (30.95%), 'Conveying of information in the languages known to you'

(31.05%), 'Care and Consideration given to your grievances' (32.46%) and Efforts taken by the bank staff to know about you and your needs' (33.24%). The average dispersion for the entire dimension stood at 29.92 per cent.

Reliability Dimension on Desired Level of Service Quality: Private Sector Banks

As seen in the Table 5.6, the reliability dimension indicates that among the various factors considered, the factor on 'Interest and willingness to help you to provide prompt service' (3.64), 'Attention given to the grievances and the follow up actions taken' (3.35), 'Care and Consideration of your property and values entrusted for safe custody ' (3.29), 'Quick provision of services' (3.18), 'Neatness and legibility of the entries in the pass book' (3.17), 'Time taken to process your grievances' (3.09), 'Skill of the staff to use computers and other modern technical devices' (3.01) and 'Appropriateness and update of the account statements provided to you' (2.68). The average score for the entire dimension stood at 3.18. In terms of coefficient of variation also this order has been maintained with 'Interest and willingness to help you to provide prompt service' (24.73%) taking up the lead in terms of least coefficient of variation. This is being followed by the factors on: 'Care and Consideration of your property and values entrusted for safe custody' (33.43%), 'Quick provision of services' (33.65%), 'Attention given to the grievances and the follow up actions taken' (34.03%), Neatness and legibility of the entries in the pass book' (35.02%), 'Time taken to process your grievances' (37.86%), 'Skill of the staff to use computers and other modern technical devices' (39.20%) and 'Appropriateness and update of the account statements provided to you' (51.49%). The average dispersion for the entire dimension stood at 35.53 per cent.

Thus from the analysis it can be concluded that under the tangibility dimension the desired level of service quality among the private sector banks has registered the highest

Table 5.6: Desired Level of Satisfaction: Private Sector Banks

Sl. No.	Factor	Average Sample Size	Total Score	Average Score	C.V.
1	2	3	4	5	6
	TANGIBILITY DIMENSION				
1.	Indication of display timings at appropriate counters:	220	984.00	4.47	28.86
2.	Indication of display boards at appropriate counters:	220	968.00	4.40	29.77
3.	Upkeep and cleanliness of the bank premises:	220	955.00	4.34	28.11
4.	Adequacy of space?	220	952.00	4.33	27.71
5.	Location of the bank	220	937.00	4.26	28.40
6.	Usage of computers and other modern technology to provide service:	220	939.00	4.27	26.93
7.	Image of your bank among the public:	220	925.00	4.20	26.90
	TOTAL		**951.43**	**4.32**	**28.24**
	ASSURANCE DIMENSION				
8.	Usage of technical terms when speaking with you:	220	935.00	4.25	27.53
9.	Proficiency of the staff on the work they carry out for you:	220	904.00	4.11	27.49

(Contd...)

1	2	3	4	5	6
10.	Confidence and perfection of the services provided to you:	220	910.00	4.14	27.05
	TOTAL		**916.33**	**4.17**	**27.34**
	RESPONSIVENESS DIMENSION				
11.	Attitude, responsiveness and courtesy of the staff:	220	898.00	4.08	28.19
12.	Responsiveness to your comments and suggestions:	220	860.00	3.91	29.92
13.	Transfer of money from your bank to other bank:	220	880.00	4.00	28.75
14.	Treatment of your need and urgency with care and seriousness:	220	864.00	3.93	30.53
15.	Response of the staff when there is a grievance:	220	887.00	4.03	27.30
16.	Dependability and accuracy of the services provided to you:	220	875.00	3.98	27.89
17.	Promptness of the services carried out	220	851.00	3.87	28.42
	TOTAL		**873.57**	**3.97**	**28.72**
	EMPATHY DIMENSION				
18.	Reaction of the bank staff if a scheduled appointment is missed by you	220	865.00	3.93	27.23

(Contd...)

1	2	3	4	5	6
19.	Efforts taken by the bank staff to know about you and your needs	220	813.00	3.70	33.24
20.	Recognition of the bank staff to call you by your name	220	843.00	3.83	27.94
21.	Accessibility of the staff in the bank to contact by email	220	823.00	3.74	28.61
22.	Conveying of information in the languages known to you	220	772.00	3.51	31.05
23.	Accessibility of staff in the bank by telephone	220	775.00	3.52	30.40
24.	Accessibility of the branch manager or higher officials	220	776.00	3.53	29.75
25.	Accessibility and contact of staff in the bank	220	788.00	3.58	30.17
26.	Care and Consideration given to your grievances	220	758.00	3.45	32.46
27.	Convenience of timing of the office hours of the bank	220	795.00	3.61	27.98
28.	Prompt opening/closing of the branch as per time	220	740.00	3.36	30.95
	TOTAL		**795.27**	**3.61**	**29.92**
	RELIABILITY DIMENSION				
29.	Interest and willingness to help you to provide prompt service:	220	800.00	3.64	24.73
30.	Time taken to process your grievances	220	680.00	3.09	37.86

(Contd...)

1	2	3	4	5	6
31.	Attention given to the grievances and the follow up actions taken:	220	738.00	3.35	34.03
32.	Care and Consideration of your property and values entrusted for safe custody	220	724.00	3.29	33.43
33.	Appropriateness and update of the account statements provided to you:	220	589.00	2.68	51.49
34.	Neatness and legibility of the entries in the pass book:	220	698.00	3.17	35.02
35.	Quick provision of services:	220	700.00	3.18	33.65
36.	Skill of the staff to use computers and other modern technical devices	220	662.00	3.01	39.20
	TOTAL		**698.88**	**3.18**	**35.53**

Source: Computed from Primary Data

value in the case of 'Indication of display timings at appropriate counters' while in terms of the coefficient of variation, the factor on 'Image of your bank among the public' formed the least dispersion. The private sector banks under the assurance dimension on the desired level of service quality, the highest value has been recorded by the factor on 'Usage of technical terms when speaking with you' while in terms of dispersion, the factor on 'Confidence and perfection of the services provided to you' recorded the least. Under the responsiveness dimension the factor on 'Attitude, responsiveness and courtesy of the staff'has registered the highest value. Under empathy dimension, in terms of average and coefficient of variation, the factor on 'Reaction of the bank staff if a scheduled appointment is missed by you' is in favourable position when compared to all other factors. The factor on 'Interest and willingness to help you to provide prompt service' formed the highest score as well as the minimum variance, under reliability dimension indicating the consistency of the customers towards the preference for this factor.

SECTION III

Perceived and Desired Level of Satisfaction: A Gap Analysis

The earlier two sections provided a detailed view on the customers' level of satiation on e-Banking and other services for the entire sample banks as a whole and by public and private sector banks. This analysis has provided the perceived and desired levels of satisfaction in isolation. But as provided in the literature, the success of the bank depends greatly on the difference between the two. Higher the difference (gap) between the two higher is the level of dissatisfaction and hence the banks would be in a position to improve the level of satisfaction by reducing the gap. Hence, an understanding of the extent of gap in the case of each of the dimension and the difference in each of the factors and in the present section such an attempt is being made. To identify the significance of the difference, the't' test is being attempted.

Service Quality Gap: All Banks

In the subsequent paragraphs it is attempted to provide a view on the customers' opinion on the service quality gap of all sample banks.

Service Quality Gap in Tangibility Dimension: All Banks

As it could be seen in table 5.7 (*See on pages 162-165*), the service quality gap in the case of tangibility dimension is found to be negative for all the factors indicating the higher desired level than the perceived level of satisfaction. This again indicates that the banks have into increase their services to improve the level of satisfaction of their customers. The table indicates that the service quality gap is more in the case of 'Indication of display timings at appropriate counters (-2.82), followed by 'Indication of display boards at appropriate counters' (-2.64), Upkeep and cleanliness of the bank premises(-2.62), Adequacy of space (-2.60), Location of the bank (-2.58), Usage of computers and other modern technology to provide service (-2.54) and Image of your bank among the public (-2.52). The gap indicates that the serviced quality gap is found to be higher with regard to the location, space, display board etc., while the gap is lower in the case of service related factors like the use of computes. This implies that the banks could rise to the expectations of the customers considerably.

Service Quality Gap in Assurance Dimension: All Banks

As it could be seen in the Table 5.7, in the case of assurance dimension the total scores as well as the scores of the individual factors have turned out to be negative indicating the higher desired level of service quality than the perceived level. Factor wise, the highest negative value could be found in the case of the factor on 'Usage of technical terms when speaking with you (-2.42), followed by the factor on 'Proficiency of the staff on the work they carry out for you' (-2.30) and 'Confidence and perfection of the services provided to you' (-2.22). The discussion provides the conclusion that the banks could provide a higher level of service quality nearing to the expectations of the customers in terms of perfection in the services provided.

Service Quality Gap in Responsive Dimension: All Banks

As it could be seen in the Table 5.7, in the case of responsiveness dimension, the highest service quality gap could be seen on 'Attitude, responsiveness and courtesy of the staff' (-2.04). The order of other factors is: 'Responsiveness to your comments and suggestions (-1.79), 'Promptness of the services carried out (-1.79), Transfer of money from your bank to other bank' (-1.75), Dependability and accuracy of the services provided to you (-1.75), Treatment of your need and urgency with care and seriousness (-1.73) and Response of the staff when there is a grievance (-1.73). The overall service quality gap is also found to be negative indicating the higher desired level of service of the customers than the perceived level in the case of responsiveness dimension. The lower gap recorded in the case of the factor on 'Response of the staff when there is a grievance' which indicates that the employees of the bank are attending to the customers' grievances immediately. This is an indication of the better service provision of the sample banks.

Service Quality Gap in Empathy Dimension: All Banks

As given in the Table 5.7, the entire dimension on empathy has recorded the negative gap indicating the higher desired level when compared to the perceived level of service quality. Factor-wise, the highest level of gap could be found in the case of 'Reaction of the bank staff if a scheduled appointment is missed by you' (-1.64), followed by 'Efforts taken by the bank staff to know about you and your needs' (-1.58), Recognition of the bank staff to call you by your name' (-1.44), 'Accessibility of the staff in the bank to contact by email' (-1.32), 'Conveying of information in the languages known to you:' (-1.2), 'Accessibility of staff in the bank by telephone' (-1.14), 'Accessibility of the branch manager or higher officials' (-1.08), 'Accessibility and contact of staff in the bank' (-1.02), 'Convenience of timing of the office hours of the bank' (-1.00), 'Care and Consideration given to your grievances' (-0.92) and 'Prompt opening/closing of the branch as per time' (-0.76).

Service Quality Gap in Reliability Dimension: All Banks

As it could be seen in the Table 5.7, the factor on 'Interest and willingness to help you to provide prompt service' recorded the least negative gap of -0.64. The next lowest gap could be found in the case of the factor on 'Attention given to the grievances and the follow up actions taken (-0.52). The order of the other negative factors is: Care and Consideration of your property and values entrusted for safe custody' (-0.36), Time taken to process your grievances (-0.26), Appropriateness and update of the account statements provided to you (-0.14), and Neatness and legibility of the entries in the pass book (-0.12). It is interesting to note that the factor on 'Quick provision of services' recorded a zero gap indicating the perfect matching of the desired level of service quality with the perceived level of service quality. It is heartening to note that the facto on 'Skill of the staff to use computers and other modern technical devices'(0.02) recorded a positive service quality gap indicating the higher level of perceived service quality than the desired service quality.

Thus from the analysis it can be concluded that the gap is found to be more in the case of location while it is lower in

Table 5.7: Comparison of Perceived and Desired Level of Satisfaction of All Banks: A Gap Analysis All Banks

Sl. No.	Factor	Perceived	Desired	GAP	Combined Standard Deviation	t Value
1	2	3	4	5	6	7
	TANGIBILITY DIMENSION					
1.	Indication of display timings at appropriate counters:	1.59	4.41	-2.82	1.72	-3.64*
2.	Indication of display boards at appropriate counters:	1.68	4.32	-2.64	1.70	-3.55*
3.	Upkeep and cleanliness of the bank premises:	1.69	4.31	-2.62	1.66	-3.58*
4.	Adequacy of space?	1.7	4.3	-2.60	1.62	-3.60*
5.	Location of the bank	1.71	4.29	-2.58	1.63	-3.58*
6.	Usage of computers and other modern technology to provide service:	1.73	4.27	-2.54	1.58	-3.61*
7.	Image of your bank among the public:	1.74	4.26	-2.52	1.57	-3.61*
	TOTAL	**1.69**	**4.31**	**-2.62**	**1.64**	**-3.60***
	ASSURANCE DIMENSION:					
8.	Usage of technical terms when speaking with you:	1.79	4.21	-2.42	1.56	-3.56*

(Contd...)

1	2	3	4	5	6	7
9.	Proficiency of the staff on the work they carry out for you:	1.85	4.15	-2.30	1.53	-3.50*
10.	Confidence and perfection of the services provided to you:	1.89	4.11	-2.22	1.53	-3.46*
	TOTAL	**1.88**	**4.16**	**-2.28**	**1.52**	**-3.50***
	RESPONSIVENESS DIMENSION					
11.	Attitude, responsiveness and courtesy of the staff:	1.98	4.02	-2.04	1.48	-3.38*
12.	Responsiveness to your comments and suggestions:	2.18	3.97	-1.79	1.38	-3.29*
13.	Transfer of money from your bank to other bank:	2.16	3.91	-1.75	1.40	-3.25*
14.	Treatment of your need and urgency with care and seriousness:	2.15	3.88	-1.73	1.42	-3.22*
15.	Response of the staff when there is a grievance:	2.12	3.85	-1.73	1.43	-3.21*
16.	Dependability and accuracy of the services provided to you:	2.09	3.84	-1.75	1.43	-3.22*
17.	Promptness of the services carried out	2.03	3.82	-1.79	1.44	-3.25*
	TOTAL	**2.1**	**3.9**	**-1.80**	**1.43**	**-3.26***

(Contd...)

1	2	3	4	5	6	7
	EMPATHY DIMENSION					
18.	Reaction of the bank staff if a scheduled appointment is missed by you	2.18	3.82	-1.64	1.37	-3.19*
19.	Efforts taken by the bank staff to know about you and your needs	2.21	3.79	-1.58	1.35	-3.17*
20.	Recognition of the bank staff to call you by your name	2.28	3.72	-1.44	1.33	-3.08*
21.	Accessibility of the staff in the bank to contact by email	2.34	3.66	-1.32	1.31	-3.01*
22.	Conveying of information in the languages known to you	2.4	3.6	-1.20	1.28	-2.94*
23.	Accessibility of staff in the bank by telephone	2.43	3.57	-1.14	1.28	-2.89*
24.	Accessibility of the branch manager or higher officials	2.46	3.54	-1.08	1.27	-2.85*
25.	Accessibility and contact of staff in the bank	2.49	3.51	-1.02	1.27	-2.80*
26.	Care and Consideration given to your grievances	2.54	3.46	-0.92	1.26	-2.73*
27.	Convenience of timing of the office hours of the bank	2.5	3.5	-1.00	1.27	-2.79*
28.	Prompt opening/closing of the branch as per time	2.62	3.38	-0.76	1.25	-2.61*
	TOTAL	**2.4**	**3.6**	**-1.20**	**1.30**	**-2.93***
	RELIABILITY DIMENSION					
29.	Interest and willingness to help you to provide prompt service:	2.676	3.32	-0.64	1.23	-2.52*

(Contd...)

1	2	3	4	5	6	7
30.	Time taken to process your grievances	2.868	3.13	-0.26	1.18	-2.22*
31.	Attention given to the grievances and the follow up actions taken:	2.744	3.26	-0.52	1.25	-2.41*
32.	Care and Consideration of your property and values entrusted for safe custody	2.822	3.18	-0.36	1.19	-2.30*
33.	Appropriateness and update of the account statements : provided to you	2.932	3.07	-0.14	1.18	-2.12*
34.	Neatness and legibility of the entries in the pass book:	2.938	3.06	-0.12	1.20	-2.10*
35.	Quick provision of services:	2.998	3	0.00	1.18	-2.00*
36.	Skill of the staff to use computers and other modern technical devices	3.006	2.99	0.02	1.16	-1.99*
	TOTAL	**2.873**	**3.13**	**-0.26**	**1.19**	**-2.22***

* Indicates significant at % per cent Level
Source: Computed from Primary Data

the case of service related factors. In terms of the perfection in the services provided the banks satisfy the customers' expectations to a greater extent. The employees of the bank are attending to the customers' grievances immediately. The customers are highly satisfied over the provision of the facility on prompt opening and closing of the bank branch as per the time. The factor on 'Quick provision of services' recorded a zero gap indicating the perfect matching of the desired level of service quality with the perceived level of service quality. It is heartening to note that the facto on 'Skill of the staff to use computers and other modern technical devices'(0.02) recorded a positive service quality gap indicating the higher level of perceived service quality than the desired service quality. The service quality gap is found to be positive for a majority of the factors on service charges. The sample customer respondents are more than satisfied over the provision of e-Banking facilities.

Service Quality Gap on Tangibility Dimension: Public Sector Banks

In the subsequent paragraphs it is attempted to provide a view on the customers' opinion on the service quality gap of public private sector banks.

Service Quality Gap in Tangibility Dimension: Public Sector Banks

As it could be seen in Table 5.8 (*See on page 170-173*), the service quality gap in the case of tangibility dimension on the public sector banks is found to be negative for all the factors indicating the higher desired level than the perceived level of satisfaction. This again indicates that the banks have into increase their services to improve the level of satisfaction of their customers. The table indicates that the service quality gap is more in the case of 'Indication of display timings at appropriate counters (-3.89), followed by Location of the bank (-3.8), Image of your bank among the public (-3.78), Adequacy of space (-3.74), 'Upkeep and cleanliness of the bank premises (-3.73), 'Usage of computers and other modern technology to provide service' (-3.73), Indication of display boards at appropriate counters (-3.67). The overall service quality gap on the tangibility dimension stood at -3.76. The gap indicates that the serviced quality gap is found to be higher with regard to the location, space, display board etc., while the gap is lower in the case of service related factors like the use of computes. This implies that the banks could rise to the expectations of the customers considerably.

Service Quality Gap in Assurance Dimension: Public Sector Banks

As it could be seen in the Table 5.8, in the case of assurance dimension for the public sector banks, the total as well as the scores of the individual factors has turned out to be negative indicating the higher desired level of service quality than the perceived level. Factor wise, the highest negative value could be found in the case of the factor on 'Usage of technical terms when speaking with you:' (-3.53), 'Proficiency of the staff on the work they carry out for you' (-3.48), Confidence and perfection of the services provided to you' (-3.31). The average score stood at -3.39. The discussion provides the conclusion that the customers have confidence on the services provided.

Service Quality Gap in Responsive Dimension: Public Sector Banks

As it could be seen in the Table (5.8), in the case of responsiveness dimension, the highest service quality gap could be seen on 'Responsiveness to your comments and suggestions' (-4.35). The order of the other factors is: Transfer of money from your bank to other bank: (-2.72), Treatment of your need and urgency with care and seriousness (-2.72), Promptness of the services carried out (-2.63), Dependability and accuracy of the services provided to you (-2.49) and Response of the staff when there is a grievance' (-2.44). The lower gap recorded in the case of the factor on 'Response of the staff when there is a grievance' which indicates that the employees of the public sector bank are attending to the customers' grievances immediately. This is an indication of the better service provision of the sample banks.

Service Quality Gap in Empathy Dimension: Public Sector Banks

As given in the Table (5.8), the entire dimension on empathy has recorded the negative service quality gap indicating the higher desired level when compared to the perceived level of service quality. Factor wise, the highest level of gap in the public sector banks could be found in the case of 'Efforts taken by the bank staff to know about you and your needs' (-2.77), 'Reaction of the bank staff if a scheduled appointment is missed by you' (-2.46), Conveying of information in the languages known to you (-2.32), Recognition of the bank staff to call you by your name' (-2.27), Accessibility of staff in the bank by telephone (-2.21), Accessibility of the staff in the bank to contact by email (-2.19), 'Accessibility of the branch manager or higher officials' (-2.09), Care and Consideration given to your grievances' (-1.89), 'Accessibility and contact of staff in the bank' (-1.86), 'Convenience of timing of the office hours of the bank' (-1.75) and 'prompt opening/closing of the branch as per time' (-1.72). The overall service quality gap is recorded as -2.14. This analysis provides the conclusion that the customers are highly satisfied over the provision of the facility on prompt opening and closing of the bank branch as per the time.

Service Quality Gap in Reliability Dimension: Public Sector Banks

As it could be seen in the Table (5.8), the factor on 'Appropriateness and update of the account statements provided to you' (-1.67), recorded the least negative gap.

The next lowest gap could be found in the case of the factor on 'Attention given to the grievances and the follow up actions taken' (-1.23), 'Time taken to process your grievances' (-1.19), 'Care and Consideration of your property and values entrusted for safe custody' (-1.02), 'Interest and willingness to help you to provide prompt service' (1.00), 'Skill of the staff to use computers and other modern technical devices' (-0.78), 'Neatness and legibility of the entries in the pass book' (-0.76) and 'Quick provision of services' (-0.5).

It can also be noted that in the case of the analysis of the over all banking performance, a majority of the factors indicated a positive value while in the case of the public sector banks all the factors shows a negative value indicating the poor performance of the public sector banks which is below average. However, among the factors considered under the reliability dimension the factor on 'Quick provision of services' recorded the least gap. This indicates that the difference between the perceived and desired level of service quality is much narrowed.

Thus from the analysis it can be concluded that the gap is found to be more in the case of location while it is lower in the case of service related factors. In terms of the perfection in the services provided the banks satisfy the customers' expectations to a greater extent. The employees of the bank are attending to the customers' grievances immediately. The customers are highly satisfied over the provision of the facility on prompt opening and closing of the bank branch as per the time. The analysis of the over all banking performance, a majority of the factors indicated a positive value while in the case of the public sector banks all the factors shows a negative value indicating the poor performance of the public sector banks which is below average. However, among the factors considered under the reliability dimension the factor on 'Quick provision of services' recorded the least gap. This indicates that the difference between the perceived and desired level of service quality is much narrowed.

Table 5.8: Service Quality Gap: Public Sector Banks

Sl. No.	Factor	Perceived	Desired	GAP	Combined Standard Deviation	t Value
1	2	3	4	5	6	7
	TANGIBILITY DIMENSION					
1.	Indication of display timings at appropriate counters:	1.65	5.54	-3.89	1.68	-4.32*
2.	Indication of display boards at appropriate counters:	1.76	5.43	-3.67	1.64	-4.24*
3.	Upkeep and cleanliness of the bank premises:	1.72	5.45	-3.73	1.64	-4.28*
4.	Adequacy of space?	1.7	5.44	-3.74	1.59	-4.35*
5.	Location of the bank	1.69	5.49	-3.80	1.62	-4.35*
6.	Usage of computers and other modern technology to provide service:	1.72	5.45	-3.73	1.56	-4.39*
7.	Image of your bank among the public:	1.7	5.48	-3.78	1.56	-4.43*
	TOTAL	**1.71**	**5.47**	**-3.76**	**1.61**	**-4.34***
	ASSURANCE DIMENSION					
8.	Usage of technical terms when speaking with you:	1.79	5.32	-3.53	1.52	-4.33*
9.	Proficiency of the staff on the work they carry out for you:	1.83	5.31	-3.48	1.52	-4.28*

(Contd...)

1	2	3	4	5	6	7
10.	Confidence and perfection of the services provided to you:	1.9	5.21	-3.31	1.51	-4.19*
	TOTAL	**1.89**	**5.28**	**-3.39**	**1.49**	**-4.27***
	RESPONSIVENESS DIMENSION					
11.	Attitude, responsiveness and courtesy of the staff:	2.04	5.05	-3.01	1.41	-4.13*
12.	Responsiveness to your comments and suggestions:	0.76	5.11	-4.35	1.61	-4.71*
13.	Transfer of money from your bank to other bank:	2.16	4.88	-2.72	1.40	-3.94*
14.	Treatment of your need and urgency with care and seriousness:	2.16	4.88	-2.72	1.35	-4.02*
15.	Response of the staff when there is a grievance:	2.29	4.73	-2.44	1.35	-3.81*
16.	Dependability and accuracy of the services provided to you:	2.26	4.75	-2.49	1.28	-3.94*
17.	Promptness of the services carried out	2.19	4.82	-2.63	1.30	-4.02*
	TOTAL	**1.98**	**4.89**	**-2.91**	**1.38**	**-4.10***
	EMPATHY DIMENSION					
18.	Reaction of the bank staff if a scheduled appointment is missed by you	2.28	4.74	-2.46	1.32	-3.87*

(Contd...)

1	2	3	4	5	6	7
19.	Efforts taken by the bank staff to know about you and your needs	2.14	4.91	-2.77	1.24	-4.23*
20.	Recognition of the bank staff to call you by your name	2.36	4.63	-2.27	1.27	-3.79*
21.	Accessibility of the staff in the bank to contact by email	2.4	4.59	-2.19	1.25	-3.76*
22.	Conveying of information in the languages known to you	2.34	4.66	-2.32	1.26	-3.84*
23.	Accessibility of staff in the bank by telephone	2.39	4.6	-2.21	1.26	-3.76*
24.	Accessibility of the branch manager or higher officials	2.44	4.53	-2.09	1.27	-3.65*
25.	Accessibility and contact of staff in the bank	2.54	4.4	-1.86	1.22	-3.52*
26.	Care and Consideration given to your grievances	2.53	4.42	-1.89	1.22	-3.55*
27.	Convenience of timing of the office hours of the bank	2.59	4.34	-1.75	1.26	-3.39*
28.	Prompt opening/closing of the branch as per time	2.6	4.32	-1.72	1.29	-3.33*
	TOTAL	**2.42**	**4.56**	**-2.14**	**1.26**	**-3.70***
	RELIABLITY DIMENSION					
29.	Interest and willingness to help you to provide prompt service:	2.92	3.92	-1.00	1.25	-2.80*

(Contd...)

1	2	3	4	5	6	7
30.	Time taken to process your grievances	2.84	4.03	-1.19	1.16	-3.02*
31.	Attention given to the grievances and the follow up actions taken:	2.82	4.05	-1.23	1.21	-3.02*
32.	Care and Consideration of your property and values entrusted for safe custody	2.91	3.93	-1.02	1.16	-2.88*
33.	Appropriateness and update of the account statements provided to you:	2.63	4.3	-1.67	1.11	-3.50*
34.	Neatness and legibility of the entries in the pass book:	3.03	3.79	-0.76	1.20	-2.63*
35.	Quick provision of services:	3.14	3.64	-0.50	1.21	-2.41*
36.	Skill of the staff to use computers and other modern technical devices	3.02	3.8	-0.78	1.13	-2.69*
	TOTAL	**2.91**	**3.93**	**-1.02**	**1.18**	**-2.86***

* Indicates significant at 5% per cent Level

Source: Computed from Primary Data

Service Quality Gap Private Sector Banks

In the present and in the subsequent paragraphs it is attempted to examine the service quality gap of private sector banks.

Service Quality Gap in Tangibility Dimension: Private Sector Banks

As it could be seen in Table 5.9 (*See on pages 177-180*), the service quality gap in the case of tangibility dimension on the private sector banks is found to be negative for all the factors indicating the higher desired level than the perceived level of satisfaction. This again indicates that the banks have into increase their services to improve the level of satisfaction of their customers. The table indicates that the service quality gap is more in the case of 'Indication of display timings at appropriate counters (2.94), 'indication of display boards at appropriate counters' (2.84), Upkeep and cleanliness of the bank premises' (-2.68), 'Adequacy of space (-2.63), 'Usage of computers and other modern technology to provide service' (-2.54), 'Location of the bank' (-2.52), 'Image of your bank among the public' (-2.40). The average level of service quality gap is found to be -2.65. The gap indicates that the serviced quality gap is found to be higher in the case of private sector banks with regard to the location, space, display board etc., while the gap is lower in the case of service related factors like the use of computes. This implies that the banks could rise to the expectations of the customers considerably.

Service Quality Gap in Assurance Dimension Private Sector Banks

As it could be seen in Table 5.9, in the case of assurance dimension for the private sector banks, the total as well as the scores of the individual factors has turned out to be negative indicating the higher desired level of service quality than the perceived level. Factor wise, the highest negative value could be found in the case of the factor on 'Usage of technical terms when speaking with you:' (-2.45), "Confidence and perfection of the services provided to you' (-2.28) and 'Proficiency of the staff on the work they carry out for you' (-2.22), the average score stood at -2.30. The discussion provides the conclusion that the customers have confidence on the services provided.

Service Quality Gap in Responsive Dimension Private Sector Banks

As it could be seen in Table 5.9, in the case of responsiveness dimension, the highest service quality gap could be seen on 'Attitude, responsiveness and courtesy of the staff (-2.16). The order of other factors is: 'Response of the staff when there is a grievance' (-2.06), 'Transfer of money from your bank to other bank' (-2.00), 'Dependability and accuracy of the services provided to you' (-1.96), 'Treatment of your need and urgency with care and seriousness' (-1.86), Promptness of the services carried out' (-1.72) and Responsiveness to your comments and suggestions (-0.26). The lower gap recorded in the case of the factor on 'Responsiveness to your comments and suggestions' (-0.26) which indicates that the employees of the public sector bank are responding to the comments and suggestion of the customers. This is an indication of the private sector banks' attempt to satisfy the customers after having understood their service requirements.

Service Quality Gap in Empathy Dimension Private Sector Banks

As given in Table 5.9, the entire dimension on empathy has recorded the negative gap indicating the higher desired level when compared to the perceived level of service quality. Factor wise, the highest level of gap in the public sector banks could be found in the case of 'Reaction of the bank staff if a scheduled appointment is missed by you' (-1.86), Recognition of the bank staff to call you by your name (-1.66), Accessibility of the staff in the bank to contact by email (-1.48), 'Efforts taken by the bank staff to know about you and your needs (-1.40), 'Convenience of timing of the office hours of the bank (-1.22), 'Accessibility and contact of staff in the bank' (-1.16), Accessibility of the branch manager or higher officials (-1.06), Accessibility of staff in the bank by telephone (-1.04), 'Conveying of information in the languages known to you (-1.02), Care and Consideration given to your grievances' (-0.90) and Prompt opening/closing of the branch as per time (-0.72).This analysis provides the conclusion that the customers of private sector banks on the average, have a higher satisfaction on the provision of the facility on prompt opening and closing of the bank branch as per the time.

Service Quality Gap in Reliability Dimension Private Sector Banks

As it could be seen in Table 5.9, the factor on 'Interest and willingness to help you to provide prompt service (-1.28), Attention given to the grievances and the follow up actions taken (-0.70), Care and Consideration of your property and values entrusted for safe custody (-0.58), Quick provision of services (-0.36), Neatness and legibility of the entries in the pass book' (-0.34), Time taken to process your grievances (-0.18), 'Skill of the staff to use computers and other modern technical devices' (-0.02), 'Appropriateness and update of the account statements provided to you (0.64).

Thus from the analysis it can be concluded that the gap is found to be more in private sector banks in the case of location while it is lower in the case of service related factors. In terms of the perfection in the services provided the banks satisfy the customers' expectations to a greater extent. The employees of the private sector banks are listening to the comments and suggestions of the customers immediately. The customers of private sector banks on the average have a higher satisfaction on the provision of the facility on prompt opening and closing of the bank branch as per the time. The customers are satisfied over the provision of the updated accounts and maintenance.

Table 5.9: Service Quality Gap: Private Sector Banks

Sl. No.	Factor	Perceived	Desired	GAP	Combined Standard Deviation	t Value
1	2	3	4	5	6	7
	TANGIBILITY DIMENSION					
1.	Indication of display timings at appropriate counters:	1.53	4.47	-2.94	1.77	-3.66*
2.	Indication of display boards at appropriate counters:	1.56	4.4	-2.84	1.77	-3.61*
3.	Upkeep and cleanliness of the bank premises:	1.66	4.34	-2.68	1.68	-3.59*
4.	Adequacy of space?	1.7	4.33	-2.63	1.67	-3.58*
5.	Location of the bank	1.74	4.26	-2.52	1.65	-3.52*
6.	Usage of computers and other modern technology to provide service:	1.73	4.27	-2.54	1.61	-3.58*
7.	Image of your bank among the public:	1.8	4.2	-2.40	1.58	-3.52*
	TOTAL	**1.67**	**4.32**	**-2.65**	**1.67**	**-3.58***
	ASSURANCE DIMENSION					
8.	Usage of technical terms when speaking with you:	1.80	4.25	-2.45	1.61	-3.52*
9.	Proficiency of the staff on the work they carry out for you:	1.89	4.11	-2.22	1.54	-3.44*

(Contd...)

1	2	3	4	5	6	7
10.	Confidence and perfection of the services provided to you:	1.86	4.14	-2.28	1.55	-3.47*
	TOTAL	**1.87**	**4.17**	**-2.30**	**1.56**	**-3.47***
	RESPONSIVENESS DIMENSION					
11.	Attitude, responsiveness and courtesy of the staff:	1.92	4.08	-2.16	1.55	-3.39*
12.	Responsiveness to your comments and suggestions:	3.65	3.91	-0.26	1.23	-2.21*
13.	Transfer of money from your bank to other bank:	2	4	-2.00	1.52	-3.31*
14.	Treatment of your need and urgency with care and seriousness:	2.07	3.93	-1.86	1.54	-3.21*
15.	Response of the staff when there is a grievance:	1.97	4.03	-2.06	1.50	-3.38*
16.	Dependability and accuracy of the services provided to you:	2.02	3.98	-1.96	1.48	-3.32*
17.	Promptness of the services carried out	2.15	3.87	-1.72	1.45	-3.19*
	TOTAL	**2.26**	**3.97**	**-1.71**	**1.47**	**-3.17***
	EMPATHY DIMENSION					
18.	Reaction of the bank staff if a scheduled appointment is missed by you	2.07	3.93	-1.86	1.44	-3.29*

(Contd...)

1	2	3	4	5	6	7
19.	Efforts taken by the bank staff to know about you and your needs	2.3	3.7	-1.40	1.49	-2.94*
20.	Recognition of the bank staff to call you by your name	2.17	3.83	-1.66	1.41	-3.18*
21.	Accessibility of the staff in the bank to contact by email	2.26	3.74	-1.48	1.37	-3.08*
22.	Conveying of information in the languages known to you	2.49	3.51	-1.02	1.30	-2.78*
23.	Accessibility of staff in the bank by telephone	2.48	3.52	-1.04	1.29	-2.81*
24.	Accessibility of the branch manager or higher officials	2.47	3.53	-1.06	1.28	-2.83*
25.	Accessibility and contact of staff in the bank	2.42	3.58	-1.16	1.32	-2.88*
26.	Care and Consideration given to your grievances	2.55	3.45	-0.90	1.31	-2.69*
27.	Convenience of timing of the office hours of the bank	2.39	3.61	-1.22	1.28	-2.95*
28.	Prompt opening/closing of the branch as per time	2.64	3.36	-0.72	1.21	-2.60*
	TOTAL	**2.39**	**3.61**	**-1.22**	**1.34**	**-2.91***
	RELIABLITY DIMENSION					
29.	Interest and willingness to help you to provide prompt service:	2.36	3.64	-1.28	1.21	-3.06*

(Contd...)

1	2	3	4	5	6	7
30.	Time taken to process your grievances	2.91	3.09	-0.18	1.21	-2.15*
31.	Attention given to the grievances and the follow up actions taken:	2.65	3.35	-0.70	1.29	-2.54*
32.	Care and Consideration of your property and values entrusted for safe custody	2.71	3.29	-0.58	1.23	-2.47*
33.	Appropriateness and update of the account statements provided to you:	3.32	2.68	0.64	1.26	-1.49
34.	Neatness and legibility of the entries in the pass book:	2.83	3.17	-0.34	1.19	-2.29*
35.	Quick provision of services:	2.82	3.18	-0.36	1.15	-2.31*
36.	Skill of the staff to use computers and other modern technical devices	2.99	3.01	-0.02	1.19	-2.02*
	TOTAL	**2.82**	**3.18**	**-0.36**	**1.21**	**-2.30***

* Indicates Significant at 5 per cent level.

Source: Computed from Primary Data.

6 Quality of Work Life and Satisfaction of Sample Employees
An Analysis

Introduction

The earlier chapter provided a detailed discussion on the customers' satisfaction on the level of services of the sample commercial banks. However, the expected service provision of the customers depends greatly on the Quality of Work Life of the employees. Since the prime objective of introducing the modern technology in service industry is to improve the level of satisfaction of the customers, it becomes pertinent on the part of the employees to acquire the required new skills and knowledge. This is said to bring about a change in the Quality of Work Life. Studies carried out in the context of developed countries could come out with the conclusion on the significant influence of the internal factors on Quality of Work Life. However, the studies did not consider the influence of the external factors. In the Indian context where family sentiments play a significant role, the Quality of Work Life is said to be influenced not only by the internal factors operating within the firm but also by the socio-economic and demographic factors like the age, education, experience, income, family background etc. which are called the external factors . Hence, the analysis of the Quality of work life is partial when only the internal factors are considered. This means it becomes pertinent to understand the relative influence of both the internal and external factors on the Quality of Work Life. The present chapter is directed towards this end.

The present chapter has been divided into *Three Sections. Section I* deals with the socio-economic profile of the sample bank employees. In *Section II,* the relative importance of the internal factors as perceived by the employees and the relationship between the selected socio-economic factors and the employees' opinion on 37 exhaustive factors pertaining to Quality of Work Life that have been identified from the literature has been examined. In *Section III,* the relative influence of the individual factors on the total scores of Quality of Work Life has been estimated and discussed.

SECTION I

Profile of the Sample Bank Employees

Differences in the distribution of sex, age, education levels, occupational status, the level of income are expected to lead to differences in the opinion on the factors determining the Quality of Work Life. Similarly, the difference in the years of experience is another important factor that determines the opinion on the factors on Quality of Work Life. A higher year of experience with monotonous nature of job leads to frustration which in turn affects the opinion on the job and the Quality of Work Life. The number of members in the family is another external factor that determines the workers' opinion on the Quality of work Life. In fact, there is an inverse relationship between the opinion on the Quality of Work Life and the number of members in the family.

The type of family is an external factor that determines the workers' opinion on the Quality of work Life. In a nuclear family the number of members is expected to be small and eventually the problems associated with the family are also expected to be small. This provides the employee the peace of mind that provides a better opinion on the factors determining the quality of work life. Hence, an understanding of the type of family of the sample employees becomes pertinent. This is because, it is expected that in an employee's family where there are more number of members and dependents the problems associated with the family is also expected to be more. This in turn affects the employees' interest at work which leads to differences in the opinion on the factors determining the Quality of Work Life. Hence, an understanding of the number of dependents in the families of sample employees becomes pertinent and in the present paragraph such an analysis is being made.

As it could be seen in Table 6.1, among the 200 sample bank respondents selected, 146, that is 73 per cent are males while the remaining 27 per cent are females. An examination of the number of sample respondents by distribution of age indicates that the highest share of 38.50 per cent of the sample respondents are from the age group of 35-45 years. As high as 30.50 per cent of the respondents have their post graduation general degree that includes the post graduation degrees in Arts, Science and Commerce. There are 15.50 per cent of the worker respondents who have completed their technical post graduation degrees. There are 38.50 per cent are from professional category of managers. Among the sample respondents of 200, a lion's share namely 31 per cent have an experience of 10-15 years in their present job. The data given in the table on the distribution of income of the sample respondents indicate that 37 per cent have a monthly income ranging from Rs.10,000-15,000. Among the worker respondents, the highest 50.50 per cent of the sample employees have 2-4 member families. The data on the type

Table 6.1: Distribution of Sample Workers by Socio-economic and Demographic Profile

Distribution	No. of Sample Employees	Percentage
1	2	3
DISTRIBUTION OF SEX		
Male	146	73.00
Female	54	27.00
DISTRIBUTION OF AGE		
less than 25	7	3.50
25-35	54	27.00
35-45	77	38.50
45-55	39	19.50
55 and above	23	11.50
DISTRIBUTION OF EDUCATION		
General Graduates	25	12.50
General Post Graduates	61	30.50
Technical Graduates	43	21.50
Technical Post Graduates	31	15.50
Professional Graduates	29	14.50
Professional Post Graduates	11	5.50
DISTRIBUTION OF PROFESSION		
Clerks	58	29.00
Middle Level Managers	77	38.50
Top Level Managers	51	25.50
System Administrators	14	7.00
DISTRIBUTION OF YEARS OF EXPERIENCE		
less than 5	6	3.00

(Contd...)

1	2	3
5-10	47	23.50
10-15	62	31.00
15-25	32	16.00
20-25	26	13.00
above 25	27	13.50
DISTRIBUTION OF INCOME		
Less than 10,000	21	10.50
10000-15000	74	37.00
15000-20000	67	33.50
20000-25000	32	16.00
above 25000	6	3.00
DISTRIBUTION OF NUMBER OF MEMBERS IN THE FAMILY		
1	7	3.50
2-4	101	50.50
4-6	57	28.50
6-8	23	11.50
above 8	12	6.00
DISTRIBUTION BY TYPE OF FAMILY		
Nuclear	147	73.50
Joint	53	26.50
DISTRIBUTION BY NUMBER OF DEPENDENTS		
2-4	160	80.00
4-6	25	12.50
above 6	15	07.50

Source: Computed from Primary Data.

of family indicates that as high as 73.50 per cent have nuclear families, while the remaining 26.50 per cent have joint family. As it could also be seen in Table 6.1, 80 per cent of families of the sample workers have 2-4 dependents.

Thus from the analysis it can be concluded that: (1) Male respondents constitute the major share of respondents; (2) The respondents in the age group of 35-45 years form the highest; (3) Employee respondents who completed their general Post graduation forms the highest; (4) A major share of respondents is middle level managers; (5) The respondents who have put 10-15 years of experience form the highest; (6) The respondents who earn a monthly income of Rs.10000-15000 constitute the highest; (7) A majority of the respondents' family have the family size of 2-4 members; (8) A majority of the sample respondents belong to nuclear family; and (9) In a majority of the sample respondents' families, the number of dependents constitute 2-4 members.

SECTION II

Relationship between Internal Factors and Socio-economic Status

As noted earlier, it is assumed that there is a relationship between the opinion on quality of work and the employees' socio-economic status. In the present section it is being attempted to examine the significance of this relationship.

Correlation Matrix

To understand the nature of relationship among the 37 service quality variables considered a simple correlation analysis is being attempted.

As it could be seen in Table 6.2, the simple correlation coefficients worked out for the selected 37 variables indicate that a majority of the variables are significant at 5 per cent level indicating a strong relationship among the variables considered.

Table 6.2: Inter Correlation Matrix of Factors Determining Quality of Work Life

	Increase Output	Increse Quality of Work	Make work easier	Save time	Saves Costs	Data Storage	Report generation	Analysis & decisions	Letter Writing	Reduce Paper Usage	Use of computers at Work	Computer's Help in Work	Hours spent on computers	Planning and Scheduling	Interate data base	Operating Computers Personally	Financial Incentives	Reduce Repetitive Work	Adequately trained
1	2	3	4	5	6	7	8	9	10	11	12	13	14	15	16	17	18	19	20
Increase Output	1.00	0.93*	0.95*	0.94*	0.91*	0.89*	0.85*	0.84*	0.80*	0.76*	0.80*	0.75*	0.60**	0.63**	0.63**	0.63**	0.50**	0.57**	0.56**
Increase Quality of Work		1.00	0.93*	0.90*	0.87*	0.87*	0.86*	0.79*	0.77*	0.71*	0.77*	0.75*	0.55**	0.62**	0.63**	0.62**	0.46**	0.57**	0.54**
Make work easier			1.00	0.97**	0.97*	0.95*	0.92*	0.90*	0.85*	0.79*	0.84*	0.78*	0.64*	0.69**	0.69**	0.68*	0.57*	0.62**	0.60**
Save time				1.00	0.97	0.97*	0.96*	0.95*	0.90*	0.85*	0.88*	0.81*	0.74*	0.76*	0.75*	0.75**	0.64*	0.67**	0.65**
Saves Costs					1.00	0.97*	0.96*	0.96*	0.90*	0.84*	0.87*	0.81*	0.73*	0.75*	0.75*	0.73*	0.65*	0.66**	0.65**
Data Storage						1.00	0.98*	0.97*	0.94*	0.88*	0.89*	0.83*	0.76*	0.81*	0.78*	0.78*	0.68*	0.70*	0.69**
Report generation							1.00	0.97*	0.94*	0.88*	0.89*	0.84*	0.77*	0.82*	0.80*	0.79*	0.70**	0.71*	0.69**
Analysis and Decisions								1.00	0.96*	0.91*	0.91*	0.83*	0.81*	0.83*	0.80*	0.80*	0.73**	0.72*	0.72**
Letter Writing									1.00	0.95*	0.94*	0.89*	0.86*	0.89*	0.83*	0.84*	0.78*	0.79*	0.80*
Reduce Paper Usage										1.00	0.96*	0.92*	0.93*	0.93*	0.86*	0.88*	0.87*	0.83*	0.82*

(Contd...)

1	2	3	4	5	6	7	8	9	10	11	12	13	14	15	16	17	18	19	20
Use of computers at Work											1.00	0.94*	0.90*	0.92*	0.89*	0.90*	0.86*	0.84*	0.79*
Computer's Help in Work												1.00	0.90*	0.95*	0.92*	0.92*	0.90*	0.90*	0.83*
Hours spent on computers													1.00	0.95*	0.90	0.89*	0.96*	0.86*	0.82*
Planning and Scheduling														1.00	0.94	0.94*	0.95*	0.91*	0.85*
Integrate data base															1.00	0.97*	0.91*	0.93*	0.89*
Operating Computers Personally																1.00	0.90*	0.95*	0.89*
Financial Incentives																	1.00	0.89*	0.82*
Reduce Repetitive Work																		1.00	0.92*
Adequately trained																			1.00
Learn Computer Skills																			
Training Programmes																			
Extent of Work Computerized																			
Health Problem																			
Losing of Autonomy																			
Boredom																			
Isolation																			
Helplessness																			
Delays																			

1	2	3	4	5	6	7	8	9	10	11	12	13	14	15	16	17	18	19	20
Read about computers																			
Orientation Programmes																			
Fear of Loss of Data/Files																			
Powerfailure																			
Dead Locks/shutdowns																			
Virus Threat																			
Assurance																			
Consultation/ Counseling																			
Observed Others																			

Table 6.2—(Contd...)

1	Learn Computer Skills 2	Training Programmes 3	Extent of Work Computerized 4	Health Problem 5	Losing of Autonomy 6	Boredom 7	Isolation 8	Helplessness 9	Delays 10	Read about computers 11	Orientation Programmes 12	Fear of Loss of Data/Files 13	Power failure 14	Dead Locks/ shutdowns 15	Virus Threat 16	Assurance 17	Consultation/ Counselling 18	Observed Others 19.
Increase Output	0.47**	0.55**	0.52**	0.52**	0.46**	0.42**	0.33**	0.31**	0.26**	0.20	0.18	0.15	0.13	0.12	0.11	0.11	0.13	0.11
Increase Quality of Work	0.44**	0.50**	0.52**	0.48**	0.42**	0.38**	0.30**	0.28**	0.24**	0.19	0.17	0.14	0.12	0.11	0.10	0.10	0.12	0.10
Make work easier	0.54**	0.62**	0.56**	0.59**	0.52**	0.47**	0.37**	0.35**	0.29**	0.23	0.20	0.17	0.15	0.14	0.13	0.13	0.14	0.13
Save time	0.62**	0.69**	0.59**	0.64**	0.60**	0.55**	0.43**	0.40**	0.34**	0.27	0.24	0.20	0.18	0.16	0.15	0.15	0.16	0.15
Saves Costs	0.62**	0.70**	0.58**	0.66**	0.60**	0.55**	0.43**	0.40**	0.34**	0.27	0.24	0.20	0.18	0.16	0.15	0.15	0.16	0.15
Data Storage	0.68**	0.73**	0.61**	0.68**	0.66**	0.60**	0.47**	0.44**	0.37**	0.29	0.26	0.21	0.19	0.18	0.16	0.16	0.18	0.16
Report generation	0.70**	0.75**	0.62**	0.68**	0.67**	0.61**	0.48**	0.45**	0.38**	0.30**	0.26	0.22	0.20	0.18	0.17	0.17	0.18	0.17
Analysis and Decisions	0.73**	0.78**	0.61**	0.71**	0.72**	0.65**	0.51**	0.48**	0.41**	0.32**	0.28	0.23	0.21	0.19	0.18	0.18	0.20	0.18
Letter Writing	0.81**	0.83**	0.67**	0.74**	0.79**	0.73**	0.59**	0.55**	0.47**	0.37**	0.32**	0.27**	0.24	0.22	0.20	0.21	0.23	0.20
Reduce Paper Usage	0.89**	0.87**	0.75**	0.81**	0.88**	0.79**	0.69**	0.66**	0.57**	0.45**	0.39**	0.33**	0.29	0.27**	0.25**	0.25**	0.28**	0.25**
Use of computers at Work	0.85**	0.86**	0.80**	0.82**	0.83**	0.79**	0.67**	0.62**	0.58**	0.47**	0.41**	0.34**	0.31**	0.28**	0.26**	0.26**	0.29**	0.26**

(Contd...)

1	2	3	4	5	6	7	8	9	10	11	12	13	14	15	16	17	18	19
Computer's Help in Work	0.86**	0.89**	0.86**	0.84**	0.83**	0.81**	0.74**	0.69**	0.63**	0.55**	0.48**	0.40**	0.36**	0.33**	0.30**	0.31**	0.34**	0.30**
Hours spent on computers	0.95**	0.91**	0.83**	0.88**	0.90**	0.85**	0.79**	0.75**	0.69**	0.56**	0.49**	0.40**	0.36**	0.34**	0.31**	0.31**	0.34**	0.31**
Planning and Scheduling	0.94**	0.94**	0.86**	0.87**	0.91**	0.86**	0.81**	0.75**	0.67**	0.59**	0.52**	0.43**	0.39**	0.36**	0.33**	0.33**	0.36**	0.33**
Integrate data base	0.89**	0.92**	0.90**	0.92**	0.89**	0.87**	0.82**	0.79**	0.74**	0.67**	0.62**	0.59**	0.53**	0.49**	0.44**	0.45**	0.50**	0.44**
Operating Computers Personally	0.90**	0.92**	0.91**	0.91**	0.91**	0.89**	0.83**	0.79**	0.75**	0.69**	0.63**	0.59**	0.55**	0.51**	0.46**	0.47**	0.52**	0.46**
Financial Incentives	0.95**	0.95**	0.89**	0.91**	0.91**	0.88**	0.85**	0.79**	0.74**	0.65**	0.57**	0.47**	0.43**	0.40**	0.36**	0.36**	0.40**	0.36**
Reduce Repetitive Work	0.89**	0.93**	0.92**	0.91**	0.91**	0.87**	0.89**	0.84**	0.78**	0.72**	0.69**	0.64**	0.60**	0.55**	0.50**	0.51**	0.56**	0.50**
Adequately trained	0.86**	0.89**	0.83**	0.88**	0.90**	0.89**	0.87**	0.88**	0.81**	0.75**	0.72***	0.72**	0.68**	0.65**	0.61**	0.61**	0.65**	0.61**
Learn Computer Skills	1.00	0.92**	0.83**	0.90**	0.96**	0.89p	0.87**	0.84**	0.79**	0.64**	0.58**	0.54**	0.50**	0.48**	0.43**	0.44**	0.48**	0.43**
Training Programmes		1.00	0.88**	0.93**	0.92**	0.91**	0.88**	0.83**	0.77**	0.72**	0.65**	0.58**	0.55**	0.53**	0.50**	0.50**	0.52**	0.49**
Extent of Work Computerized			1.00	0.91**	0.83**	0.89**	0.89**	0.83**	0.84**	0.81*	0.77*	0.66**	0.62**	0.58**	0.55**	0.56**	0.59**	0.55**
Health Problem				1.00	0.90**	0.90**	0.89**	0.88**	0.87**	0.78*	0.74**	0.69**	0.65**	0.61**	0.58**	0.58**	0.62**	0.58**
Losing of Autonomy					1.00	0.92**	0.89**	0.88**	0.81**	0.69**	0.66**	0.63**	0.60**	0.57**	0.51**	0.53**	0.58**	0.53**
Boredom						1.00	0.90**	0.89**	0.87**	0.83*	0.77**	0.69**	0.67**	0.65**	0.64**	0.63**	0.65**	0.63**
Isolation							1.00	0.95**	0.91**	0.87*	0.86**	0.80*	0.76**	0.74**	0.72**	0.72**	0.74**	0.71**
Helplessness								1.00	0.94**	0.89*	0.86*	0.86*	0.83*	0.80*	0.77*	0.77*	0.80*	0.77*

1	2	3	4	5	6	7	8	9	10	11	12	13	14	15	16	17	18	19
Delays									1.00	0.93*	0.89*	0.87*	0.86*	0.86*	0.83*	0.83*	0.86*	0.82*
Read about computers										1.00	0.94*	0.89*	0.90*	0.89*	0.89*	0.88*	0.87*	0.87*
Orientation Programmes											1.00	0.90*	0.90*	0.89*	0.87*	0.87*	0.89*	0.88*
Fear of Loss of Data/Files												1.00	0.97*	0.96*	0.93*	0.94*	0.96*	0.94*
Powerfailure													1.00	0.98*	0.96*	0.97*	0.97*	0.96*
Dead Locks/shutdowns														1.00	0.97*	0.98*	0.99*	0.97*
Virus Threat															1.00	0.99*	0.94*	0.97*
Assurance																1.00	0.96*	0.99*
Consultation/Counselling																	1.00	0.97*
Observed Others																		1.00

* and ** indicate significant at 1% and 5% level respectively.

Among them, the factors on driving force and organizational incentives and stumbling blocks are found to be highly correlated indicating that the workers consider the factors on. driving forces and organizational incentives as the positive factors determining the Quality of Work Life, while the factors on stumbling blocks as the most important negative factors of Quality of Work Life.

Thus from the correlation matrix it can be concluded that the factors considered under Quality Work Life are not independent among them but are dependent.

Factors on Quality of Work Life by Average and Dispersion

As it is given in Table 6.3 (*See on next page*), among the individual factors that determine the quality of work life either positively or negatively, the factor on Increase Output (1.13) received the highest preference for the application of computers among the sample banks. The next foremost reason for the application of new technology in banking industry is the Increase Quality of Work (1.34). The order of other factors in terms of the preference of the workers to use computes in the work place are: Make work easier (1.42), Save time (1.48), Saves Costs (1.51), Data Storage (1.54), Report generation (1.64), Analysis and Decisions (1.72), Letter Writing (1.78), Reduce Paper Usage (1.91), Use of computers at Work (1.99), Computer's Help in Work (2.17), Hours spent on computers (2.27), Planning and Scheduling (2.34), Integrate data base (2.44), Operating Computers Personally (2.64), Financial Incentives (2.83), Reduce Repetitive Work (2.97), Adequately trained (3.15), Learn Computer Skills (3.36), Training Programmes (3.54), Extent of Work Computerized (3.62), Losing of Autonomy (3.7), Health Problem (3.7), Boredom (3.74), Isolation (3.8), Helplessness (3.81), Delays (3.88), Read about computers (3.92), Orientation Programmes (4.01), Power failure (4.02), Dead Locks/shutdowns (4.06), Fear of Loss of Data/Files

(4.07), Virus Threat (4.19), Assurance (4.2), Consultation/ Counselling (4.26) and Observed Others (4.41).

Table 6.3: Distribution of Factors on Quality of Work Life

Sl.No.	Factors	Mean	STD	CV (%)
1	2	3	4	5
I.	**DRIVING FORCE**			
1.	Make work easier	1.42	1.06	75.22
2.	Increase Quality of Work	1.34	0.99	73.88
3.	Save time	1.48	1.07	72.45
4.	Increase Output	1.13	0.56	49.44
5.	Reduce Repetitive Work	2.97	1.48	49.84
6.	Integrate data base	2.44	1.50	61.43
		1.80	1.11	61.67
II.	**LEARNING**			
7.	Read about computers	3.92	1.20	30.73
8.	Learn Computer Skills	3.36	1.25	37.33
9.	Adequately trained	3.15	1.38	43.87
10.	Observed Others	4.41	0.92	20.94
		3.71	1.19	32.01
III.	**APPLICATIONS**			
11.	Analysis and Decisions	1.72	1.21	70.79
12.	Planning and Scheduling	2.34	1.46	62.43
13.	Report generation	1.64	1.15	70.05
14.	Data Storage	1.54	1.06	68.98
15.	Letter Writing	1.78	1.22	68.38
		1.80	1.22	67.78
IV.	**COMMON COMPLAINTS**			
16.	Losing of Autonomy	3.70	1.16	31.29
17.	Boredom	3.74	1.17	31.21

1	2	3	4	5
18.	Isolation	3.80	1.15	30.42
19.	Delays	3.88	1.15	29.67
20.	Helplessness	3.81	1.16	30.50
21.	Health Problem	3.70	1.15	31.00
		2.49	1.16	46.45
V.	**ORGANIZATIONAL INCENTIVE**			
22.	Orientation Programmes	4.01	1.11	27.75
23.	Consultation/Counselling	4.26	0.97	22.91
24.	Assurance	4.20	1.03	24.62
25.	Training Programmes	3.54	1.18	33.46
26.	Financial Incentives	2.83	1.48	52.32
		3.77	1.15	30.61
VI.	**PROXIMITY**			
27.	Extent of Work Computerized	3.62	1.17	32.34
28.	Use of Computers at Work	1.99	1.35	68.05
29.	Hours spent on computers	2.27	1.44	63.49
30.	Operating Computers Personally	2.64	1.51	57.08
31.	Computer's Help in Work	2.17	1.40	64.37
		2.54	1.64	64.72
VII.	**STUMBLING BLOCKS**			
32.	Power failure	4.02	1.08	27.00
33.	Dead Locks/shutdowns	4.06	1.08	26.71
34.	Virus Threat	4.19	1.01	24.03
35.	Fear of Loss of Data/Files	4.07	1.07	26.41
		4.09	1.06	25.92
VIII.	**ECONOMIES**			
36.	Saves Costs	1.51	1.05	69.77
37.	Reduce Paper Usage	1.91	1.29	67.49
		1.71	1.17	68.42

Source: Computed from Primary Data.

The discussion made above clearly vindicates that in the case of the internal factors, the workers are most dissatisfied with the factors on stumbling block. They viewed that the factors on stumbling block are significant in influencing their productivity negatively.

Thus from the analysis it can be concluded that as viewed by the sample bank employees, the factors on stumbling block influence their productivity negatively to a major extent.

Factors on Quality of Work Life by Sex

In the present paragraph it is attempted to discuss whether there is any difference in the opinion about the factors on Quality of Work life between male and female workers.

As given in Table 6.4, in the case of male employees the factor on Make work easier (1.39) constituted the highest factor of preference. This is being followed by the factor on Increase Output (1.12).

The order of other factors is: Increase Quality of Work (1.3), Save time (1.44), Data Storage (1.46), Saves Costs (1.48), Report generation (1.55), Analysis and Decisions (1.69), Use of computers at Work (1.69), Letter Writing (1.7), Reduce Paper Usage (1.88), Computer's Help in Work (2.00), Planning and Scheduling (2.15), Hours spent on computers (2.2), Integrate data base (2.39), Operating Computers Personally (2.5), Financial Incentives (2.7), Reduce Repetitive Work (2.8), Adequately trained (3.1), Learn Computer Skills (3.22), Training Programmes (3.25), Extent of Work Computerized (3.5), Losing of Autonomy (3.6), Boredom (3.6), Isolation (3.62), Health Problem (3.63), Helplessness (3.65), Delays (3.8), Read about computers (3.84), Orientation Programmes (3.96), Power failure (3.98), Fear of Loss of Data/Files (4.01), Dead Locks/shutdowns (4.02), Assurance (4.15), Virus Threat (4.15), Consultation/ Counseling (4.27) and Observed Others (4.38).

Table 6.4: Distribution of Factors on Quality of Work Life by Sex

Sl.No.	Factors	Male	Female	CV (Male)	CV (Feamle)	F Ratio
1	2	3	4	5	6	7
I.	**DRIVING FORCE**					
1.	Make work easier	1.39	1.44	10.05	11.2	12.63*
2.	Increase Quality of Work	1.3	1.36	9.93	10.26	14.78*
3.	Save time	1.44	1.51	10.2	12.38	21.75*
4.	Increase Output	1.12	1.15	9.67	9.68	20.83*
5.	Reduce Repetitive Work	2.8	3.03	23.79	28.52	24.23*
6.	Integrate data base	2.39	2.47	18.75	25.49	32.45*
II.	**LEARNING**					
7.	Read about computers	3.84	3.98	69.44	72.33	31.45*
8.	Learn Computer Skills	3.22	3.45	32.45	30.03	13.33*
9.	Adequately trained	3.1	3.21	28.45	29.33	12.36*
10.	Observed Others	4.38	4.43	91.42	65.42	14.89*
III.	**APPLICATIONS**					
11.	Analysis and Decisions	1.69	1.74	11.07	18.35	15.86*
12.	Planning and Scheduling	2.15	2.42	18.29	23.47	16.47*
13.	Report generation	1.55	1.72	10.42	17.42	17.71*
14.	Data Storage	1.46	1.59	10.38	16.98	121.22*
15.	Letter Writing	1.7	1.81	11.45	18.92	141.28*
IV.	**COMMON COMPLAINTS**					
16.	Losing of Autonomy	3.6	3.79	42.39	34.33	97.67*
17.	Boredom	3.6	3.85	51.34	37.98	67.88*
18.	Isolation	3.62	3.95	55.49	51.54	54.38*
19.	Delays	3.8	3.95	64.55	67.92	45.91*
20.	Helplessness	3.65	3.99	61.39	50.38	33.45*
21.	Health Problem	3.63	3.87	40.54	33.22	37.87*

(Contd...)

1	2	3	4	5	6	7
V.	**ORGANIZATIONAL INCENTIVE**					
22.	Orientation Programmes	3.96	4.07	70.34	74.36	27.35*
23.	Consultation/ Counseling	4.27	4.28	89.48	92.11	29.38*
24.	Assurance	4.15	4.24	88.57	84.38	14.33*
25.	Training Programmes	3.25	3.78	37.42	31.23	16.17*
26.	Financial Incentives	2.7	2.94	23.48	22.38	99.22*
VI.	**PROXIMITY**					
27.	Extent of Work Computerized	3.5	3.72	42.41	32.33	127.32*
28.	Use of computers at Work	1.69	2.22	12.09	19.99	187.38*
29.	Hours spent on computers	2.2	2.32	17.29	22.22	112.34*
30.	Operating Computers Personally	2.5	2.67	18.97	27.9	36.38*
31.	Computer's Help in Work	2	2.34	12.17	21.28	44.54*
VII.	**STUMBLING BLOCKS**					
32.	Power failure	3.98	4.05	77.39	79.42	57.68*
33.	Dead Locks/shutdowns	4.02	4.09	81.49	69.42	87.87*
34.	Virus Threat	4.15	4.27	83.49	88.54	64.55*
35.	Fear of Loss of Data/Files	4.01	4.09	74.83	77.38	35.45*
VIII.	**ECONOMIES**					
36.	Saves Costs	1.48	1.53	10.27	14.57	78.87*
37.	Reduce Paper Usage	1.88	1.94	11.95	19.47	64.54*

*Indicate significant at 5 per cent level.

Source: Computed from Primary Data.

In terms of the coefficient of variation registered, the order is: Increase Output (9.67), Increase Quality of Work (9.93%), Make work easier (10.05%), Save time (10.2%), Saves Costs (10.27%), Data Storage (10.38%), Report generation (10.42%), Analysis and Decisions (11.07%), Letter Writing (11.45%), Reduce Paper Usage (11.95%), Use of computers at Work (12.09%), Computer's Help in Work (12.17%), Hours spent on computers (17.29%), Planning and Scheduling (18.29%), Integrate data base (18.75%), Operating Computers Personally (18.97%), Financial Incentives (23.48%), Reduce Repetitive Work (23.79%), Adequately trained (28.45%), Learn Computer Skills (32.45 per cent), Training Programmes (37.42%), Health Problem (40.54%), Losing of Autonomy (42.39%), Extent of Work Computerized (42.41%), Boredom (51.34%), Isolation (55.49%), Helplessness (61.39%), Delays (64.55%), Read about computers (69.44%), Orientation Programmes (70.34%), Fear of Loss of Data/Files (74.83%), Power failure (77.39%), Dead Locks/shutdowns (81.49%), Virus Threat (83.49%), Assurance (88.57%), Consultation/Counseling (89.48%) and Observed Others (91.42%).

In the case of females, the order of the preference for various factors determining Quality of Work Life is: Increase Output (1.15), Increase Quality of Work (1.36), Make work easier (1.44), Save time (1.51), Saves Costs (1.53), Data Storage (1.59), Report generation (1.72), Analysis and Decisions (1.74), Letter Writing (1.81), Reduce Paper Usage (1.94), Use of computers at Work (2.22), Hours spent on computers (2.32), Computer's Help in Work (2.34), Planning and Scheduling (2.42), Integrate data base (2.47), Operating Computers Personally (2.67), Financial Incentives (2.94), Reduce Repetitive Work (3.03), Adequately trained (3.21), Learn Computer Skills (3.45), Extent of Work Computerized (3.72), Training Programmes (3.78), Losing of Autonomy (3.79), Boredom (3.85), Health Problem (3.87), Isolation (3.95), Delays (3.95), Read about computers (3.98), Helplessness (3.99), Power failure (4.05), Orientation Programmes (4.07), Dead Locks/shutdowns (4.09), Fear of Loss of Data/Files (4.09), Assurance (4.24), Virus Threat (4.27), Consultation/ Counseling (4.28) and Observed Others (4.43).

The order of the coefficient of variation for female scores is: Increase Output (9.68 per cent), Increase Quality of Work (10.26%), Make work easier (11.2 per cent), Save time (12.38%), Saves Costs (14.57%), Data Storage (16.98%), Report generation (17.42%), Analysis and Decisions (18.35%), Letter Writing (18.92%), Reduce Paper Usage (19.47%), Use of computers at Work (19.99%), Computer's Help in Work (21.28%), Hours spent on computers (22.22%), Financial Incentives (22.38%), Planning and Scheduling (23.47%), Integrate data base (25.49%), Operating Computers Personally (27.9%), Reduce Repetitive Work (28.52%), Adequately trained (29.33%), Learn Computer Skills (30.03%), Training Programmes (31.23%), Extent of Work Computerized (32.33%), Health Problem (33.22%), Losing of Autonomy (34.33%), Boredom (37.98%), Helplessness (50.38%), Isolation (51.54%), Observed Others (65.42%), Delays (67.92%), Dead Locks/shutdowns (69.42%), Read about computers (72.33%), Orientation Programmes (74.36%), Fear of Loss of Data/Files (77.38%), Power failure (79.42%). Assurance (84.38%), Virus Threat (88.54%) and Consultation/ Counseling (92.11%).

The F value given in the table indicates that it is significant for all the factors considered. This implies that there is a significant difference between the opinion of males and females in terms of the factors considered.

Thus from the analysis it can be concluded that there is a significant difference between the opinion of males and females in terms of the factors considered under Quality of Work Life.

Factors on Quality of Work Life by Age

In the present paragraph it is attempted to discuss whether there is any difference in the opinion about the factors on

Quality of Work life among the different age groups. This is due to the reason that generally people from the younger age group gets themselves adopted easily to the changing technology while the old aged are reluctant. Hence, it becomes pertinent to understand whether there is any difference in the opinion about the various factors on Quality Work Life and whether there is a significant difference among the various age groups.

Table 6.5: Distribution of Factors on Quality of Work Life by Age

Factors	Less 25	25-35	35-45	45-55	Above 55	F Ratio
1	2	3	4	5	6	7
DRIVING FORCE						
Make work easier	1.45	1.43	1.44	1.38	1.36	18.95*
C.V.	71.44	60.48	61.32	79.41	81.43	
Increase Quality of Work	0.97	1.37	1.37	1.29	1.28	22.17*
C.V.	62.55	68.72	70.47	79.28	84.32	
Save time	1.43	1.45	1.47	1.40	1.39	32.63*
C.V.	67.42	68.41	63.49	78.49	83.33	
Increase Output	1.15	1.14	1.15	1.11	1.11	31.25*
C.V.	50.10	36.41	38.18	57.28	60.27	
Reduce Repetitive Work	2.88	2.99	2.98	2.88	2.86	36.35*
C.V.	53.44	47.29	47.22	51.55	52.37	
Integrate data base	2.39	2.47	2.48	2.19	2.32	48.68*
C.V.	66.12	58.44	57.88	63.59	66.42	
LEARNING						
Read about computers	3.90	3.97	3.98	3.84	3.79	47.18*
C.V.	29.99	28.45	26.21	30.31	31.30	
Learn Computer Skills	3.28	3.38	3.37	3.22	3.12	20.00*
C.V.	39.00	36.50	35.66	38.52	37.84	

(Contd...)

1	2	3	4	5	6	7
Adequately trained	3.03	3.19	3.16	3.00	3.01	18.54*
C.V.	44.87	41.27	40.55	44.29	45.87	
Observed Others	4.28	4.45	4.44	4.28	4.22	22.34*
C.V.	21.07	19.94	20.04	21.06	20.99	
APPLICATIONS						
Analysis and Decisions	1.69	1.74	1.73	1.69	1.64	23.79*
C.V.	74.45	67.23	64.38	75.25	79.28	
Planning and Scheduling	2.28	2.38	2.37	2.22	2.24	24.71*
C.V.	58.10	60.51	61.65	64.69	70.38	
Report generation	1.55	1.68	1.67	1.50	1.52	26.57*
C.V.	71.33	66.42	61.67	78.54	79.54	
Data Storage	1.41	1.57	1.56	1.48	1.48	181.83*
C.V.	67.22	62.35	61.58	71.34	77.48	
Letter Writing	1.69	1.79	1.78	1.72	1.69	211.92*
C.V.	71.66	64.29	62.55	60.42	74.77	
COMMON COMPLAINTS						
Losing of Autonomy	32.54	3.71	3.72	3.58	3.66	146.51*
C.V.	34.03	30.19	29.66	31.57	32.04	
Boredom	3.71	3.75	3.76	3.64	3.69	101.82*
C.V.	28.27	30.43	30.48	32.03	32.09	
Isolation	3.77	3.83	3.84	3.71	3.71	81.57*
C.V.	28.88	30.57	30.68	31.57	31.08	
Delays	3.67	3.89	3.90	3.74	3.77	68.87*
C.V.	31.69	29.54	28.74	30.54	31.69	
Helplessness	3.77	3.83	3.85	3.74	3.73	50.18*
C.V.	31.57	29.51	28.75	30.88	31.06	
Health Problem	3.68	3.73	3.73	3.60	3.62	56.81*
C.V.	32.00	30.16	29.87	32.17	31.58	

(Contd...)

1	2	3	4	5	6	7
ORGANIZATIONAL INCENTIVE						
Orientation Programmes	4.00	4.04	4.01	3.84	3.89	41.03*
C.V.	30.87	28.99	27.88	31.57	32.66	
Consultation/Counselling	4.22	4.28	4.29	4.12	4.08	44.07*
C.V.	22.97	21.37	20.57	24.12	25.06	
Assurance	4.19	4.22	4.18	4.10	4.18	21.50*
C.V.	24.89	23.22	23.67	24.99	25.06	
Training Programmes	3.44	3.57	3.58	3.40	3.22	24.26*
C.V.	36.11	31.42	30.69	34.22	35.31	
Financial Incentives	2.77	2.87	2.86	2.79	2.56	148.83*
C.V.	53.29	50.15	49.98	53.19	54.45	
PROXIMITY						
Extent of Work Computerized	3.58	3.66	3.67	3.51	3.48	190.98*
C.V.	33.54	30.71	30.50	33.18	33.96	
Use of computers at Work	1.69	2.01	1.99	1.90	1.8	281.07*
C.V.	70.74	62.33	60.59	73.48	70.00	
Hours spent on computers	2.19	2.29	2.30	2.11	2.12	168.51*
C.V.	60.13	61.58	60.55	64.13	64.00	
Operating Computers Personally	2.58	2.69	2.69	2.59	2.44	54.57*
C.V.	58.51	55.12	54.25	59.01	60.28	
Computer's Help in Work	2.08	2.19	2.16	2.06	2.01	66.81*
C.V.	63.12	61.22	64.91	65.00	64.23	
STUMBLING BLOCKS						
Power failure	3.98	4.07	4.08	3.97	3.91	86.52*
C.V.	29.01	26.40	25.90	28.08	28.55	
Dead Locks/shutdowns	4.01	4.08	4.09	3.94	3.99	131.81*
C.V.	27.48	25.41	26.55	28.43	26.79	

(Contd...)

1	2	3	4	5	6	7
Virus Threat	4.02	4.21	4.22	4.01	4.03	96.83*
C.V.	25.11	23.99	24.02	25.00	26.08	
Fear of Loss of Data/ Files	4.03	4.11	4.14	3.99	3.99	53.18*
C.V.	27.28	25.44	24.56	27.41	27.98	
ECONOMIES						
Saves Costs	1.49	1.52	1.53	1.46	1.44	118.31*
C.V.	69.21	68.25	69.91	70.07	70.16	
Reduce Paper Usage	1.84	1.93	1.94	1.80	1.79	96.81*
C.V.	71.55	60.48	61.22	76.81	70.48	

*Indicate significant at 5 per cent level.

Source: Computed from Primary Data.

In the case of the sample employees whose age is less than 25 years, the order of the preference factors is: Increase Quality of Work (0.97), Increase Output (1.15), Data Storage (1.41), Save time (1.43), Make work easier (1.45), Saves Costs (1.49), Report generation (1.55), Analysis and Decisions (1.69), Letter Writing (1.69), Use of computers at Work (1.69), Reduce Paper Usage (1.84), Computer's Help in Work (2.08), Hours spent on computers (2.19), Planning and Scheduling (2.28), Integrate data base (2.39), Operating Computers Personally (2.58), Financial Incentives (2.77), Reduce Repetitive Work (2.88), Adequately trained (3.03), Learn Computer Skills (3.28), Training Programmes (3.44), Extent of Work Computerized (3.58), Delays (3.67), Health Problem (3.68), Boredom (3.71), Isolation (3.77), Helplessness (3.77), Read about computers (3.9), Power failure (3.98), Orientation Programmes (4.00), Dead Locks/shutdowns (4.01), Virus Threat (4.02), Fear of Loss of Data/ Files (4.03), Assurance (4.19), Consultation/ Counselling (4.22), Observed Others (4.28) and Losing of Autonomy (32.54).

In the case of employees who age ranges between 25-35 years, the order of the factor preference is: Increase Output

(1.14), Increase Quality of Work (1.37), Make work easier (1.43), Save time (1.45), Saves Costs (1.52), Data Storage (1.57), Report generation (1.68), Analysis and Decisions (1.74), Letter Writing (1.79), Reduce Paper Usage (1.93), Use of computers at Work (2.01), Computer's Help in Work (2.19), Hours spent on computers (2.29), Planning and Scheduling (2.38), Integrate data base (2.47), Operating Computers Personally (2.69), Financial Incentives (2.87), Reduce Repetitive Work (2.99), Adequately trained (3.19), Learn Computer Skills (3.38), Training Programmes (3.57), Extent of Work Computerized (3.66), Losing of Autonomy (3.71), Health Problem (3.73), Boredom (3.75), Isolation (3.83), Helplessness (3.83), Delays (3.89), Read about computers (3.97), Orientation Programmes (4.04), Power failure (4.07), Dead Locks/shutdowns (4.08), Fear of Loss of Data/Files (4.11), Virus Threat (4.21), Assurance (4.22), Consultation/ Counselling (4.28) and Observed Others (4.45).

In the case of employees who age ranges between 35-45 the order of the preference is: Increase Output (1.15), Increase Quality of Work (1.37), Make work easier (1.44), Save time (1.47), Saves Costs (1.53), Data Storage (1.56), Report generation (1.67), Analysis and Decisions (1.73), Letter Writing (1.78), Reduce Paper Usage (1.94), Use of computers at Work (1.99), Computer's Help in Work (2.16), Hours spent on computers (2.3), Planning and Scheduling (2.37), Integrate data base (2.48), Operating Computers Personally (2.69), Financial Incentives (2.86), Reduce Repetitive Work (2.98), Adequately trained (3.16), Learn Computer Skills (3.37), Training Programmes (3.58), Extent of Work Computerized (3.67), Losing of Autonomy (3.72), Health Problem (3.73), Boredom (3.76), Isolation (3.84), Helplessness (3.85), Delays (3.90), Read about computers (3.98), Orientation Programmes (4.01), Power failure (4.08), Dead Locks/shutdowns (4.09), Fear of Loss of Data/Files (4.14), Assurance (4.18), Virus Threat (4.22), Consultation/ Counselling (4.29) and Observed Others (4.44).

Among the age group of 45-55, the order of the preference of the quality of work life factors is: Increase Output (1.11), Increase Quality of Work (1.29), Make work easier (1.38), Save time (1.4), Saves Costs (1.46), Data Storage (1.48), Report generation (1.5), Analysis and Decisions (1.69), Letter Writing (1.72), Reduce Paper Usage (1.8), Use of computers at Work (1.9), Computer's Help in Work (2.06), Hours spent on computers (2.11), Integrate data base (2.19), Planning and Scheduling (2.22), Operating Computers Personally (2.59), Financial Incentives (2.79), Reduce Repetitive Work (2.88), Adequately trained (3.00), Learn Computer Skills (3.22), Training Programmes (3.4), Extent of Work Computerized (3.51), Losing of Autonomy (3.58), Health Problem (3.6), Boredom (3.64), Isolation (3.71), Delays (3.74), Helplessness (3.74), Read about computers (3.84), Orientation Programmes (3.84), Dead Locks/shutdowns (3.94), Power failure (3.97), Fear of Loss of Data/Files (3.99), Virus Threat (4.01), Assurance (4.1), Consultation/ Counselling (4.12), Observed Others (4.28).

In the case of the worker respondents whose age above 55 years, the order of the preference is: Increase Output (1.11), Increase Quality of Work (1.28), Make work easier (1.36), Save time (1.39), Saves Costs (1.44), Data Storage (1.48), Report generation (1.52), Analysis and Decisions (1.64), Letter Writing (1.69), Reduce Paper Usage (1.79), Use of computers at Work (1.8), Computer's Help in Work (2.01), Hours spent on computers (2.12), Planning and Scheduling (2.24), Integrate data base (2.32), Operating Computers Personally (2.44), Financial Incentives (2.56), Reduce Repetitive Work (2.86), Adequately trained (3.01), Learn Computer Skills (3.12), Training Programmes (3.22), Extent of Work Computerized (3.48), Health Problem (3.62), Losing of Autonomy (3.66), Boredom (3.69), Isolation (3.71), Helplessness (3.73), Delays (3.77), Read about computers (3.79), Orientation Programmes (3.89), Power failure (3.91),Dead Locks/shutdowns (3.99), Fear of Loss of Data/

Files (3.99), Virus Threat (4.03), Consultation/ Counseling (4.08), Assurance (4.18), Observed Others (4.22).

The *F* ratio worked out among different age group indicates that they are all significant at five per cent level implying that there is a significant difference among the various age groups in terms of the opinion on the various factors determining the Quality of Work Life of the employees.

Thus from the analysis it can be concluded that there is a significant difference between the various age groups and the opinion on the various factors determining the Quality of Work Life.

Factors on Quality of Work Life by Education Qualification

In the present paragraph it is attempted to discuss whether there is any difference in the opinion about the factors on Quality of Work life among the different respondents of different educational attainment.

As it could be seen in Table 6.6, in the case of the opinion on the factors determining the quality of work life of employees by levels of education indicates that the order of the factors according to the sample employees who have their general graduation is : Increase Output (0.99), Increase Quality of Work (1.11), Saves Costs (1.44), Make work easier (1.48), Save time (1.49), Data Storage (1.5), Report generation (1.59), Analysis and Decisions (1.66), Letter Writing (1.84), Use of computers at Work (1.84), Reduce Paper Usage (1.86), Computer's Help in Work (2.03), Hours spent on computers (2.21), Planning and Scheduling (2.28), Integrate data base (2.39), Operating Computers Personally (2.54), Reduce Repetitive Work (2.67), Financial Incentives (2.77), Adequately trained (3.02), Learn Computer Skills (3.3), Training Programmes (3.48), Extent of Work Computerized (3.55), Losing of Autonomy (3.59), Helplessness (3.65), Health Problem (3.65), Boredom (3.68),

Delays (3.68), Isolation (3.7), Read about computers (3.74), Orientation Programmes (3.84), Fear of Loss of Data/Files (3.84), Power failure (3.89), Dead Locks/shutdowns (3.91), Assurance (4.03), Virus Threat (4.03), Observed Others (4.15) and Consultation/ Counselling (4.22).

Table 6.6: Distribution of Factors on Quality of Work Life by Education Qualification

Factors	General Graduates	General Post Graduates	Technical Graduates	Technical Post Graduates	Professional Graduates	Professional Post Graduates	F Ratio
1	2	3	4	5	6	7	8
DRIVING FORCE							
Make work easier	1.48	1.38	1.36	1.45	1.49	1.52	16.84*
C.V	79.49	70.52	70.14	76.54	77.29	78.50	
Increase Quality of Work	1.11	1.37	1.38	1.28	1.25	1.39	19.71*
C.V	75.26	70.18	71.27	74.22	76.59	77.66	
Save time	1.49	1.52	1.56	1.45	1.40	1.38	29.00*
C.V	74.44	70.28	71.53	77.01	75.28	76.22	
Increase Output	0.99	1.13	1.14	1.11	1.12	1.11	27.77*
C.V	48.64	49.28	41.31	42.33	45.38	52.11	
Reduce Repetitive Work	2.67	2.98	3.05	2.84	2.79	2.78	32.31*
C.V	50.06	49.22	49.34	50.09	50.15	50.34	
Integrate data base	2.39	2.47	2.49	2.38	2.28	2.29	43.27*
C.V	62.00	60.45	60.14	62.19	62.32	62.00	
LEARNING							
Read about computers	3.74	3.97	4.08	3.65	3.77	3.45	41.93*
C.V	29.52	30.54	31.36	31.96	32.04	32.17	
Learn Computer Skills	3.30	3.41	3.48	3.33	3.28	3.29	17.77*
C.V	39.05	36.98	36.55	37.87	37.87	34.00	
Adequately trained	3.02	3.19	3.21	3.11	3.09	3.07	16.48*
C.V	44.05	42.67	42.99	44.18	44.19	44.35	

(Contd...)

1	2	3	4	5	6	7	8
Observed Others	4.15	4.59	4.65	4.00	4.18	4.23	19.85*
C.V	21.54	19.98	19.54	21.54	21.38	22.08	
APPLICATIONS							
Analysis and Decisions	1.66	1.74	1.78	1.64	1.60	1.59	21.15*
C.V	73.54	68.54	69.00	71.54	71.45	74.73	
Planning and Scheduling	2.28	2.39	2.40	2.28	2.24	2.40	21.96*
C.V	63.00	62.00	61.53	62.55	62.58	62.71	
Report generation	1.59	1.67	1.68	1.53	1.58	1.69	23.61*
	71.25	68.11	66.888	72.35	70.98	73.18	
Data Storage	1.50	1.55	1.57	1.47	1.48	1.43	161.63*
C.V	69.27	66.54	66.14	70.22	71.32	70.00	
Letter Writing	1.84	1.82	1.78	1.64	1.62	1.61	188.37*
C.V	69.44	67.66	67.60	69.55	70.03	70.33	
COMMON COMPLAINTS							
Losing of Autonomy	3.59	3.76	3.79	3.64	3.69	3.63	130.23*
C.V	31.00	30.94	30.81	31.54	31.45	31.69	
Boredom	3.68	3.79	3.81	3.65	3.64	3.67	90.51*
C.V	32.00	30.21	30.12	31.84	31.45	31.99	
Isolation	3.70	3.94	3.98	3.75	3.69	3.71	72.51*
C.V	34.28	29.12	29.99	30.59	30.77	30.67	
Delays	3.68	3.93	3.99	3.55	3.65	3.69	61.21*
C.V	30.00	30.98	31.03	30.34	30.39	30.18	
Helplessness	3.65	3.89	3.98	3.74	3.68	3.57	44.60*
C.V	28.54	29.42	30.51	31.28	31.97	32.54	
Health Problem	3.65	3.75	3.79	3.63	3.59	3.54	50.49*
C.V	31.54	29.45	29.00	31.54	31.88	31.97	
ORGANIZATIONAL INCENTIVE							
Orientation Programmes	3.84	4.08	4.12	3.79	3.91	3.83	36.47*
C.V	30.88	28.45	29.11	31.08	31.54	30.88	

(Contd...)

1	2	3	4	5	6	7	8
Consultation/Counselling	4.22	4.39	4.45	4.00	4.03	4.18	39.17*
C.V	23.00	22.01	22.18	23.91	23.02	23.65	
Assurance	4.03	4.28	4.36	4.05	4.00	3.77	19.11*
C.V	24.98	24.00	24.87	24.99	25.00	25.09	
Training Programmes	3.48	3.59	3.62	3.33	3.43	3.48	21.56*
C.V	34.44	32.48	32.22	34.12	33.97	33.82	
Financial Incentives	2.77	2.89	2.91	2.81	2.80	2.74	132.29*
C.V	53.00	50.98	51.06	52.88	52.74	52.99	
PROXIMITY							
Extent of Work Computerized	3.55	3.71	3.78	3.58	3.51	3.49	169.76*
C.V	33.15	31.00	31.12	32.48	32.74	33.08	
Use of computers at Work	1.84	2.03	2.08	1.94	1.89	1.93	249.84*
C.V	69.06	67.28	67.94	68.74	68.98	69.00	
Hours spent on computers	2.21	2.28	2.31	2.24	2.22	2.18	149.79*
C.V	64.87	62.99	62.55	64.11	64.18	65.00	
Operating Computers Personally	2.54	2.68	2.71	2.53	2.58	2.54	48.51*
C.V.	58.00	56.49	56.59	57.88	57.98	57.23	
Computer's Help in Work	2.03	2.19	2.20	2.12	2.11	2.13	59.39*
C.V	65.33	63.88	63.64	65.98	65.48	65.13	
STUMBLING BLOCKS							
Power failure	3.89	4.15	4.16	3.89	3.99	3.75	76.91*
C.V	28.00	26.45	26.89	27.49	27.55	27.94	
Dead Locks/shutdowns	3.91	4.19	4.21	3.94	3.98	3.89	117.16*
C.V	27.00	25.98	26.00	27.21	26.89	26.98	
Virus Threat	4.03	4.25	4.28	4.06	4.09	4.01	86.07*
C.V	25.06	22.94	23.68	23.55	23.57	23.77	

1	2	3	4	5	6	7	8
Fear of Loss of Data/Files	3.84	4.15	4.19	3.94	3.89	3.99	47.27*
C.V	26.15	26.00	27.09	26.94	26.85	26.99	
ECONOMIES							
Saves Costs	1.44	1.53	1.55	1.43	1.44	1.47	105.16*
C.V	70.24	68.54	67.22	71.26	72.55	73.28	
Reduce Paper Usage	1.86	1.95	1.99	1.84	1.82	1.88	86.05*
C.V	69.55	65.22	65.39	70.00	68.77	68.43	

* Indicate significant at 5 per cent level.
Source: Computed from Primary Data.

As given in the same table, the order of the opinion of the general post graduate sample employees is: Increase Output (1.13), Increase Quality of Work (1.37), Make work easier (1.38), Save time (1.52), Saves Costs (1.53), Data Storage (1.55), Report generation (1.67), Analysis and Decisions (1.74), Letter Writing (1.82), Reduce Paper Usage (1.95), Use of computers at Work (2.03), Computer's Help in Work (2.19), Hours spent on computers (2.28), Planning and Scheduling (2.39), Integrate data base (2.47), Operating Computers Personally (2.68), Financial Incentives (2.89), Reduce Repetitive Work (2.98), Adequately trained (3.19), Learn Computer Skills (3.41), Training Programmes (3.59), Extent of Work Computerized (3.71), Health Problem (3.75), Losing of Autonomy (3.76), Boredom (3.79), Helplessness (3.89), Delays (3.93), Isolation (3.94), Read about computers (3.97, Orientation Programmes (4.08), Power failure (4.15), Fear of Loss of Data/Files (4.15), Dead Locks/shutdowns (4.19), Virus Threat (4.25), Assurance (4.28), Consultation/ Counselling (4.39) and Observed Others (4.59).

As given in the same table, the order of the opinion on the factors determining the quality of work life of employees who have completed their technical education indicates that the Increase Output (1.14) forms the major factor of preference. This is being followed by the factors on: Make work easier (1.36), Increase Quality of Work (1.38), Saves Costs (1.55), Save time (1.56), Data Storage (1.57), Report generation (1.68), Analysis and Decisions (1.78), Letter Writing (1.78), Reduce Paper Usage (1.99), Use of computers at Work (2.08), Computer's Help in Work (2.2), Hours spent on computers (2.31), Planning and Scheduling (2.4), Integrate data base (2.49), Operating Computers Personally (2.71), Financial Incentives (2.91), Reduce Repetitive Work (3.05), Adequately trained (3.21), Learn Computer Skills (3.48), Training Programmes (3.62), Extent of Work Computerized (3.78), Losing of Autonomy (3.79), Health Problem (3.79), Boredom (3.81), Isolation (3.98), Helplessness (3.98), Delays (3.99), Read about computers (4.08), Orientation Programmes (4.12), Power failure (4.16), Fear of Loss of Data/Files (4.19), Dead Locks/shutdowns (4.21), Virus Threat (4.28), Assurance (4.36), Consultation/ Counselling (4.45) and Observed Others (4.65).

As seen in the table, according to the opinion of the Technical Post Graduates sample employees, Increase Output (1.11) forms the foremost factor of preference. This is being followed by the factor on: Increase Quality of Work (1.28). The order of other factors is: Saves Costs (1.43), Make work easier (1.45), Save time (1.45), Data Storage (1.47), Report generation (1.53), Analysis and Decisions (1.64), Letter Writing (1.64), Reduce Paper Usage (1.84), Use of computers at Work (1.94), Computer's Help in Work (2.12), Hours spent on computers (2.24), Planning and Scheduling (2.28), Integrate data base (2.38), Operating Computers Personally (2.53), Financial Incentives (2.81), Reduce Repetitive Work (2.84), Adequately trained (3.11), Learn Computer Skills (3.33), Training Programmes (3.33), Delays (3.55), Extent of Work Computerized (3.58), Health Problem (3.63), Losing of Autonomy (3.64), Read about computers (3.65), Boredom (3.65), Helplessness (3.74), Isolation (3.75), Orientation Programmes (3.79), Power failure (3.89), Dead Locks/ shutdowns (3.94), Fear of Loss of Data/Files (3.94), Observed

Others (4.00), Consultation/Counselling (4.00), Assurance (4.05) and Virus Threat (4.06).

As seen in Table 6.6, the opinion of the professional graduate sample employees indicates that the factor on 'Increase Output (1.12)' forms the major factor of preference. The order of other factors is: Increase Quality of Work (1.25), Save time (1.40), Saves Costs (1.44), Data Storage (1.48), Make work easier (1.49), Report generation (1.58), Analysis and Decisions (1.60), Letter Writing (1.62), Reduce Paper Usage (1.82), Use of computers at Work (1.89), Computer's Help in Work (2.11), Hours spent on computers (2.22), Planning & Scheduling (2.24), Integrate data base (2.28), Operating Computers Personally (2.58), Reduce Repetitive Work (2.79), Financial Incentives (2.80), Adequately trained (3.09), Learn Computer Skills (3.28), Training Programmes (3.43), Extent of Work Computerized (3.51), Health Problem (3.59), Boredom (3.64), Delays (3.65), Helplessness (3.68), Losing of Autonomy (3.69), Isolation (3.69), Read about computers (3.77), Fear of Loss of Data/Files (3.89), Orientation Programmes (3.91), Dead Locks/shutdowns (3.98), Power failure (3.99), Assurance (4.00), Consultation/ Counselling (4.03), Virus Threat (4.09) and Observed Others (4.18).

As given in the Table, the opinion of the Professional Post Graduate sample employees indicates that 'Increase Output (1.11)' forms the major factor of preference. This is being followed by the factor on: Save time (1.38). The order of other factor is: Increase Quality of Work (1.39), Data Storage (1.43), Saves Costs (1.47), Make work easier (1.52), Analysis and Decisions (1.59), Letter Writing (1.61), Report generation (1.69), Reduce Paper Usage (1.88), Use of computers at Work (1.93), Computer's Help in Work (2.13), Hours spent on computers (2.18), Integrate data base (2.29), Planning and Scheduling (2.40), Operating Computers Personally (2.54), Financial Incentives (2.74), Reduce Repetitive Work (2.78), Adequately trained (3.07), Learn

Computer Skills (3.29), Read about computers (3.45), Training Programmes (3.48), Extent of Work Computerized (3.49), Health Problem (3.54), Helplessness (3.57), Losing of Autonomy (3.63), Boredom (3.67), Delays (3.69), Isolation (3.71), Assurance (3.77), Orientation Programmes (3.83), Dead Locks/shutdowns (3.89), Fear of Loss of Data/Files (3.99), Virus Threat (4.01), Consultation/ Counselling (4.18), Observed Others (4.23) and Power failure (3.75).

The *F* values provided in Table 6.13 indicate that they are significant at 5 per cent levels. This provides the inference that there is a significant difference between the level of education of the sample employees and their opinion.

Thus from the analysis it can be concluded that irrespective of the level of educational attainment of the sample employees, the opinion indicated that increasing the output forms the major reason for the adoption of computerization in work place.

Factors on Quality of Work Life by Profession

In the present paragraph it is attempted to discuss whether there is any significant difference in the opinion about the factors on Quality of Work life among the different respondents of different profession.

Table 6.7: Distribution of Factors on Quality of Work Life by Profession

Variables	Clerks	Middle Level Managers	Top Level Managers	System Administrators	F Ratio
1	2	3	4	5	6
DRIVING FORCE					
Make work easier	1.48	1.35	1.36	1.52	28.32*
C.V.	70.22	77.38	76.54	74.32	
Increase Quality of Work	1.38	1.32	1.333	1.41	33.14*
C.V.	70.25	74.23	75.00	71.08	

(Contd...)

1	2	3	4	5	6
Save time	1.51	1.44	1.41	1.52	48.77*
C.V.	71.22	72.89	72.98	71.21	
Increase Output	1.17	1.08	1.10	1.16	46.70*
C.V.	48.34	49.88	49.00	48.03	
Reduce Repetitive Work	3.07	2.86	2.89	3.06	54.33*
C.V.	47.03	50.04	51.00	48.34	
Integrate data base	2.55	2.21	2.09	2.47	72.76*
C.V.	60.44	61.89	62.00	61.08	
LEARNING					
Read about computers	3.99	3.74	3.86	3.97	70.52*
C.V.	28.15	30.75	31.23	28.19	
Learn Computer Skills	3.74	3.03	3.12	3.49	29.89*
C.V.	37.01	37.98	38.54	37.00	
Adequately trained	3.24	3.10	3.08	3.28	27.71*
C.V.	41.54	44.58	44.79	43.08	
Observed Others	4.87	4.06	4.12	4.49	33.39*
C.V.	19.91	21.65	21.67	20.67	
APPLICATIONS					
Analysis and Decisions	1.84	1.63	1.53	1.82	35.56*
C.V.	70.00	71.09	71.25	70.12	
Planning and Scheduling	2.68	2.13	2.28	2.47	36.93*
C.V.	61.25	62.87	62.98	62.00	
Report generation	1.76	1.54	1.48	1.75	39.71*
C.V.	69.13	70.88	70.89	69.28	
Data Storage	1.69	1.45	1.54	1.71	271.79*
C.V.	67.00	69.00	68.45	68.73	
Letter Writing	1.81	1.68	1.76	1.82	316.77*
C.V.	66.18	69.00	68.65	68.44	

(Contd...)

1	2	3	4	5	6
COMMON COMPLAINTS					
Losing of Autonomy	3.88	3.69	3.58	3.79	218.99*
C.V.	31.10	31.67	31.76	31.66	
Boredom	3.84	3.60	3.64	3.79	152.20*
C.V.	30.00	31.75	31.86	31.10	
Isolation	3.98	3.79	3.69	3.87	121.93*
C.V.	30.11	31.12	31.27	29.76	
Delays	3.97	3.68	3.79	3.93	102.94*
C.V.	28.22	29.88	29.87	28.50	
Helplessness	3.97	3.64	3.50	3.86	75.00*
C.V.	29.50	30.89	31.12	29.65	
Health Problem	3.91	3.68	3.36	3.81	84.91*
C.V.	29.99	31.75	32.21	29.74	
ORGANIZATIONAL INCENTIVE					
Orientation Programmes	4.25	3.65	3.76	4.08	61.32*
C.V.	26.11	27.99	28.47	27.00	
Consultation/ Counselling	4.31	4.20	4.22	4.33	65.87*
C.V.	20.98	23.54	23.00	22.00	
Assurance	4.38	4.12	4.18	4.44	32.13*
C.V.	23.55	25.68	27.91	23.67	
Training Programmes	3.78	3.31	3.28	3.83	36.26*
C.V.	31.54	35.68	37.75	32.12	
Financial Incentives	2.98	2.74	2.76	2.99	222.47*
C.V.	50.12	53.54	54.00	50.32	
PROXIMITY					
Extent of Work Computerized	3.77	3.54	3.66	3.81	285.47*
C.V.	31.22	33.28	34.12	31.58	

(Contd...)

1	2	3	4	5	6
Use of computers at Work	2.13	1.84	1.76	2.09	420.13*
C.V.	66.58	68.99	68.77	67.24	
Hours spent on computers	2.69	2.01	1.97	2.45	251.88*
C.V.	61.22	65.78	67.53	60.55	
Operating Computers Personally	2.76	2.54	2.23	2.69	81.57*
C.V.	55.17	57.98	58.15	56.44	
Computer's Help in Work	2.28	2.02	2.14	2.22	99.87*
C.V.	63.12	65.18	66.22	64.10	
STUMBLING BLOCKS					
Power failure	4.34	3.78	3.92	4.12	129.33*
C.V.	26.11	27.77	28.22	26.43	
Dead Locks/shutdowns	4.12	3.98	3.85	4.20	197.02*
C.V.	25.31	27.38	27.88	26.03	
Virus Threat	4.36	4.02	4.07	4.21	144.73*
C.V.	23.45	24.94	24.88	23.12	
Fear of Loss of Data/Files	4.12	4.01	3.77	4.13	79.48*
C.V.	26.11	26.79	27.15	26.09	
ECONOMIES					
Saves Costs	1.58	1.44	1.34	1.67	176.84*
C.V.	68.11	70.28	71.65	69.00	
Reduce Paper Usage	1.99	1.45	1.64	2.09	144.71*
C.V.	65.55	68.12	67.87	66.38	

Source: Computed from Primary Data.

As it could be seen in Table 6.7, among the sample employees, the professional category of clerks viewed 'Increase Output (1.17)' as the foremost reason for the introduction of computers in work place. Increase Quality of Work (1.38) forms the next foremost reason. The order of other factors is: Make work easier (1.48), Save time (1.51), Saves Costs (1.58), Data Storage (1.69), Report generation (1.76), Letter Writing (1.81), Analysis and Decisions (1.84), Reduce Paper Usage (1.99), Use of computers at Work (2.13), Computer's Help in Work (2.28), Integrate data base (2.55), Planning and Scheduling (2.68), Hours spent on computers (2.69), Operating Computers Personally (2.76), Financial Incentives (2.98), Reduce Repetitive Work (3.07), Adequately trained (3.24), Learn Computer Skills (3.74), Extent of Work Computerized (3.77), Training Programmes (3.78), Boredom (3.84), Losing of Autonomy (3.88), Health Problem (3.91), Delays (3.97), Helplessness (3.97), Isolation (3.98), Read about computers (3.99), Dead Locks/shutdowns (4.12), Fear of Loss of Data/Files (4.12), Orientation Programmes (4.25), Consultation/ Counseling (4.31), Power failure (4.34), Virus Threat (4.36), Assurance (4.38), Observed Others (4.87).

In the case of middle level managers, 'Increase Output (1.08)' forms the top most preference for the introduction of computers in the work place. The order of other factors is: Increase Quality of Work (1.32), Make work easier (1.35), Save time (1.44), Saves Costs (1.44), Data Storage (1.45), Reduce Paper Usage (1.45), Report generation (1.54), Analysis and Decisions (1.63), Letter Writing (1.68), Use of computers at Work (1.84), Hours spent on computers (2.01), Computer's Help in Work (2.02), Planning and Scheduling (2.13), integrate data base (2.21), Operating Computers Personally (2.54), Financial Incentives (2.74), Reduce Repetitive Work (2.86), Learn Computer Skills (3.03), Adequately trained (3.1), Training Programmes (3.31), Extent of Work Computerized (3.54), Boredom (3.6), Helplessness (3.64), Orientation Programmes (3.65), Delays (3.68), Health Problem (3.68), Losing of Autonomy (3.69), Read about computers (3.74), Power failure (3.78), Isolation (3.79), Dead Locks/shutdowns (3.98), Fear of Loss of Data/ Files (4.01), Virus Threat (4.02), Observed Others (4.06), Assurance (4.12), Consultation/ Counselling (4.2).

As it could be seen in the same table, according to the top level managers' view, 'Increase Output (1.10)' constitutes the primary reason for the introduction of computers in the work place. The order of other factors is: Increase Quality of Work (1.33), Saves Costs (1.34), Make work easier (1.36), Save time (1.41), Report generation (1.48), Analysis and Decisions (1.53), Data Storage (1.54), Reduce Paper Usage (1.64), Letter Writing (1.76), Use of computers at Work (1.76), Hours spent on computers (1.97), Integrate data base (2.09), Computer's Help in Work (2.14), Operating Computers Personally (2.23), Planning and Scheduling (2.28), Financial Incentives (2.76), Reduce Repetitive Work (2.89), Adequately trained (3.08), Learn Computer Skills (3.12), Training Programmes (3.28), Health Problem (3.36), Helplessness (3.5), Losing of Autonomy (3.58), Boredom (3.64), Extent of Work Computerized (3.66), Isolation (3.69), Orientation Programmes (3.76), Fear of Loss of Data/Files (3.77), Delays (3.79), Dead Locks/shutdowns (3.85), Read about computers (3.86), Power failure (3.92), Virus Threat (4.07), Observed Others (4.12), Assurance (4.18) and Consultation/ Counseling (4.22).

As perceived by the system administrators, 'Increase Output (1.16)' constitutes the primary factor of preference for the introduction of computers n work place. The order of other factors is: Increase Quality of Work (1.41), Make work easier (1.52), Save time (1.52), Saves Costs (1.67), Data Storage (1.71), Report generation (1.75), Analysis and Decisions (1.82), Letter Writing (1.82), Use of computers at Work (2.09), Reduce Paper Usage (2.09), Computer's Help in Work (2.22), Hours spent on computers (2.45), Integrate data base (2.47), Planning and Scheduling (2.47), Operating Computers Personally (2.69), Financial Incentives (2.99), Reduce Repetitive Work (3.06), Adequately trained (3.28), Learn Computer Skills (3.49), Losing of Autonomy (3.79), Boredom (3.79), Health Problem (3.81), Extent of Work Computerized (3.81), Training Programmes (3.83),

Helplessness (3.86), Isolation (3.87), Delays (3.93), Read about computers (3.97), Orientation Programmes (4.08), Power failure (4.12), Fear of Loss of Data/Files (4.13), Dead Locks/shutdowns (4.2), Virus Threat (4.21), Consultation/ Counselling (4.33), Assurance (4.44) and Observed Others (4.49).

The *F* values given in Table 6.7 also indicate that they are significant at 5 per cent levels providing the inference that there is a significant difference between the professional category of the sample employees and their opinion.

Thus from the analysis it can be concluded that irrespective of the category of profession of the sample employees, the opinion indicated that increasing the output forms the major reason for the adoption of computerization in work place.

Factors on Quality of Work Life by Years of Expereince

In the present paragraph it is attempted to discuss whether there is any significant difference in the opinion about the factors on Quality of Work life among the different respondents by years of experience.

Table 6.8: Distribution of Factors on Quality of Work Life By Years of Experience

Factors	less than 5	5-10	10-15	15-25	20-25	Above 25	F Ratio
1	2	3	4	5	6	7	8
DRIVING FORCE							
Make work easier	1.38	1.45	1.48	1.37	1.36	1.29	19.61*
C.V.	75.00	74.22	74.97	75.49	75.99	76.19	
Increase Quality of Work	1.17	1.58	1.64	1.12	1.24	1.33	22.95*
C.V.	73.99	72.02	71.87	74.03	74.22	74.18	
Save time	1.22	1.54	1.55	1.32	1.22	1.34	33.77*
C.V.	73.44	71.03	71.44	73.44	73.18	73.88	

(Contd...)

1	2	3	4	5	6	7	8
Increase Output	1.01	1.29	1.24	1.02	0.98	1.02	32.34*
C.V.	50.27	48.42	48.29	49.78	49.97	49.88	
Reduce Repetitive Work	2.22	3.08	3.15	2.77	2.64	2.68	37.62*
C.V.	50.13	48.12	48.77	49.97	50.17	50.49	
Integrate data base	2.24	2.68	2.79	2.13	2.33	2.19	50.39*
C.V.	62.14	60.02	60.88	62.12	61.98	61.87	
LEARNING							
Read about computers	3.77	3.99	4.08	3.80	3.74	3.78	48.84*
C.V.	30.87	30.02	30.14	31.12	31.44	31.54	
Learn Computer Skills	3.21	3.45	3.41	3.28	3.14	3.17	20.70*
C.V.	38.00	37.00	36.45	38.45	38.71	39.12	
Adequately trained	2.99	3.23	3.27	3.00	2.98	2.98	19.19*
C.V.	44.99	43.00	42.98	44.08	44.67	44.21	
Observed Others	4.02	4.54	4.65	4.12	4.13	4.19	23.12*
C.V.	21.12	20.58	20.74	21.22	21.44	21.38	
APPLICATIONS							
Analysis and Decisions	1.64	1.87	1.98	1.55	1.44	1.36	24.63*
C.V.	72.00	70.00	71.87	71.69	72.08	72.14	
Planning and Scheduling	2.12	2.47	2.49	2.11	2.03	2.22	25.57*
C.V.	63.45	62.00	62.11	63.15	63.45	63.22	
Report generation	1.52	1.75	1.78	1.54	1.47	1.34	27.50*
C.V.	71.05	69.22	69.78	71.45	71.22	71.38	
Data Storage	1.41	1.71	1.66	1.21	1.14	1.29	188.23*
C.V.	69.00	68.00	68.21	69.12	69.45	69.44	
Letter Writing	1.70	1.89	1.99	1.64	1.54	1.45	219.38*
C.V.	68.00	67.00	66.45	70.03	69.28	69.47	

(Contd...)

1	2	3	4	5	6	7	8
COMMON COMPLAINTS							
Losing of Autonomy	3.44	3.98	3.74	3.54	3.62	3.68	151.66*
C.V.	32.45	30.02	30.19	32.08	31.47	31.11	
Boredom	3.55	3.87	3.98	3.66	3.51	3.48	105.40*
C.V.	32.11	30.18	30.22	31.87	31.99	32.03	
Isolation	3.71	3.81	3.88	3.72	3.80	3.74	84.44*
C.V.	31.00	30.00	29.74	30.99	30.45	30.54	
Delays	3.65	3.98	4.08	3.65	3.44	3.35	71.29*
C.V.	29.00	28.45	28.71	29.77	29.87	30.08	
Helplessness	3.15	3.88	4.07	3.66	3.56	3.58	51.94*
C.V.	31.14	29.88	29.74	30.75	30.85	31.07	
Health Problem	3.25	3.84	3.78	3.54	3.67	3.69	58.80*
C.V.	32.04	29.15	29.78	32.17	32.56	32.19	
ORGANIZATIONAL INCENTIVE							
Orientation Programmes	3.78	4.14	4.37	3.88	3.79	3.97	42.47*
C.V.	28.45	26.78	26.99	27.98	27.99	28.08	
Consultation/Counselling	4.00	4.45	4.59	4.28	4.37	4.49	45.62*
C.V.	23.47	22.00	22.14	23.14	23.57	23.60	
Assurance	4.12	4.37	4.57	4.00	4.17	4.16	22.25*
C.V.	25.15	24.11	24.45	25.44	26.14	26.49	
Training Programmes	3.12	3.78	3.77	3.36	3.39	3.43	25.11*
C.V.	33.98	32.08	32.19	33.54	33.78	33.97	
Financial Incentives	2.64	2.97	3.09	2.66	3.55	3.44	154.07*
C.V.	52.87	51.02	51.45	52.87	52.88	53.14	
PROXIMITY							
Extent of Work Computerized	3.47	3.63	3.78	3.45	3.57	3.55	197.70*
C.V.	33.45	32.00	31.78	32.87	32.47	32.77	

(Contd...)

1	2	3	4	5	6	7	8
Use of computers at Work	1.74	2.09	2.17	1.74	1.68	1.87	290.96*
C.V.	69.74	67.24	67.87	68.71	68.41	38.56	
Hours spent on computers	2.00	2.71	2.68	2.11	2.08	2.14	174.44*
C.V.	64.14	63.00	63.13	63.78	63.84	63.99	
Operating Computers Personally	2.14	2.71	2.79	2.97	2.18	2.41	56.49*
C.V.	58.12	56.58	56.67	56.99	57.97	58.00	
Computer's Help in Work	2.01	2.52	2.47	2.02	1.97	1.94	69.16*
C.V.	65.00	63.14	63.78	65.02	65.47	65.11	
STUMBLING BLOCKS							
Power failure	3.87	4.15	4.27	3.78	3.76	3.84	89.57*
C.V.	28.00	26.45	26.41	27.88	27.14	27.64	
Dead Locks/shutdowns	3.97	4.17	4.21	3.78	3.78	3.66	136.44*
C.V.	27.00	26.00	25.97	26.89	27.05	27.14	
Virus Threat	4.00	4.24	4.37	3.97	3.89	3.74	100.23*
C.V.	25.02	23.64	23.59	24.12	24.31	24.51	
Fear of Loss of Data/ Files	3.99	4.37	4.41	3.87	3.78	3.81	55.05*
C.V.	27.12	25.14	25.87	26.94	26.74	27.45	
ECONOMIES							
Saves Costs	1.40	1.57	1.68	1.38	1.4	1.23	122.47*
C.V.	70.44	69.12	69.14	70.02	70.14	70.24	
Reduce Paper Usage	1.74	2.32	2.23	1.78	1.64	1.66	100.22*
C.V.	68.14	67.00	67.21	68.22	68.74	68.00	

*Indicate significant at 5 per cent level.

Source: Computed from Primary Data.

The above table indicates the opinion of the employees on the various Quality of Work Life related factors by experience in bank. As it could be seen in the table, in the experience group of less than 5 years, the highest preference was given to the factor on Increase Output (1.01). The order of the other variables is: Increase Quality of Work (1.17), Save time (1.22), Make work easier (1.38), Saves Costs (1.4), Data Storage (1.41), Report generation (1.52), Analysis and Decisions (1.64), Letter Writing (1.7), Use of computers at Work (1.74), Reduce Paper Usage (1.74), Hours spent on computers (2.00), Computer's Help in Work (2.01), Planning and Scheduling (2.12), Operating Computers Personally (2.14), Reduce Repetitive Work (2.22), Integrate data base (2.24), Financial Incentives (2.64), Adequately trained (2.99), Training Programmes (3.12), Helplessness (3.15), Learn Computer Skills (3.21), Health Problem (3.25), Losing of Autonomy (3.44), Extent of Work Computerized (3.47), Boredom (3.55), Delays (3.65), Isolation (3.71), Read about computers (3.77), Orientation Programmes (3.78), Power failure (3.87), Dead Locks/shutdowns (3.97), Fear of Loss of Data/Files (3.99), Consultation/ Counselling (4.00), Virus Threat (4.00), Observed Others (4.02) and Assurance (4.12).

In the case of the experience group of 5-10 years, the factor on Increase Output (1.29) could be identified as the foremost factor of preference. The order of other factors is: Make work easier (1.45), Save time (1.54), Saves Costs (1.57), Increase Quality of Work (1.58), Data Storage (1.71), Report generation (1.75), Analysis and Decisions (1.87), Letter Writing (1.89), Use of computers at Work (2.09), Reduce Paper Usage (2.32), Planning and Scheduling (2.47), Computer's Help in Work (2.52), Integrate data base (2.68), Hours spent on computers (2.71), Operating Computers Personally (2.71), Financial Incentives (2.97), Reduce Repetitive Work (3.08), Adequately trained (3.23), Learn Computer Skills (3.45), Extent of Work Computerized (3.63), Training Programmes (3.78), Isolation (3.81), Health

Problem (3.84), Boredom (3.87), Helplessness (3.88), Losing of Autonomy (3.98), Delays (3.98), Read about computers (3.99), Orientation Programmes (4.14), Power failure (4.15), Dead Locks/shutdowns (4.17), Virus Threat (4.24), Assurance (4.37), Fear of Loss of Data/Files (4.37), Consultation/ Counselling (4.45) and Observed Others (4.54).

In the case of the experience group of 10-15 years, the order of the factors is: Increase Output (1.24), Make work easier (1.48), Save time (1.55), Increase Quality of Work (1.64), Data Storage (1.66), Saves Costs (1.68), Report generation (1.78), Analysis and Decisions (1.98), Letter Writing (1.99), Use of computers at Work (2.17), Reduce Paper Usage (2.23), Computer's Help in Work (2.47), Planning and Scheduling (2.49), Hours spent on computers (2.68), Integrate data base (2.79), Operating Computers Personally (2.79), Financial Incentives (3.09), Reduce Repetitive Work (3.15), Adequately trained (3.27), Learn Computer Skills (3.41), Losing of Autonomy (3.74), Training Programmes (3.77), Health Problem (3.78), Extent of Work Computerized (3.78), Isolation (3.88), Boredom (3.98), Helplessness (4.07), Read about computers (4.08), Delays (4.08), Dead Locks/shutdowns (4.21), Power failure (4.27), Orientation Programmes (4.37, Virus Threat (4.37), Fear of Loss of Data/Files (4.41), Assurance (4.57), Consultation/ Counselling (4.59)and Observed Others (4.65).

For the experience group of 15-25 years the most preferred factor is: Increase Output (1.02). The other factors in the order is: Increase Quality of Work (1.12), Data Storage (1.21), Save time (1.32), Make work easier (1.37), Saves Costs (1.38), Report generation (1.54), Analysis and Decisions (1.55), Letter Writing (1.64), Use of computers at Work (1.74), Reduce Paper Usage (1.78), Computer's Help in Work (2.02), Planning and Scheduling (2.11), Hours spent on computers (2.11), Integrate data base (2.13), Financial Incentives (2.66), Reduce Repetitive Work (2.77), Operating Computers Personally (2.97), Adequately trained (3.00), Learn Computer

Skills (3.28), Training Programmes (3.36), Extent of Work Computerized (3.45), Losing of Autonomy (3.54), Health Problem (3.54), Delays (3.65), Boredom (3.66), Helplessness (3.66), Isolation (3.72), Power failure (3.78), Dead Locks/ shutdowns (3.78), Read about computers (3.80), Fear of Loss of Data/Files (3.87), Orientation Programmes (3.88), Virus Threat (3.97), Assurance (4.00), Observed Others (4.12), Consultation/ Counselling (4.28).

As it could be seen in the table, in the experience group of 20-25 years, Increase Output (0.98) again forms the foremost factor of preference. The order of other factors is: Data Storage (1.14), Save time (1.22), Increase Quality of Work (1.24), Make work easier (1.36), Saves Costs (1.4), Analysis and Decisions (1.44), Report generation (1.47), Letter Writing (1.54), Reduce Paper Usage (1.64), Use of computers at Work (1.68), Computer's Help in Work (1.97), Planning and Scheduling (2.03), Hours spent on computers (2.08), Operating Computers Personally (2.18), Integrate data base (2.33), Reduce Repetitive Work (2.64), Adequately trained (2.98), Learn Computer Skills (3.14), Training Programmes (3.39), Delays (3.44), Boredom (3.51), Financial Incentives (3.55), Helplessness (3.56), Extent of Work Computerized (3.57), Losing of Autonomy (3.62), Health Problem (3.67), Read about computers (3.74), Power failure (3.76), Dead Locks/shutdowns (3.78), Fear of Loss of Data/ Files (3.78), Orientation Programmes (3.79), Isolation (3.8), Virus Threat (3.89), Observed Others (4.13), Assurance (4.17) and Consultation/ Counselling (4.37).

As it could be seen in the table, in the experience group of Above 25 years the factor or Increase Output (1.02) forms the highest preference. The other factors in their order is: Saves Costs (1.23), Make work easier (1.29), Data Storage (1.29), Increase Quality of Work (1.33), Save time (1.34), Report generation (1.34), Analysis and Decisions (1.36), Letter Writing (1.45), Reduce Paper Usage (1.66), Use of computers at Work (1.87), Computer's Help in Work (1.94),

Hours spent on computers (2.14), Integrate data base (2.19), Planning and Scheduling (2.22), Operating Computers Personally (2.41), Reduce Repetitive Work (2.68), Adequately trained (2.98), Learn Computer Skills (3.17), Delays (3.35), Training Programmes (3.43), Financial Incentives (3.44), Boredom (3.48), Extent of Work Computerized (3.55), Helplessness (3.58), Dead Locks/shutdowns (3.66), Losing of Autonomy (3.68), Health Problem (3.69), Isolation (3.74), Virus Threat (3.74), Read about computers (3.78), Fear of Loss of Data/Files (3.81), Power failure (3.84), Orientation Programmes (3.97), Assurance (4.16), Observed Others (4.19) and Consultation/ Counselling (4.49).

The *F* values given in Table 6.8 also indicate that they are significant at 5 per cent levels providing the inference that there is a significant difference between the years of experience of the sample employees and their opinion on Quality of Work Life.

Thus from the analysis it can be concluded that there is a significant difference between the years of experience of the sample employees and their opinion on the Quality of Work Life.

Factors on Quality of Work Life by Monthly Income

In the present paragraph it is attempted to discuss whether there is any significant difference in the opinion about the factors on Quality of Work life among the different respondents by years of experience.

Table 6.9: Distribution of Factors on Quality of Work Life by Monthly Income

Factors	Less than 10,000	10000-15000	15000-20000	20000-25000	above 25000	F Ratio
1	2	3	4	5	6	7
DRIVING FORCE						
Make work easier	1.34	1.38	1.41	1.44	1.48	18.21*
C.V.	77.29	76.54	75.46	75.21	74.12	

(Contd...)

1	2	3	4	5	6	7
Increase Quality of Work	1.27	1.29	1.31	1.34	1.36	21.31*
C.V.	75.49	74.29	73.54	72.91	71.54	
Save time	1.35	1.39	1.42	1.47	1.52	31.36*
C.V.	73.15	73.02	72.76	72.41	71.26	
Increase Output	1.01	1.08	1.10	1.13	1.17	30.03*
C.V.	51.22	50.27	50.13	49.98	49.12	
Reduce Repetitive Work	2.34	2.56	2.76	2.94	2.99	34.94*
C.V.	49.00	49.61	49.52	49.47	48.35	
Integrate data base	2.14	2.26	2.37	2.41	3.67	46.79*
C.V.	62.57	62.43	61.00	60.66	60.18	
LEARNING						
Read about computers	3.21	3.44	3.68	3.77	4.05	45.35*
C.V.	31.54	31.28	31.07	30.67	30.02	
Learn Computer Skills	3.03	3.14	3.27	3.37	3.84	19.22*
C.V.	39.55	38.12	37.00	37.12	36.54	
Adequately trained	2.97	3.01	3.17	3.21	3.27	17.82*
C.V.	44.57	43.12	43.03	42.97	42.12	
Observed Others	4.08	4.14	4.21	4.37	4.57	21.47*
C.V.	21.41	21.08	20.87	20.54	19.97	
APPLICATIONS						
Analysis and Decisions	1.23	1.45	1.57	1.78	1.91	22.87*
C.V.	72.03	71.08	70.54	70.21	70.03	
Planning and Scheduling	2.04	2.11	2.27	2.39	2.45	23.75*
C.V.	63.07	62.97	62.85	62.54	62.01	
Report generation	1.31	1.41	1.57	1.62	1.71	25.54*
C.V.	71.00	70.97	70.65	70.41	69.88	

(Contd...)

1	2	3	4	5	6	7
Data Storage	1.12	1.34	1.47	1.53	1.61	174.78*
C.V.	69.44	68.87	68.77	68.21	67.87	
Letter Writing	1.47	1.67	1.71	1.79	1.84	203.71*
C.V.	69.33	69.11	69.00	68.76	68.23	
COMMON COMPLAINTS						
Losing of Autonomy	3.22	3.47	3.87	3.97	4.07	140.83*
C.V.	33.18	32.74	32.12	31.77	30.27	
Boredom	3.12	3.48	3.57	3.73	3.89	97.87*
C.V.	32.45	32.12	32.00	31.54	30.11	
Isolation	3.22	3.47	3.54	3.79	4.21	78.41*
C.V.	31.79	31.65	31.41	31.01	29.57	
Delays	3.55	3.69	3.80	3.91	4.08	66.20*
C.V.	31.23	30.74	30.65	30.00	28.77	
Helplessness	3.44	3.67	3.71	3.79	4.12	48.23*
C.V.	32.12	31.54	30.97	30.43	29.46	
Health Problem	3.21	3.33	3.78	3.83	3.98	54.60*
C.V.	32.12	31.66	31.57	31.02	30.40	
ORGANIZATIONAL INCENTIVE						
Orientation Programmes	3.67	3.79	3.84	4.09	4.23	39.43*
C.V.						
Consultation/ Counselling	3.97	4.03	4.21	4.29	4.47	42.36*
C.V.	23.87	23.64	23.00	22.87	22.41	
Assurance	4.01	4.12	4.27	4.34	4.57	20.66*
C.V.	25.37	25.07	24.97	24.51	23.19	
Training Programmes	2.97	3.21	3.41	3.58	3.97	23.31*
C.V.	34.57	34.21	34.02	33.51	33.00	
Financial Incentives	2.66	2.79	2.84	2.96	3.00	143.06*
C.V.	53.21	53.01	52.97	52.45	52.03	

(Contd...)

1	2	3	4	5	6	7
PROXIMITY						
Extent of Work Computerized	3.44	3.56	3.71	3.83	3.97	183.58*
C.V.	33.12	33.00	32.54	32.28	33.12	
Use of computers at Work	1.44	1.67	1.97	2.04	2.31	270.18*
C.V.	69.71	69.04	68.54	68.00	67.41	
Hours spent on computers	2.04	2.18	2.37	2.48	2.49	161.98*
C.V.	64.11	63.77	63.54	63.22	63.12	
Operating Computers Personally	2.23	2.29	2.38	2.71	2.99	52.45*
C.V.	58.04	57.74	57.64	57.22	56.44	
Computer's Help in Work	1.97	2.01	2.12	2.23	2.27	64.22*
C.V.	65.98	65.64	64.77	64.22	63.12	
STUMBLING BLOCKS						
Power failure	3.77	3.87	3.91	4.11	4.22	83.17*
C.V.	29.45	29.00	28.54	27.10	26.31	
Dead Locks/shutdowns	3.78	3.99	4.01	4.11	4.19	126.70*
C.V.	27.71	27.22	27.00	26.12	25.30	
Virus Threat	3.77	3.99	4.08	4.21	4.28	93.07*
C.V.	25.31	25.07	24.11	23.71	23.00	
Fear of Loss of Data/ Files	3.66	3.79	3.91	4.10	4.21	51.11*
C.V.	27.13	26.64	26.00	25.91	25.21	
ECONOMIES						
Saves Costs	1.12	1.22	1.37	1.67	1.71	113.72*
C.V.	71.25	70.64	69.77	69.41	67.22	
Reduce Paper Usage	1.45	1.69	1.93	1.98	2.14	93.06*
C.V.	69.21	68.45	67.71	67.54	66.83	

Source: Computed from Primary Data.

As it could be seen in Table 6.9, among the 37 factors considered, the factor on 'Increase Output (1.01)' constituted the highest preference by the income group of Less than 10,000. The order of other variables is: Data Storage (1.12), Saves Costs (1.12), Analysis and Decisions (1.23), Increase Quality of Work (1.27), Report generation (1.31), Make work easier (1.34), Save time (1.35), Use of computers at Work (1.44), Reduce Paper Usage (1.45), Letter Writing (1.47), Computer's Help in Work (1.97), Planning and Scheduling (2.04), Hours spent on computers (2.04), Integrate data base (2.14), Operating Computers Personally (2.23), Reduce Repetitive Work (2.34), Financial Incentives (2.66), Adequately trained (2.97), Training Programmes (2.97), Learn Computer Skills (3.03), Boredom (3.12), Read about computers (3.21), Health Problem (3.21), Losing of Autonomy (3.22), Isolation (3.22), Helplessness (3.44), Extent of Work Computerized (3.44), Delays (3.55), Fear of Loss of Data/ Files (3.66), Orientation Programmes (3.67), Power failure (3.77), Virus Threat (3.77), Dead Locks/shutdowns (3.78), Consultation/ Counselling (3.97), Assurance (4.01) and Observed Others (4.08).

In the case of income Rs.10000-15000, Increase Output (1.08), Saves Costs (1.22), Increase Quality of Work (1.29), Data Storage (1.34), Make work easier (1.38), Save time (1.39), Report generation (1.41), Analysis and Decisions (1.45), Letter Writing (1.67), Use of computers at Work (1.67), Reduce Paper Usage (1.69), Computer's Help in Work (2.01), Planning and Scheduling (2.11), Hours spent on computers (2.18), Integrate data base (2.26), Operating Computers Personally (2.29), Reduce Repetitive Work (2.56), Financial Incentives (2.79), Adequately trained (3.01), Learn Computer Skills (3.14), Training Programmes (3.21), Health Problem (3.33), Read about computers (3.44), Losing of Autonomy (3.47),Isolation (3.47), Boredom (3.48), Extent of Work Computerized (3.56), Helplessness (3.67), Delays (3.69), Orientation Programmes (3.79), Fear of Loss of Data/Files

(3.79), Power failure (3.87), Dead Locks/shutdowns (3.99), Virus Threat (3.99), Consultation/ Counselling (4.03), Assurance (4.12) and Observed Others (4.14).

In the case of the income group of Rs. 15,000-20,000, the order of the factor preference is: Increase Output (1.1), Increase Quality of Work (1.31), Saves Costs (1.37), Make work easier (1.41), Save time (1.42), Data Storage (1.47), Analysis and Decisions (1.57), Report generation (1.57), Letter Writing (1.71), Reduce Paper Usage (1.93), Use of computers at Work (1.97), Computer's Help in Work (2.12), Planning and Scheduling (2.27), Integrate data base (2.37), Hours spent on computers (2.37), Operating Computers Personally (2.38), Reduce Repetitive Work (2.76), Financial Incentives (2.84), Adequately trained (3.17), Learn Computer Skills (3.27), Training Programmes (3.41), Isolation (3.54), Boredom (3.57), Read about computers (3.68), Helplessness (3.71), Extent of Work Computerized (3.71), Health Problem (3.78), Delays (3.8), Orientation Programmes (3.84), Losing of Autonomy (3.87), Power failure (3.91), Fear of Loss of Data/Files (3.91), Dead Locks/shutdowns (4.01), Virus Threat (4.08), Observed Others (4.21), Consultation/ Counselling (4.21) and Assurance (4.27).

In the case of the income group of 20000-25000 the order of the preference is: Increase Output (1.13), Increase Quality of Work (1.34), Make work easier (1.44), Save time (1.47), Data Storage (1.53), Report generation (1.62), Saves Costs (1.67), Analysis and Decisions (1.78), Letter Writing (1.79), Reduce Paper Usage (1.98), Use of computers at Work (2.04), Computer's Help in Work (2.23), Planning and Scheduling (2.39), Integrate data base (2.41), Hours spent on computers (2.48), Operating Computers Personally (2.71), Reduce Repetitive Work (2.94), Financial Incentives (2.96), Adequately trained (3.21), Learn Computer Skills (3.37), Training Programmes (3.58), Boredom (3.73), Read about computers (3.77), Isolation (3.79), Helplessness (3.79), Health Problem (3.83), Extent of Work Computerized (3.83), Delays

(3.91), Losing of Autonomy (3.97), Orientation Programmes (4.09), Fear of Loss of Data/Files (4.10), Power failure (4.11), Dead Locks/shutdowns (4.11), Virus Threat (4.21), Consultation/Counselling (4.29), Assurance (4.34) and Observed Others (4.37).

In the case of the income group of above 25000 the order of the preference is: Increase Output (1.17), Increase Quality of Work (1.36), Make work easier (1.48), Save time (1.52), Data Storage (1.61), Report generation (1.71), Saves Costs (1.71), Letter Writing (1.84), Analysis and Decisions (1.91), Reduce Paper Usage (2.14), Computer's Help in Work (2.27), Use of computers at Work (2.31), Planning and Scheduling (2.45), Hours spent on computers (2.49), Reduce Repetitive Work (2.99), Operating Computers Personally (2.99), Financial Incentives (3.00), Adequately trained (3.27), Integrate data base (3.67), Learn Computer Skills (3.84), Boredom (3.89), Training Programmes (3.97), Extent of Work Computerized (3.97), Health Problem (3.98), Read about computers (4.05), Losing of Autonomy (4.07), Delays (4.08), Helplessness (4.12), Dead Locks/shutdowns (4.19), Isolation (4.21), Fear of Loss of Data/Files (4.21), power failure (4.22), Orientation Programmes (4.23), Virus Threat (4.28), Consultation/Counselling (4.47), Observed Others (4.57), Assurance (4.57).

Thus from the analysis it can be concluded that there is a significant difference between the distribution of income of the sample employees and their opinion on the Quality of Work Life.

SECTION III

Impact of Individual Factors on the Quality of Work Life

The earlier section provided a detailed view on the significance of the relationship between the selected socio economic factors and the employees' opinion on the factors determining the Quality of Work Life due to the introduction of computers. Though the analysis could provide the significance of the relationship among the variables determining the Quality of Work Life, it fails to provide the relative importance of these factors on Quality of Work Life. To fill this void, in the present section it is attempted to estimate the relative influence of the individual factors on Quality of Work Life. For this purpose, a full log multiple regression function has been applied.

Linear Regression Results of Factors Determining Qulaity of Work Life

As it could be seen in Table 6.10, the adjusted R^2 value is 0.995 which indicates that the included variables could explain 99 per cent of the changes in the total score. Among the broad categories, the factors on stumbling block could explain the highest changes in the total score. The slope coefficient of 1.865 indicates that every 100 per cent changes in the variable on stumbling block could bring about 185 per cent change in the total scores. The negative value indicates that the variable on stumbling block influence the level of satisfaction on Quality of Work Life negatively.The the next highest factor of influence is economies. The slope coefficient of 1.465 indicates that it could bring about 147 per cent change in total scores for every 100 per cent change. The order of other factors in terms of influence is: economies, common complaints, applications, learning and driving force. The factor on organizational incentives influences the total scores negatively. This indicates that the organizational incentives are not on par with the expectations and productivity of the employees. It can also be seen in the table that all the factors are significant at 5 per cent level. The F value is also significant at 5 per cent level.

Thus from the analysis it can be concluded that all the eight factors considered have significant influence on the quality of work life.

Table 6.10: Linear Regression Results: Dependent Variable – Quality Work Life

Independent Variables	Coefficients
Constant	-0.0273 (0.2680)
Driving force	0.581* (0.094)
Learning	1.105* (0.181)
Applications	1.136* (0.121)
Common Complaints	1.248* (0.185)
Organization Incentives	-.774* (0.213)
Proximity	1.324* (0.098)
Stumbling Blocks	-1.865* (0.112)
Economies	1.465* (0.128)
R^2	0.99
Adjusted R^2	0.99
F	4395.722*
N	200
D.F.	191

*Indicates Significant at 5 per cent level.
Figures in parentheses indicate standard error of Estimates.
Source: Computed from Primary Data.

Regression Results of the Scores on Driving Force

The earlier discussion provided a view on the impact of individual dimensions on the total scores on the opinion on

Quality Work Life. In the present and in the subsequent paragraphs it is attempted to discuss the influence of the individual factors on the respective dimension.

As it could be seen in table 6.11, the adjusted R^2 value is 0.998 which indicates that the included variables could explain almost 100 per cent of the changes in the total score. Among the various individual factors determining the total

Table 6.11: Linear Regression Results: Dependent Variable – Scores of Driving Force

Independent Variables	Coefficients
Constant	0.772* (0.002)
Make work easier	0.122* (0.011)
Increase Quality of Work	0.121* (0.009)
Save time	0.171* (0.008)
Increase Output	0.102* (0.009)
Reduce Repetitive Work	0.251* (0.009)
Integrate data base	0.227* (0.009)
R^2	0.99
Adjusted R^2	0.99
F	15946.07*
N	200
D.F.	193

*Indicates Significant at 5 per cent level.

Figures in parentheses indicate standard error of Estimates.

Source: Computed from Primary Data.

scores on driving force, the factors on Reduce Repetitive Work could explain the highest changes in the total score. The slope coefficient of 0.251 indicates that every 100 per cent changes in this variable could bring about 25.10 per cent change in the total scores on driving force. The next highest factor of influence is 'Integrate data base'.

The slope coefficient of 0.227 indicates that it could bring about 22.70 per cent change in total scores of driving force for every 100 per cent change in it. The order of other factors in terms of influence is: Save time, make work easier, Increase Quality of Work and Increase Output. It can also be seen in the table that all the factors are significant at 5 per cent level. The *F* value is also significant at 5 per cent level.

Thus from the analysis it can be concluded that all the factors are significantly influence over the total scores on driving force.

Regression Results of the Scores on Learning

As seen in Table 6.12, among the four factors that influence 'learning', the factor on 'observed others forms the highest influence. For every 100 per cent increase in this factor, the factor on 'learning' increases by 33.70 per cent. The next highest contributing factor is 'read about computers. This variable influences the 'learning' learning variable by 24.50 per cent. The influence of other factors is 'adequately trained' and learns computers. These factors contribute to 23.50 per cent and 17.20 per cent change. The adjusted R^2 value is 0.998 which indicates that the included variables could explain 99.80 per cent of the changes in the scores on 'learning'.

Thus from the analysis it can be concluded that all the factors are significantly influencing over the scores on 'learning'.

Table 6.12: Linear Regression Results: Dependent Variable—Scores of Learning

Independent Variables	Coefficients
Constant	0.608* (0.006)
Read about computers	0.245* (0.008)
Learn Computer Skills	0.172* (0.003)
Adequately trained	0.235* (0.007)
Observed Others	0.337* (0.015)
R^2	0.998
Adjusted R^2	0.998
F	23698.49*
N	200
D.F.	195

* Indicates Significant at 5 per cent level.
Figures in parentheses indicate standard error of Estimates.
Source: Computed from Primary Data.

Regression Results of the Scores on Application

As provided in Table 6.13, of the five factors that influence 'application', the factor on 'planning and scheduling' influences the dependent variable namely 'application; to the highest extent. For every 100 per cent change in the variable on 'planning and scheduling', the variable on 'application' changes by 29.20 per cent. The next highest influence measured in terms of the slope coefficient appears in the variable on 'Data Storage'. For every 100 per cent change in this variable, the value of the dependent variable changes by 16.70 per cent. The order of other variables in terms of their contribution is: Report generation (15.80 per cent), Letter Writing (1.93 per cent) and Analysis and Decisions (1.84 per cent). The adjusted R^2 value indicates that there is almost 100 per cent influence from the included variable. The F value is also significant at 5 per cent level.

Table 6.13: Linear Regression Results: Dependent Variable—Scores of Applications

Independent Variables	Coefficients
Constant	0.699* (0.001)
Analysis and Decisions	0.0184* (0.008)
Planning and Scheduling	0.292* (0.012)
Report generation	0.158* (0.12)
Data Storage	0.167* (0.12)
Letter Writing	0.0193* (0.005)
R^2	1.00
Adjusted R^2	1.00
F	67811.81*
N	200
D.F.	194

* Indicates Significant at 5 per cent level.
Figures in parentheses indicate standard error of Estimates.
Source: Computed from Primary Data.

Thus from the analysis it can be concluded that all the factors are significantly influencing over the scores on 'applications'.

Regression Results of the Scores on Common Complaints

Table 6.14: Linear Regression Results: Dependent Variable—Scores of Common Complaints

Independent Variables	Coefficients
Constant	0.788* (0.001)
Losing of Autonomy	0.184* (0.003)
Boredom	0.168* (0.004)
Isolation	0.136* (0.005)
Delays	0.220* (0.006)
Helplessness	.0127* (0.007)
Health Problem	0.151 (0.004)
R^2	1.00
Adjusted R^2	1.00
F	90476.90
N	200
D.F.	193

* Indicates Significant at 5 per cent level.

Figures in parentheses indicate standard error of Estimates.

Source: Computed from Primary Data.

A close look at the coefficients of independent variables given in Table 6.14 indicates that the influence of the independent variable namely, 'delays' constitutes the highest with 0.220. This means for every 100 per cent change in this variable, the value of the dependent variable namely, 'common complaints' changes by 22.00 per cent. The next highest influence comes from the variable on 'losing of autonomy'. The value of the coefficient is 0.184. This means for every 100 per cent change in the independent variable,

Regression Results of the Scores on Organisational Incentives

Table 6.15: Linear Regression Results: Dependent Variable—Scores of Organisational Incentives

Independent Variables	Coefficients
Constant	0.691* (0.011)
Orientation Programmes	0.220* (0.017)
Consultation/Counselling	0.305* (0.035)
Assurance	0.178* (0.023)
Training Programmes	0.220* (0.009)
Financial Incentives	.00811* (0.006)
R^2	0.996
Adjusted R^2	0.996
F	10364.71*
N	200
D.F.	194

* Indicates Significant at 5 per cent level.

Figures in parentheses indicate standard error of Estimates.

Source: Computed from Primary Data.

the factor on 'common complaints' increases by 18.40 per cent. The order of other independent variables in terms of its coefficients is: Boredom (16.80 per cent), Health Problem (15.00 per cent), Isolation (13.60 per cent) and Helplessness (1.27 per cent). The adjusted R^2 value indicates that there is a 100 per cent influence from the included variable. The *F* value is also significant at 5 per cent level.

Thus from the analysis it can be concluded that all the factors are significantly influencing over the scores on 'common complaints'.

As given in Table 6.15, the slope coefficient of the highest influencing independent variable over the dependent variable is 0.305. This indicates that for every 100 per cent change in the independent variable namely, consultation/ counseling, the value of the dependent variable namely 'organizational incentives' changes by 30.50 per cent. The next highest influence comes from the variables on 'orientation programme' and 'Training Programme'. These variables contribute to 22 per cent of the changes in the dependent variable namely 'organizational incentives'. The order of the other independent variables in terms of its coefficients is: Assurance (17.80 and Financial Incentives (0.81 per cent). The adjusted R^2 value indicates that the included independent variables could explain the changes in the dependent variable to 100 per cent. The *F* value is also significant at 5 per cent level.

Thus from the analysis it can be concluded that all the factors are significantly influencing the scores on 'organizational incentives'.

Regression Results of the Scores on Proximity

A close look at the data provided in Table 6.16 would indicate that among the five independent variables identified, the influence of the variable on 'Extent of Work Computerized' forms the highest with 0.249. This means, every 100 per cent increase in this variable, brings about 24.90 per cent change in the dependent variable identified namely, 'proximity'. The next highest influence comes from 'Operating Computers Personally'. Its slope coefficient indicates that every 100 per cent increase brings about 24.50 per cent increase in the dependent variable namely, 'proximity'. The order of the other variables in terms of its coefficients is: Hours spent on computers (16.30 per cent), Use of computers at Work (13.70 per cent) and Computer's Help in Work (1.96 per cent).

Table 6.16: Linear Regression Results: Dependent Variable—Scores of Proximity

Independent Variables	Coefficients
Constant	0.702* (0.001)
Extent of Work Computerized	0.249* (0.005)
Use of computers at Work	0.137* (0.005)
Hours spent on computers	0.163* (0.004)
Operating Computers Personally	0.245* (0.005)
Computer's Help in Work	.0196* (0.005)
R^2	0.999
Adjusted R^2	0.999
F	71963.36*
N	200
D.F.	194

* Indicates Significant at 5 per cent level.

Figures in parentheses indicate standard error of Estimates.

Source: Computed from Primary Data.

The adjusted R^2 value indicates that the included independent variables could explain the changes in the dependent variable by almost 100 per cent. The F value is also significant at 5 per cent level.

Thus from the analysis it can be concluded that all the factors are significantly influencing the scores on 'proximity'.

Regression Results of the Scores on Stumbling Blocks

As given in Table 6.17, in the case of the dependent variable on stumbling blocks, the independent variables identified

Table 6.17: Linear Regression Results: Dependent Variable—Scores of Stumbling Blocks

Independent Variables	Coefficients
Constant	0.603* (0.001)
Power failure	0.218* (0.010)
Dead Locks/shutdowns	0.408* (0.010)
Virus Threat	0.185* (0.003)
Fear of Loss of Data/Files	0.185* (0.006)
R^2	1.00
Adjusted R^2	1.00
F	231259.4*
N	200
D.F.	195

* Indicates Significant at 5 per cent level.

Figures in parentheses indicate standard error of Estimates.

Source: Computed from Primary Data.

are: Dead Locks/shutdowns, Power failure, Virus Threat and Fear of Loss of Data/Files. In terms of the slope coefficient among the independent variables identified, the influence of the independent variable namely, Dead Locks/shutdowns forms the highest with 0.408.

This means, every 100 per cent increase in the value of the variable brings about 40.80 per cent increase in the dependent variable. The order of the other variables is: Power failure (21.80 per cent), Virus Threat (18.50 per cent) and Fear of Loss of Data/Files (18.50 per cent).

The adjusted R^2 value indicates that the included independent variables could explain the changes in the dependent variable by 100 per cent. The F value is also significant at 5 per cent level.

Regression Results of the Scores on Economy

Table 6.18: Linear Regression Results: Dependent Variable—Scores on Economy

Independent Variables	Coefficients
Constant	0.299* (0.0004)
Saves Costs	0.388* (0.002)
Reduce Paper Usage	0.613* (0.002)
R^2	1.00
Adjusted R^2	1.00
F	362051.9*
N	200
D.F.	197

* Indicates Significant at 5 per cent level.

Figures in parentheses indicate standard error of Estimates.

Source: Computed from Primary Data.

Thus from the analysis it can be concluded that all the factors are significantly influencing the scores on 'stumbling blocks'.

As it could be seen in Table 6.18, two variables namely saves costs and reduce paper usage have been identified as the influencing variable over the dependent variable namely the 'economy'. In terms of the slope coefficient among the independent variables identified, the influence of reduce paper usage found to be the highest with 0.613. This means, every 100 per cent increase in the value of the variable brings about 61.30 percent increases in the dependent variable. The influence of the other variable namely saves cost could contribute to 38.80 per cent of the changes in the economy.

The adjusted R^2 value indicates that the included independent variables could explain the changes in the dependent variable by 100 per cent. The F value is also significant at 5 per cent level.

Thus from the analysis it can be concluded that both the included variables significantly influence the scores on 'economy'.

Inter Correlation Analysis

Job satisfaction means satisfaction relating to work related dimension also. Three are a number of factors that determine the level of job satisfaction. In the present paragraph, 12 such factors were consolidated from a set of 37 already identified and analyzed.

Inter correlation matrix has been carried out in order to understand the inter-correlation among job variables for all employees identified as samples. For this purpose, Carl Pearson's coefficients of correlation have been worked out and are given in the form of matrix and are given in Table 6.19.

It is evident from the table that almost all the variables are positive and statistically significant at 5 per cent level indicating the presence of close association among the job related variables selected. This implies that one job related variable has a direct influence on the other related variable.

Table 6.19: Correlation Matrix of Factors on Job Satisfaction

Job Related Variables	Var1	Var2	Var3	Var4	Var5	Var6	Var7	Var8	Var9	Var10	Var11	Var12
Satisfaction in Job (Var1)	1.00											
Use of Skill (Var1)	0.34	1.00										
Responsibilities given (Var1)	0.39*	0.33*	1.00									
Security of Job (Var1)	0.35*	0.34*	0.31*	1.00								
Advancement (Var1)	0.36*	0.39*	0.32*	0.30*	1.00							
Recognition (Var1)	0.26*	0.38*	0.36*	0.30*	0.51*	1.00						
Social Values (Var1)	0.44*	0.33*	0.32*	0.55*	0.28*	0.35*	1.00					
Work environment (Var1)	0.49*	0.30*	0.47*	0.25*	0.51*	0.43*	0.45*	1.00				
Salaries and other Benefits (Var1)	0.40*	0.26*	0.36*	0.51*	0.41*	0.32*	0.46*	0.45*	1.00			
Administrative policies (Var1)	0.39*	0.35*	0.36*	0.39*	0.51*	0.55*	0.31*	0.42*	0.33*	1.00		
Computerization of work (Var1)	0.38*	0.29*	0.47*	0.58*	0.66*	0.67*	0.61*	0.48*	0.69*	0.58*	1.00	
Relationship with co-officials and the administrator (Var1)	0.50*	0.43*	0.34*	0.34*	0.53*	0.52*	0.51*	0.36*	0.30*	0.56*	0.68*	1.00

*Indicates Significant at 5 per cent level.

Source: Computed from Primary Data

It is also suggests that that there is a inter term agreement among individual's score for the variable selected.

Factor Analysis

The technique adopted for analyzing job variables in respect of identifying the variables regarding job satisfaction is 'Factor analysis". The final outcome of a factor analysis is called rotation Factor Matrix, a table of coefficients that expresses the ratios between the variables and the underlying factors. They express the correlation between the variables and the factor. The sum of squares of the factor loadings of a variable is called communalities (h^2).

Table 6.20: Rotation Factor Matrix

Job Related Variables	F_1	F_2	F_3	h^2
Administrative policies	0.56	0.13	0.202	0.6292
Advancement	0.738	0.102	0.252	0.6186
Relationship with co-officials and the administrator	0.34	0.069	0.203	0.5847
Recognition	0.74	0.275	0.135	0.6036
Work environment	0.707	0.098	0.148	0.5314
Satisfaction in Job	0.086	0.719	0.152	0.5474
Computerization of work	0.208	0.704	-0.151	0.5617
Use of Skill	0.091	0.701	0.455	0.7067
Security of Job	0.316	-0.052	0.77	0.6955
Social Values	0.048	0.137	0.738	0.5657
Salaries and other Benefits	0.397	-0.106	0.716	0.6815
Responsibilities given	0.271	0.262	0.708	0.6433
Percentage Variance Measured (Cumulative)	25.247	37.735	54.462	

The communality of a variable is its common factor variances. The variables with factor loadings of 0.70 or greater are considered significant variables. This limit was chosen because it had been judged that variables with less than 50 per cent common variation with the rotated factor pattern were too weak to report.

In the present study, the Principal Factor Analysis Method with Orthogonal Varimax rotation was used.

Table 6.20 gives the factor loadings received by the variables under factor F_1, F_2 and F_3.

From the table it can be concluded that Administrative policies (0.76) advancement (0.74), interpersonal relationship (0.73), recognition (0.71) and work environment (0.73) are the variables with high loadings on Factor 1. As these variables relate work environment and administrative structure, F_1 is characterized as 'Organizational Structure' and environment. Jon itself (0.72), modernization (0.70) and use of skill (0.70) are the variables with high loading on Factor II (F_2). F_2 hence is termed as 'Attitude towards job'. The remaining variables that show high loadings on Factor III (F_3) are job security (0.770), Social Values (0.74), Salaries and other benefits (0.72) and Responsibilities (0.71).

As these variables represent salaries, benefits and job security, the factor can be termed as 'Security and Status'. The highest loadings obtained by the selected variables are provided in Table 6.21.

Table 6.21: Variables with Highest Factor Loading

	Selected Variables	Factor Loading
F_1 Organization Structure and Environment	Administrative Policies	0.756
F_2 Attitude towards Job	Job itself	0.719
F_3 Security and Status	Job Security	0.770

Impact of Job Related Factors on the Level of Job Satisfaction: Logit Model

A multiple linear regression model has been run to estimate the impact of job related variables on the level of job

Table 6.22: Impact of Job Related Factors on the Level of Job Satisfaction: Logit Model

Intercept	11.168* (3.3955)
Use of Skill	1.002* (0.1056)
Responsibilities given	0.970* (0.0950)
Security of Job	1.068* (0.1056)
Advancement	1.186* (0.1031)
Recognition	1.146* (0.0998)
Social Values	1.053* (0.1032)
Work environment	1.028* (0.1022)
Salaries and other Benefits	1.121* (0.1178)
Administrative policies	1.192* (0.847)
Computerization of work	1.062* (0.116)
Relationship with co officials and the administrator	-1.052* (0.0084)
R^2	0.99
Adjusted R^2	0.94
F Value	2073.06*
No. of Observations	500
Degrees of Freedom	488

*Indicates Significant at 5 per cent level.

Figures in parentheses indicate standard error of Estimates.

Source: Computed from Primary Data

satisfaction. The identified job related variables are treated as independent variable – the proxy for overall satisfaction and the level of job satisfaction as the dependent variable. The estimate coefficients for the independent are given in table 6.22. As it could be seen in the table, the R_2 value of the model fit is 0.99. This indicates that the included variables could explain as high as 99 per cent of the variation in the level of job satisfaction. The variables indicate that the highest slope coefficient of 1.192 has been registered by the variable on administrative policies. This is being followed by the variable on Advancement (1.186). the order of other variables in terms of the coefficients can be give as : Recognition (1.146), Salaries and other Benefits (1.121), Security of Job (1.068), Computerization of work (1.062), Social Values (1.053), Work environment (1.028), Use of Skill (1.002), Responsibilities given (0.97) and Relationship with co officials and the administrator (-1.052).

Thus from the analysis it can be concluded that all the variables are highly significant and they explain as high as 99 per cent of the variation in the level of job satisfaction of the employees of the banks.

Conclusion

Thus from the analysis made in this chapter it can be concluded that all the 37 variable identified under eight broad categories of Quality of Work Life have been found significantly influence the opinion on the quality of Work Life of the sample bank employees. From the analysis it could also be concluded that the differences in the socio economic status of the employees lead to differences in the opinion of the employees on the Quality of Work Life significantly.

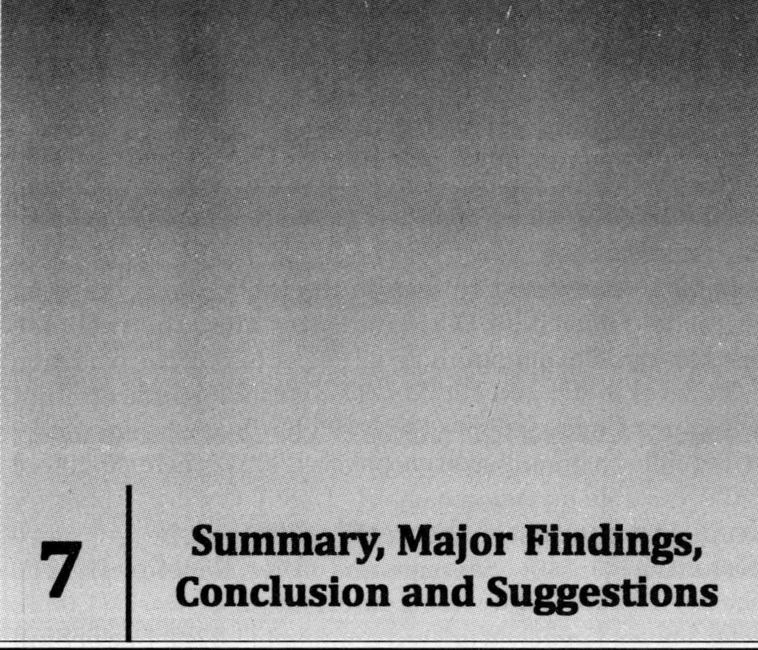

7 Summary, Major Findings, Conclusion and Suggestions

Summary

Since the introduction of New Economic Reforms in 1991, the Indian economy has been gaining momentum in the sphere of service sector playing a vital role. Of the various service sector activities, the banking industry in India has greater importance as it forms the life line of economic activity. However, the liberalization process has resulted in the increased competition among the commercial banks including the public and private sector banks with that of the foreign banks. This has necessitated the Indian banks to adopt new technology in services. However, the private sector banks are found to be fast absorbers of new technologies while the public sector banks are the slow absorbers due to various reasons. This is expected to depress their profitability considerably as, with the increasing competition, the banks have to sustain their customers with the improved service quality which should be in tune with their increased expectations. Also, the adoption of new technologies requires acquiring of new skills by the employees which in turn brings about a change in the Quality Work Life. Hence, globalization has brought about a paradigm shift in the functions and operations of the Indian commercial banks with a changing attitude of the employees to adapt to the changing needs of the business and satisfying the expectations of the customers. With the commercial banks as the absorbers of huge amount of government's funds, if the performance of the banks is not up to the mark, the negative impact could be felt not only the bank it terms of bankruptcy and closure, but also on the performance of the economy. This is a serious issue which requires an immediate concern particularly in the case of the developing countries like India where the economy's monetary impulses work only through commercial banks.

Hence, an understanding of the customers' level of satisfaction on the services and the adaptability of the employees to the changing needs of business environment and the resultant improvement in the Quality of Work Life and the opinion of the customers on the services provided under new technology becomes pertinent. The present study attempts to examine these issues in the micro level in the context of a few sample banks namely public and private sector banks operating in the urban areas of Coimbatore district, which is industrially well developed and called as the "Manchester of South India.

In this context, the following issues pertaining to technology and other related factors were identified: (1) What are the services the customers of public and private sector utilise the most?; (2) In a competitive environment, to what extent the customers of public and private sector banks are satisfied with the services of their banks; (3) to what extent the there is a difference in the level of satisfaction between the public and private sector banks; (4) What is the opinion of the bank employees on the Quality of Work Life prevailing in their banks?; and (5) Is the socio economic status of the bank employees has an influence over the opinion on Quality of Work Life?

Based on the above mentioned issues, the following objectives were framed for the present study: (1) to study the type of banking services utilized by the customers of public and private sector banks; (2) to trace out the opinion of the customers of the public and private sector banks on the perceived and desired level of service quality of their banks; (3) to estimate the Service Quality Gap between the public and private sector banks; (4) to understand the opinion of the employees of public and private banks on the quality work life; (5) to identify the relationship between the socio-economic status of the employees and their opinion on quality work life; and 6) to offer suitable suggestions on the basis of the findings of the study.

Based on the above issues the hypothesis formulated for the study were: (1) there is a significant difference between the customers of the public and private sector banks on the perceived and desired level of service quality; (2) the influence of the administrative policies of the bank on the employees' job satisfaction is higher and significant; (3) there is a significant relationship between the factors determining the Quality of work Life and the Employees' socio economic status; and (4) the impact of 'stumbling Block' on the Quality of Work Life is significant.

The prime focus of the present piece of research is to examine the opinion of the bank employees on the Quality of Work Life on the one hand and the customers' opinion on the service quality of their banks on the other. This required the collection of the primary data from both the bank officials and the customers of the banks from the study area and the universe of the study was selected as the urban areas of Coimbatore District were selected.

To collect the primary data from the customers and from the bank employees, as sample banks, 25 banks were selected at random. From the selected banks, 500 customer respondents with 280 respondents from public sector banks and 220 respondents from private sector banks and 200 bank employees with 8 employees selected from each of the 25 sample banks were selected at random. The selected sample customer respondents and employee respondents were met personally and the required data were collected with the help of two questionnaires - one for customer respondents (questionnaire I) and another one for bank employees (questionnaire II).

More specifically, to identify the customers' level of satisfaction on the quality of services provided, 25 customers from each of the sample banks were selected randomly from the list of customers obtained from each of the sample banks. The selected customer respondents were met in person and the data pertaining to 23 factors which can be categorized under six broad dimensions namely: (1) Tangibility; (2) Reliability; (3) Responsiveness; (4) Security; (5) Technology; and (6) Accessibility were collected.

To identify the employees' opinion on the 'Quality of Work Life, a list of bank employees working in each of the selected sample banks was prepared and from the list 8 employees were selected randomly covering a wide range of experience as it was felt that the years of experience is a major determining of the opinion of the employees on quality of Work life. The selected employee respondents were approached and the data pertaining to thirty seven factors identified under seven broad dimensions namely: (1) Driving Force; (2) Learning Applications; (3) Common Complaints; (4) Organizational Incentive; (5) Proximity; (6) Stumbling Blocks; and (7) Economies were collected.

Before the field survey was conducted the consistency of the information to had become essential to be tested for this purpose, a pilot survey was also conducted.

The collected data were analyzed using the simple percentage method, simple arithmetic mean, standard deviation and coefficient of variation, simple correlation, multiple regression, *T* test, *F* test, Principle component analysis and logit model and the modified version of SERVQUAL Model.

Major Findings of the Study

The analysis of the data has yielded the following findings:

(1) A majority of the sample respondents fall in the age group of 35-45 years.

(2) A majority of the respondents are males.

(3) A majority of the sample respondents are graduates.

(4) A majority of the sample respondents have a monthly income of Rs. 10,000-15,000.

(5) A majority of the sample respondents are businessmen.

(6) A majority of the respondents are savings account holder.

(7) A majority of the respondents are customers of the bank for the past 6-10 years.

(8) A majority of the respondents maintain their account for the better services provided.

(9) A majority of the respondents have come to know of their banks through friends.

(10) A majority of the respondents operate their accounts once in every 15 days.

(11) A majority of the respondents visit their banks to withdraw cash.

(12) According to a majority of the respondents it takes 10-15 minutes to provide the services of accepting deposits or making payments.

(13) A majority of the respondents have utilized the facility of clearing the local cheques.

(14) A majority of the respondents, it takes atleast five days to get their cheque amount realized.

(15) A majority of the respondents utilize the facility of clearing the outstation cheques.

(16) According to a majority of the sample respondents, it takes atleast three days for their banks to clear their outstation cheques.

(17) According to a majority of the respondents their banks did not send any reminders for the maturity of their deposits or to any other related matters.

(18) A majority of the respondents do not have ATM facility.

(19) A majority of the respondents use their cards once in every month.

(20) A majority of the respondents are either not using the e banking facility or it is not available.

(21) A majority of the respondents use the e banking facility as and when it is required.

(22) A majority of the respondents are not using the credit card facility.

(23) According to a majority of the respondents, they use their credit card facility once in every 15 days.

(24) Only a minority of the respondents hold a debit card and a majority of the respondents use their debit cards once in a month.

(25) According to a majority of the respondents, the banks where they are customers, are not working on Sundays.

(26) A majority of the respondents use the convenience banking facility once in every 15 days.

(27) Perceived Level of Service Quality: All Banks

From the discussion made on perceived level of service quality of all banks the following findings emerge:

(*a*) In the case of tangibility dimension, the factor on 'Image of your bank among the public' as the most important perceived level of service quality.

(*b*) Under assurance dimension, the customers view the factor on 'Confidence and perfection of the services provided to you' as the most important perceived service quality variable.

(*c*) Under responsive dimension of all banks, 'Responsiveness to your comments and suggestions' has recorded the highest score.

(*d*) Under empathy dimension of all banks the factor on 'Prompt opening/closing of the branch as per time' recorded the highest score.

(*e*) Under reliability dimension, the factor on 'Skill of the staff to use computers and other modern technical devices' formed the highest score.

(28) Perceived Level of Service Quality: Public Sector Banks

From the discussion made on perceived level of service quality of public sector banks the following findings emerge:

(*a*) In the case of tangibility dimension, the factors on 'Upkeep and cleanliness of the bank premises and Usage of computers and other modern technology to provide service" have recorded the highest scores in the perceived level of service quality.

(*b*) Under assurance dimension, the customers view the factor on 'Confidence and perfection of the services provided to you' was considered as most important perceived service quality variable.

(*c*) Under responsive dimension of all banks, 'Response of the staff when there is a grievance' has recorded the highest score.

(*d*) Under empathy dimension of public sector banks the factor on 'Prompt opening/closing of the branch as per time' recorded the highest score.

(*e*) Under reliability dimension, the factor on 'Quick provision of services' formed the highest score.

(29) Perceived Level of Service Quality: Private Sector Banks

From the discussion made on perceived level of service quality of private sector banks the following findings emerge:

(*a*) In the case of tangibility dimension, the factor on 'Image of your bank among the public" as the most important perceived level of service quality.

(*b*) Under assurance dimension, the customers view the factor on 'Proficiency of the staff on the work they carry out for you' was considered as most important perceived service quality variable.

(*c*) Under responsive dimension of private sector banks, 'Responsiveness to your comments and suggestions' has recorded the highest score.

(*d*) Under empathy dimension of private sector banks the factor on 'Prompt opening/closing of the branch as per time' recorded the highest score.

(*e*) Under reliability dimension, the factor on 'Appropriateness and update of the account statements provided to you, formed the highest score.

(30) Desired Level of Service Quality: All Banks

From the discussion made on desired level of service quality of all banks the following findings emerge:

(*a*) In the case of tangibility dimension, the factor on 'Indication of display timings at appropriate counters' as the most important desired level of service quality.

(*b*) Under assurance dimension, the customers viewed the factor on 'Usage of technical terms when speaking with you' was considered as most important perceived service quality variable.

(*c*) Under responsive dimension of all banks, 'Attitude, responsiveness and courtesy of the staff' has recorded the highest score.

(*d*) Under empathy dimension of all banks the factor on 'Reaction of the bank staff if a scheduled appointment is missed by you' recorded the highest score.

(*e*) Under reliability dimension, the factor on 'Interest and willingness to help you to provide prompt service' formed the highest score.

(31) Desired Level of Service Quality: Public Sector Banks

From the discussion made on desired level of service quality of public sector banks the following findings emerge:

(*a*) In the case of tangibility dimension, the factor on 'Indication of display timings at appropriate counters' as the most important desired level of service quality.

(*b*) Under assurance dimension, the customers viewed the factor on 'Usage of technical terms when speaking with you' was considered as most important perceived service quality variable.

(*c*) Under responsive dimension of public sector banks, 'Responsiveness to your comments and suggestions' has recorded the highest score.

(*d*) Under empathy dimension of public sector banks the factor on 'Efforts taken by the bank staff to know about you and your needs' recorded the highest score.

(*e*) Under reliability dimension, the factor on 'Appropriateness and update of the account statements provided to you' formed the highest score.

(32) Desired Level of Service Quality: Private Sector Banks

From the discussion made on desired level of service quality of private sector banks the following findings emerge:

(*a*) In the case of tangibility dimension, the factor on 'Indication of display timings at appropriate counters' as the most important desired level of service quality.

(*b*) Under assurance dimension, the customers viewed the factor on 'Usage of technical terms when speaking with you' was considered as most important desired level of service quality variable.

(*c*) Under responsive dimension of all banks, 'Attitude, responsiveness and courtesy of the staff' has recorded the highest score.

(*d*) Under empathy dimension of private sector banks the factor on 'Reaction of the bank staff if a scheduled appointment is missed by you' recorded the highest score.

(*e*) Under reliability dimension, the factor on 'Interest and willingness to help you to provide prompt service' formed the highest score.

(33) Service Quality Gap: All Banks

From the discussion made on the service quality gap the following findings emerged:

(*a*) In the case of tangibility dimension of all banks, service quality gap is more in the case of 'Indication of display timings at appropriate counters'.

(*b*) Under assurance dimension of all banks, the service quality gap is more in the case of 'Usage of technical terms when speaking with you

(*c*) Under responsive dimension of all banks, 'Attitude, responsiveness and courtesy of the staff' has recorded the highest score.

(*d*) Under empathy dimension of all banks, the factor on 'Reaction of the bank staff if a scheduled appointment is missed by you' recorded the highest score.

(*e*) Under reliability dimension, the factor on 'Interest and willingness to help you to provide prompt service' recorded the highest negative gap.

(34) Service Quality Gap: Public Sector Banks

From the discussion made on the service quality gap the following findings emerged:

(*a*) In the case of tangibility dimension of public sector banks, service quality gap is more in the case of 'Indication of display timings at appropriate counters'.

(*b*) Under assurance dimension of public sector banks, the service quality gap is more in the case of 'Usage of technical terms when speaking with you.

(*c*) Under responsive dimension of public sector banks, 'Responsiveness to your comments and suggestions' the highest score.

(*d*) Under empathy dimension of public sector banks, the factor on 'Efforts taken by the bank staff to know about you and your needs' recorded the highest score.

(*e*) Under reliability dimension of public sector banks the factor on 'Appropriateness and update of the account statements provided to you' recorded the highest negative gap.

(35) Service Quality Gap: Private Sector Banks

From the discussion made on the service quality gap the following findings emerged:

(*a*) In the case of tangibility dimension of private sector banks, service quality gap is more in the case of 'Indication of display timings at appropriate counters'.

(*b*) Under assurance dimension of private sector banks, the service quality gap is more in the case of 'Usage of technical terms when speaking with you

(*c*) Under responsive dimension of private sector banks, 'Attitude, responsiveness and courtesy of the staff has recorded the highest score.

(*d*) Under empathy dimension of private sector banks, the factor on 'Reaction of the bank staff if a scheduled appointment is missed by you' recorded the highest score.

(*e*) Under reliability dimension of private sector banks the factor on 'Interest and willingness to help you to provide prompt service' recorded the highest negative gap.

(*f*) Male respondents constitute the major share of respondents.

(36) The analysis of the socio economic status of the sample employees indicated that:

(*a*) Male respondents constitute the major share of respondents

(*b*) The respondents in the age group of 35-45 years form the highest

(*c*) Employee respondents who completed their general Post graduation formed the highest

(*d*) A major share of respondents is middle level managers

(*e*) The respondents who have put 10-15 years of experience form the highest

(*f*) The respondents who earn a monthly income of Rs.10000-15000 constitute the highest

(*g*) A majority of the respondents' family have the family size of 2-4 members

(*h*) A majority of the sample respondents belong to nuclear family

(*i*) In a majority of the sample respondents' families, the number of dependents constitutes 2-4 members

(37) The correlation matrix indicated that the factors considered under Quality Work Life are not independent among them but are dependent.

(38) As viewed by the sample bank employees, the factors on stumbling block influence their productivity negatively to a major extent.

(39) There is a significant difference between the opinion of males and females in terms of the factors considered under Quality of Work Life.

(40) There is a significant difference between the various age groups and the opinion on the various factors determining the Quality of Work Life.

(41) Irrespective of the level of educational attainment of the sample employees, the opinion indicated that

increasing the output forms the major reason for the adoption of computerization in work place.

(42) Irrespective of the category of profession of the sample employees, the opinion indicated that increasing the output forms the major reason for the adoption of computerization in work place.

(43) There is a significant difference between the years of experience of the sample employees and their opinion on the Quality of Work Life.

(44) There is a significant difference between the distribution of income of the sample employees and their opinion on the Quality of Work Life.

(45) All the eight factors considered have significant influence on the quality of work life.

(46) All the factors significantly influence the total scores on driving force.

(47) All the factors are significantly influencing over the scores on 'learning'.

(48) All the factors are significantly influencing over the scores on 'applications'.

(49) All the factors are significantly influencing over the scores on 'common complaints'

(50) All the factors are significantly influencing the scores on 'organizational incentives'.

(51) All the factors are significantly influencing the scores on 'proximity'.

(52) All the factors are significantly influencing the scores on 'stumbling blocks'.

(53) The included variables significantly influence the scores on 'economy'

(54) There is a inter term agreement among individual's score for the variable selected.

(55) The variables like, Organization Structure and Environment, Attitude towards Job and Security and Status have received highest factor loading.

(56) All the included variables are highly significant and they explain as high as 99 per cent of the variation in the level of job satisfaction of the employees of the banks.

Hypotheses Testing

The present project formulated four hypotheses for testing:

The *first hypothesis is that "there is a significant difference between the customers of the public and private sector banks on the perceived and desired level of service quality"*.

This means, the first hypothesis pertains to the testing of the significance of the difference between the customers' view on the what is being supplied by banks in terms of services (perceived) and what is being expected (desired).

As it has already been explained, the levels of satisfaction are scaled from 1 to 7 and the opinions are quantified to arrive at arithmetic mean, and standard deviation for each factor. The difference between two means namely, the perceived and desired levels of satisfaction has been calculated. This is termed as 'Service Quality Gap'. .Since the mean values of the desired level of satisfaction are found to be higher for all the factors than the perceived level of satisfaction measuring the five broad service quality dimensions, the service quality gap is found to be negative. Hence, the significance of the service quality gap is the difference between the perceived and desired level of satisfaction. To test the significance of the difference, the 't' statistics has been used. The 't' value is found to be significance for all the factors which indicates that there is a significant difference between the perceived and desired level of satisfaction.

This helped to accept the first Hypothesis that "there is a significant difference between the customers of the public and private sector banks on the perceived and desired level of service quality".

Hence, *the Hypothesis that there is a significant difference between the customers of the public and private sector banks on the perceived and desired level of service quality" has been proved.*

The *second hypothesis formulated was "The influence of the administrative policies of the banks on the employees' job satisfaction is higher and significant".*

To estimate the impact of employees' opinion on service quality initially, 37 broad factors were identified. Based on the literature these 37 variables were narrowed down to have 11 variables which are crucial in determining the satisfaction on job. These include the variables like, Use of Skill, Responsibilities given, Security of Job, Advancement, Recognition, Social Values, Work environment, Salaries and other Benefits, Administrative policies, Computerization of work and Relationship with co-officials and the administrator.

Since all the included independent and the dependent variables are qualitative in nature, the logit model which is commonly used to estimate the impact of the quality variables which are converted into dummy variables and which take the values of either zero or one.

The coefficients of the independent variables indicated that among the 11 included variables, the coefficient of the variable on 'administrative policies' is found to be higher and highly significant.

This implies that the second hypothesis formulated namely "The influence of the administrative policies of the banks on the employees' job satisfaction is higher and significant has been proved and accepted.

The *third hypothesis is that "There is a significant relationship between the factors determining the Quality of work Life and the Employees' socio-economic status".*

To test this hypothesis, 37 factors considered under the seven broad dimensions determining the quality of work life has been related using the *F* ratio with the broad socio economic factors like, sex, age education qualification, profession, years of experience and monthly income. The F test used was found to be significant at 5 per cent level for all the 37 variables considered implying the rejection of Null Hypothesis framed as "there is no relationship between the factors determining the Quality of work Life and the Employees' socio-economic status'.

Hence, *the third Hypothesis that 'there is significant relationship between the factors determining the Quality of work Life and the Employees' socio-economic status' has been proved.*

The *fourth hypothesis framed is 'the impact of the variable on 'stumbling block' on quality of work life is significant".*

It was identified form the literature that there are eight broad factors that influence the 'Quality of work Life' of employees. These include: Driving force, Learning, Applications, Common Complaints, Organization Incentives, Proximity, Stumbling Blocks and Economies. To examine the relative influence of each of the factors on 'Quality of work Life', a multiple regression model has been adopted. A five point scale has been used for the variables considered. The coefficient for each of the variables has been estimated. The estimated coefficient has been tested with the help of't' test for its significance. The estimated coefficients indicated that among all other variables that have been identified and estimated, the coefficient of the variable on 'Stumbling Block' is higher and significant.

Thus the fourth hypothesis framed is 'the impact of the variable on 'stumbling block' on quality of work life is significant" has been proved.

Conclusion

The prime focus of the present piece of research was to examine the impact of new technologies of services in commercial banks on the quality of work life and the level of satisfaction of the customers on the service provision. This is because, it was also felt that the introduction of New Economic Reforms has brought about a change in the functions of the banks through a change in the 'Quality of Work life' of the employees on the one hand and the customers' attitude on the other. Hence, it was felt that an understanding of the customers' opinion on the perceived and desired levels of service quality and the employees' opinion on the changes in 'Quality of Work Life' due to changes in the work environment was pertinent.

To study these two broad objectives, primary data were collected from 200 employees and 500 customers selected at random from 14 public sector and 11 private sector banks (total of 25 banks). The required data were obtained with the help of two questionnaires prepared—one for the bank employees and the other one for the customers of the banks). While the questionnaire on Quality of Work Life included information on 37 factors determining the Quality of Work Life, the customers' perceived and desired level of Service Quality have been examined with the help of the information on 36 factors included in the questionnaire.

The collected data were analysed using the tools and techniques like, Correlation matrix, Simple Percentage Method, Standard Deviation, Co-Efficient Of Variation, Principal Component Analysis, Simple Arithmetic Mean, SERVQUAL , multiple regression model and the logit model.

Suggestions

In order to improve the quality of Work Life and the level of satisfaction of customers of sample banks the following suggestions are provided:

(1) A study on the quality of work life indicated that the between the productivity of the employees and the factors determining the Quality of work life indicated that employees considered stumbling block as the major factor determining the 'Quality of Work Life' while driving force as the least important. This implies that while the employees considers the computer related problems and power shut down as the major factor determining the quality of work life, the factors relating to the introduction of computers in office as least important. Hence, the banks should take utmost care to see that the computers do not get shut down. Also, care should be taken to see that there are no power failures. For customer satisfaction, apart from providing a variety of services, making the customers to wait less time for obtaining the services is an important factor determining the customer satisfaction. Hence the bank officials can be given training on the effective utilization of the computer facilities available.

(2) An analysis on the relationship between the Quality of Work Life and the Socio economic Status indicated that the Socio economic Status has a significant influence on Quality of Work Life. Hence, the management of the banks can understand the expectations of the works by different social and economic environments and create working atmosphere in tune with their expectations. This requires the extending of the required facilities for the employees also.

(3) After sales services like, timely reminder about the maturity of term deposit, sending current account

statements promptly, crediting interest on delayed collection of cheques, delayed credit of mail transfer etc. are found to be more time taking in the case of public sector banks when compared to private sector banks and hence the public sector banks can reduce the time taken in these regard. This would increase the customer satisfaction.

(4) The banks can observe a specific day on every month, as the day of "Customer meet". This meeting could be utilized as an opportunity by the bankers to welcome suggestions and complaints from the customers, creating an awareness about the new schemes, guiding them in choosing the right scheme based on their requirements and above all in creating trust and loyalty.

(5) Though the sample banks are covered from the urban areas of Coimbatore, almost half of the banks do not have locker facilities. At present this service is necessary for the banks located in the city limits to give protection to the valuables of the customers. Hence, it is suggested that this type of services must be provided by all the banks which do not have this facility.

(6) To attract the customers from different strata of the society like, the customers from different profession, age group, sex, income groups, etc. it is suggested that the service provision must be differentiate among the customers of different socio-economic strata depending on their expectations and needs. To provide this and to have a close affinity with the customer, each bank must maintain a customer profile that is, customer data, or data warehouse. This will help the banker in analyzing and categorizing the customers. This in turn would also help the banks to plan, organize and market their products.

(7) To understand the customer needs and their grievances, to help them in opening an account for new clients, a separate cell can be created which guides the new customers and which takes care of the grievances of the customers.

(8) Increasing the number of delivery channels like, credit card, debit card, ATM, anywhere banking, multiple delivery channels, single window service, mobile banking, phone banking, e banking and service at the door steps would go a long way increasing the number of customers and the banks' businesses.

(9) Service culture is to be developed among the staff. Human Resources Development standards should be maintained in the recruitments at all levels.

(10) The study could also found that the sample banks, particularly the public sector banks are the poor users of the modern technology. Hence, attempts must be made to computerize the banks and their branches 100 per cent and concerted efforts to be made to introduce Core Banking Solutions (CBS) in at least the major branches to start with.

(11) It is found out from the study that the average value of service quality perception of public sector banks is lower than that of private sector banks. The reason being, in the case of public sector banks the customer relationship management practices are not effective as found in the case of private sector banks. This is being again proved by the comparatively lower service quality scores. Hence, the customer relationship in the case of public sector banks can be improved.

(12) Since significant differences were found between the opinion on 'Quality of Work Life' of employees and their age, gender, education, separate promotional schemes may be designed generally for the whole set

of customers of the banks. This information will lead to reduction of expenses on account of separate promotional schemes based on different segments of the market.

Scope for Future Research

The present piece of research poses certain question that can be considered for future research. They are:

(1) The present project attempted to examine the quality of work life of the employees. In this context, the study has examined the level of satisfaction or opinion on the quality of work life of the employees. However, this did not attempt to measure the risk factors associated with the work-life conflict. Hence, future research can concentrate on this relationship.

(2) The study has viewed that the socio economic factors has an influence over the opinion on the quality of work life. However, this did not measure how high levels role overload, work to family interference, family to work interference, caregiver strain and spillover from work to family affect employees and their families.

(3) Studies can be carried out to identify in the areas of improvement in customer satisfaction and loyalty ratings and differentiate themselves from the competition. For this purpose, the banks need to understand what drives satisfaction and loyalty, and whether there is greatest opportunity for improvement.

(4) Studies can be carried out by identifying the opinion and rating of the customers on relationship closeness, price (fees and charges) and value. This would help the banks to understand the areas that require improvement and price fixation for various services.

of customers of the banks. This information will lead to reduction of expenses on account of separate promotional schemes based on different segments of the market.

Scope for Future Research

The present piece of research poses certain question that can be considered for future research. They are:

(1) The present project attempted to examine the quality of work life of the employees. In this context, the study has examined the level of satisfaction or opinion on the quality of work life of the employee. However, this did not attempt to measure the risk factors associated with the work-life conflict. Hence, future research can concentrate on this relationship.

(2) The study has viewed that the socio-economic factors has an influence over the opinion on the quality of work life. However, this did not measure how high levels role overload, work to family interference, family to work interference, caregiver strain and spillover from work to family affect employees and their families.

(3) Studies can be carried out to identify in the areas of improvement in customer satisfaction and loyalty ratings and differentiate themselves from the competition. For this purpose, the banks need to understand what drives satisfaction and loyalty, and whether there is greatest opportunity for improvement.

(4) Studies can be carried out by identifying the opinion and rating of the customers on relationship closeness, price (fees and charges) and value. This would help the banks to understand the areas that require improvement and price fixation for various services.

Bibliography

Abdul Raheem. A(2005), Determinants of Banking Service Quality: An Application of Factor Analysis, *Southern Economist*, Feb., pp. 17-20.

Anu Anna Thomas (2004), Prudent Technology Investment and Its Competitive Lead in the Banking Sector, *Professional Banker*, Aug pp. 47-52.

Ashish Sen (1996), Role of Technology in Banking, *Vinimaya Special Issue*, pp. 70-74.

Ashwinini, K. Aswathi and Balaram Dogra (2006), Measuring Service Quality in Banks—An Assessment of Service Quality Dimensions, Conference on Global Competitiveness IIM Kozhikode, March, pp. 24-25.

Bhaskara.B.G.Narishmmha.T.V. and Viswanath.N.S (2000), Service Quality Management in Indian Banks, Opportunities and Challenges, *South Economist*, pp. 11-15.

Bhide, M.G. ((1997), Information Technology in Banks, *The Journal of Indian Institute of Bankers*, pp. 149-152.

Booz Allen Hamilton, (1997), Strategic Impact of Internet Banking of the Financial Service Industry, www.mfa.ee.com, pp. 1-14.

Chaitanya, V. Krishna(2005), Metamorphosis of Marketing Financial Services in India, *Journal of Services Research*, Vol. 5, No.1, April–Sep., pp. 155-166.

Chowdhury K.C. (1996), Technology in Banking: Problems and Prospects, *Vinimaya Special issue*, Oct-Dec, pp. 51-56

Daniel J. Flint (2006), Innovation Symbolic Interaction and Customer Valuing Thoughts Stemming Form A Service—Dominant Logic of Marketing, *Marketing Theory*, Col. 6 (3), pp. 349-362.

Desikan R.S. (1994), Strategic Alignment of IT future of Indian Banks, Becon,17th *Bank Economists Conference*, pp. 195-199.

Dharmalingam Venugopal (2004), Technology in Banks, Some Thoughts for the Future, *Professional Banker*, Aug., pp. 30-32.

Doreswamy. S (1996). Technology in Banking: Trends and Implications, *Vinimaya Special Issue*, Oct –Nov., pp. .38-44.

Edwyn Fernades (2004), Internet Banking: An Empirical Investigation into the Extent of Adoption by Banks and the Determinants of Customer Satisfaction in the UAE, www.arraudev.com, pp. 1-18.

Findos. T. Shroff (1998), Indian Banking Information Technology Perspectives, *Becon Canara Bank*, pp. 296-299.

Firdos T.Shroff (2004), Impact of Technology on Banking: *IBA Bulletin Special Issue*, Jan, pp. 174-181.

Ganti Subramanya (1998), Banking in the Next Millennium, *Vinimaya Special Issue*, July-Sep, pp. 15-18.

Girish Vaidya and Preetha Sundram(1997), Technology in Banking : A Global Perspective, *The Journal of Indian Institute of Bankers*, Oct-Dec, pp. 183-189

Godse.V.T (1996), Technology in Banking, *Vinimaya Special Issue*, pp. 101-105.

Gulati.V.P (2004), Technology in Banks, *Professional Banker*, Aug., pp. 22-25.

Gupta.M.P.and Rohet Sareen (2001), A Study of Consumer Concerns and Issues of Electronic Payment in India, *Global Business Review*, Jan pp. 101-119.

Hirve A.K. and Kulkarni P.R. (2002), Organizational Preparedness for Implementation of Technology Plans in Indian Banks, *Vinimaya Special Issue*, Jan-Mar, pp. 18-25.

Jabnoun N and Al-Tamimi H (2003), Measuring Perceived Service Quality at UAE Commercial Banks, *International Journal of Quality and Reliability Management*, Vol. 20, No. 4, pp. 458-472.

Jai Shankar Ganesh, Mark J.Arnold and Krishty E.Reynolds (2000), Understanding the Customer Base of Services Providers: An

Examination of the Difference Between Switchers and Stayers, *Journal of Marketing*, July, pp. 65-87.

Jani Saineen (2000), Information Technology and Developments in the Banking Sector www.cio.com.

Kalpana Arora (2003), Indian Banking: Managing Transformation through Information Technology, *IBA Bulletin Special Issues*, March pp. 134-138.

Kamath. R.J.(1996),Office Automation of Indian Banks, *Vinimaya Special Issue*, pp. 89-100.

Karti Kereem and Tallinn, (2002), *Adoption of Electronic Banking*: Underlying Consumer Behaviour and Critical Success Factors, Case of Estonia, www.insofres.com. pp. 1-12.

Kasturi Nageswara Rao (2004), IT in Banks: Indian Scenario, *Professional Banker*, Aug., pp. 27-29.

Kathiria C.G (1996), Technology Imperatives in Banks, *Vinimaya Special Issue*, Oct-Dec., pp. 45-50.

Kshirsagar S.D(2003),Financial Services in India: A New Perspective', *Management Review*, June, pp. 37 -44.

Kuppuswamy, P.T. (2004), Technology in Banks: *Professional Banker*, Aug., pp. 6-13.

Lakshmi Prasad Padhy (2003), Banking: Challenges and Prospects, *Facts for You*. Feb., pp. 34-38.

Madhavaiah.C., and Durga Rao. S (2006), Effective Measurement of Customer Service in Banks, Banking "Finance, Vol. XIX, No. 11, November.

Metta Ongkasuwan Worasri Tantichattanon (2002) A Comparative Study of Internet Banking in Thailand, www.hot.or.th.com, pp. 1-18.

Mukta Kamplikar (2006), Managing the Evidence of Service in Banks, *Vinimaya* Vol.XXVI, No.3, pp. 32-38.

Mushtaq A. Bhat and Gani. A (2003), Service Quality in Commercial Banks: A Comparative Study Paradigm, Jan-June, pp. 24-36.

Nandan.K. (1996), Application of information Technology in Banks for Competitive Edge, *Vinimaya Special Issue*, pp. 75-81.

Nandan.M.Nilekani(!998), Information technology strategy, Becon, pp. 186-189.

Narendra Kumar and Mohan Kumar (2005), A Study on Impact of Computerization on Customer Service, *South Asian Journal of Management*, March, pp. 20, 28.

Nazrral Isalam and Ezaz Ahmed(2005), A Measurement of Customer Service Quality of Banks in Dharka city of Bangladesh, *South Asian Journal of Management*, Jan –March, pp. 37-55.

Parimal Vyas(2002), Measurement of Customer Satisfaction: A Study of Banking Services Business Perspectives Jan-June Vol. 4, pp. 73-78.

Parimal Vyas(2004), Measurement of Customer Satisfaction on Information Technology Adoption in Banking Services, *PMJR*, April –Oct, pp. 7-16.

Pathrose.P.P (2003), Product Development and Marketing in Banks, *IBA Bulletin* Feb, pp. 32-34.

Pooja Malhotra and Balwinder Singh(2004), Internet Banking in India, *The Management Accountant*, Vol. 39, Nov, pp. 890-896.

Prabhakara Rao. Ch (2004), Indian Banking in 2010: *IBA Bulletin Special Issue*, Jan, pp. 170-173.

Prabhakara, S. (2003), An Insight into Service Attributes in Banking Sector, *Journal of Service Research* April-Sep., pp. 157-169.

Prabhu, A.G. (1996), Banking Technology in India: A Few Issues, *Vinimaya Special issue*, pp. 83-88

Purwar. A.K. (2004), Technology in Banks, *Professional Banker*, Aug. pp. 14-21.

Rabri N. Mishra.(2004), Technology in Banks,*Professional Banker*, Aug. pp. 26-28.

Rajagoapal, S. (1996), Vision 2000 for Indian Banking: Demands and Challenges, *Vinimaya Special Issue*, Oct-Dec., pp. .57-63.

Rajashekara.K.S(2004), Application of Information Technology in Banking, *Southern Economist*, Vol. 43, May, pp. 9-12.

Rangarjan.C(2000), Banking in the High-tech Environment Banking and Finance, April pp. 7-12.

Rawani A.M. and Gupta.M.P (2002), Role of Information Systems in Banks: An Empirical Studying the Indian Context, *Vikalpa*, Oct-Dec., pp. 69-74.

Rawani.A.M and m.P.Gupta (2000), Information Technology Initiatives in Indian Banking Sector Paradigm, Jan-June, pp. 129-143.

Rupa Rega Nisture (2004), Technology in Banks, *Professional Banker*, Aug pp. 28-32.

Sajaya S. Gaur, Abdul Wheed.K., Avish J. Kuzhimattathil, and Ashish Mahajan(2003), Perceived Benefits and Inhibitors of IT Adoption and Resulting Satisfaction, A Study in Indian BFSI Context, *The ICFAI Journal of Bank Management*, pp. 83-94.

Sanjeevaiah B.C and Venugopal, Paradigm Shift in Banks, Banking Finance, April, pp. 5-9.

Saraf.W.S (1997), Banking Technology: Agenda Ahead, *The Journal of Indian Institute of Bankers* pp. 153-162.

Shajahan.S(2005), A Study on the Level of Customers Satisfaction on Various Modes of Banking Services in India, *The ICFAI Journal of Bank Management*, Vol. IV, Feb., pp. 79-85.

Shastri, R.V (2003), Recent Trends in Banking Industry, IT Emergence, *Charted Financial Analyst*, March pp. 45-56.

Shastri, R.V(2004), Leading Issues in Banking Technology Scenario, *Professional Banker*, Aug pp. 20-26.

Shergill, G.S. and Bring Li(2003), Internet Banking: An Empirical Investigation of a Trust and Loyalty Model for New Zeland Banks, www.konganpage.com pp. 1-22.

Shetty, J.V. (1996), Customer Service in Banks, *Vinimaya Special Issue*, pp. 5-9.

Shroff, F.T (1994), Information Technology—A Tool for Development, Becon, 17th Bank Economists Conference, pp. 177-179.

Shyamala Gopinath(2005), Reserve Bank of India, at the IBA- Banking Frontiers International Conference on Retail Banking Directions Opportunities and Challenges in Mumbai , May, pp. 44-48.

Signh.S.B(2003), Marketing of Bank Services in India; An Integrated approach, *Vinimaya Special Issue*, Oct-Dec pp. 26-33.

Talwar.S.P (1999), Information Technology and Banking Seector, *Economic Developments in India*, Vol.19, pp. 119-129.

Tokunbo Simbowale Osinubu (2004), Marketing of Financial Services in Commercial Banks in Nigeria, *The ICFAI Journal of Service Marketing*, Vol. 11 Dec., pp. 37-47.

Upinder Dhar, Santosh Dhar and Abninav Jain (2004), Service with a Difference: A Comparative Analysis of Private and Public Sector Banks, *PMJR*, April, pp. 17-43.

Vepa Kamesam (2002), Changing Faces of Banking: Banking with Technology Banking Finance, Jan., pp. 9-12.

Vinod Sharma(2004), PSBs and Growing Competition, *Professional Banker*, March pp. 30-32.

Vyas Parimal, (2004), "Measurement of Customer Satisfaction on Information Technology Adoption in Banking Services", *Prestige Journal of Management and Research*, Vol. 8, Nov. 1-2, April –October.

Yash Paul Pahuja (2004), Internet Banking and Frauds, *Professional Banker*, Aug., pp. 70-71.3

Zillur Rahman (2005), Service Quality: Gaps in the Indian Banking Industry: *ICFAI Journal of Marketing Management*, Vol. IV, Feb., pp. 37-47.

Web Sites

- www.ask.com
- www.rbi.org.in
- www.canbankindia.com
- www.google.com
- www.indianbank.com
- www..iob.com
- www.stateebankindia.com
- www.researchpaper.com
- www.search.oxide.com
- www.the –paper-store.com
- www.essaytown.com
- www.indiaserver.com
- www.cio.com
- www.banknetindia.com
- www.expresindia.com

Index

S